THE CONTEXT ARCHITECT

THE ARCHITECTURAL BLUEPRINT FOR AI-ERA ORGANIZATIONS

SEAN PAN

The Context Architect

This book is a work of nonfiction. References to organizations, technologies, and regulatory environments are used for illustrative purposes. Any resemblance to specific internal systems, proprietary architectures, or confidential business practices is unintentional.

The views expressed in this book are those of the author and do not necessarily reflect the views of any current or former employer, client, or affiliated organization.

ISBN: 979-8-9946296-2-8

Printed in the United States of America

First edition

CONTENTS

DEDICATION

For my son

Author's Note

When my son chose to pursue a career in Product Management, it clarified a lesson learned over decades of building and operating complex systems: experience cannot be transferred on demand. Advice offered too early becomes instruction. Instruction rarely survives contact with reality. Judgment must be discovered, not delivered.

This book exists to preserve a set of observations about how systems fail—not because of bad intent or insufficient effort, but because responsibility is defined too late and authority is placed too far downstream. These failures are structural. They recur regardless of talent, tooling, or organizational maturity.

I wrote this so that one day he—and others entering roles of system ownership—might encounter these ideas without my voice in the room, free to test them against real constraints rather than inherited assumptions.

If this work helps Product Managers, executives, and others responsible for system ownership recognize that their role is not to coordinate execution, but to design the constraint environments in which systems operate safely, coherently, and predictably, then it has served its purpose. Anything beyond that is incidental.

PREFACE

From the Empty Room to the Architect's Blueprint

In my previous work, *The Empty Room*, I explored the philosophical crisis of the Artificial Intelligence age. Through the lens of John Searle's famous argument, we established a disquieting and operationally relevant truth: modern AI possesses near-perfect Syntactic Fluency—the ability to manipulate symbols, language, and code with extraordinary speed and accuracy—while simultaneously suffering from absolute Semantic Blindness—a complete absence of understanding regarding intent, liability, consequence, or meaning.

We diagnosed the machine as a vessel of infinite horsepower but zero direction—an "Empty Room" capable of executing any instruction placed before it while remaining structurally indifferent to outcomes. The room is not broken. The machinery functions exactly as designed. What is missing is not intelligence, creativity, or capability, but governance.

If *The Empty Room* was the diagnosis of the problem, this book is the manual for the cure. Not by attempting to "fix" the machine, and not by pretending it can reason, but by redesigning the way intent, constraint, and responsibility are imposed on the system before execution ever begins.

We are no longer asking whether the machine understands. We already know that it does not, and pretending otherwise is professionally dangerous. We are now asking a practical, career-defining question that sits at the center of modern organizations: who stands in the room?

Who provides the substitute for judgment? Who encodes legal exposure, ethical boundaries, commercial reality, and strategic intent into forms rigid enough that the machine cannot drift, reinterpret, or hallucinate its way into failure? That role is no longer a "Manager," a coordinator of handoffs, or a supervisor of tasks. It is an Architect.

This book is the blueprint for that role. It is written for the systems thinker who must step into the vacuum left by automation, assume responsibility for constraint design, and govern the ghost in the machine not through oversight, escalation, or post-hoc correction, but through structure. This transition marks a permanent shift in authority and accountability for anyone operating automated systems at scale.

A NOTE ON TECHNICAL DEPTH: TO THE NON-CODER

You do not need to be a Software Engineer to read this book. You do not need to know how to write a single line of Python, configure a server, or debug a compiler.

However, you must be willing to become a systems thinker—someone who can reason about structure, constraints, and failure modes across an entire system.

In the following chapters, you will see diagrams of JSON schemas, references to API structures, and logic flows that look like code. Do not skip them. They are not there to teach you to build the machine; they are there to teach you to govern it, audit it, and constrain it before execution.

In the age of AI, the syntax (the code) is cheap. The semantics (the logic and intent) are priceless. If you can read a legal contract, a financial spreadsheet, or a complex architectural blueprint, you can read a Context Schema, because each is a formal system designed to make intent enforceable.

We are leaving behind the era of generalities. We are entering the era of specifics. This book is technically demanding because the AI you are about to manage is technically unforgiving, and ambiguity is where automated systems fail.

The code is the machine's job. The logic is yours, and the responsibility that comes with it is non-delegable.

INTRODUCTION

THE EVOLUTION OF THE MACHINE AND THE HUMAN PIVOT

Before we dive into the core problem this book is designed to solve, I want to take you back through a decades-long professional observation that revealed the true, systemic bottleneck in innovation: the sequential product lifecycle. This bottleneck is not technological, nor is it a failure of talent. It is a structural constraint embedded in how modern organizations translate intent into execution.

Some may argue that traditional Product Management processes are already obsolete. You may be thinking: "I understand prompt engineering. My team moves fast. We generate code, content, and designs faster than ever. We don't need more process."

I hear that argument, and it is partially correct. Emerging Generative AI and parallel development have absolutely changed the playing field, making legacy workflows appear slow, bureaucratic, and outdated. But the danger lies in mistaking speed for structure. Speed without structure does not eliminate failure; it merely accelerates it. It allows organizations to arrive at the wrong answer faster, with greater confidence and higher downstream costs.

The process most teams are currently using—feeding partial specifications or loosely defined requirements into an AI system for code or content generation—is still assistance inside a single phase of a sequential lifecycle. It does not challenge the lifecycle itself. This book proposes something categorically different: not faster execution within the old structure, but AI-enabled systemic transformation that breaks the structure entirely.

The distinction matters. One approach optimizes a broken pipeline. The other replaces it with a different governing model altogether. This book is concerned only with the latter.

THE NECESSARY DISCIPLINE OF PRODUCT MANAGEMENT

It is important to address a common and dangerous counter-argument immediately: the claim that the traditional discipline of Product Management was always flawed and therefore disposable. This argument surfaces frequently during periods of technological acceleration, and it is almost always misdiagnosed.

Many executives will point to past project failures as evidence. But those failures were rarely the result of Product Management being conceptually wrong. More often, they were the predictable outcome of organizations that never implemented the strategic rigor outlined in classic Product Management texts in the first place. We are not attempting to resurrect the failures of the past. Companies that experienced negative outcomes often failed not because the discipline was incorrect, but because they lacked the maturity, focus, and organizational alignment required for proper execution—particularly in the areas of market segmentation, positioning, and prioritization, themes explored rigorously in Geoffrey Moore's *Crossing the Chasm* and *Inside the Tornado*.

The core strategic function of Product Management—the semantic ownership of the market problem, the explicit definition of the target customer, and the strategic road mapping of value—was sound then and remains non-negotiable now. These disciplines answer the most important question any organization faces—*why* a product should exist—before asking *how* it should be built.

Our focus in this book is deliberately narrow. We are not attacking strategy. We are interrogating execution. Specifically, we are isolating the sequential methodology that translates strategy into action.

Emerging Infinite Execution Velocity has strained the administrative, handoff-driven execution model of traditional Product Management to the breaking point. This book argues that while the foundational principles of Product Management are structurally sound, the sequential execution model that surrounds them is fatally inadequate for the AI era. What is required is not abandonment, but transformation: a structural upgrade that converts the Product Manager (PM) from a coordinator of phases into a Context Architect responsible for governing systems before they execute.

THE CORE PROBLEM: THE CONTEXTUAL BLIND SPOT

The reason the traditional process breaks down is not administrative; it is philosophical. For centuries, thinkers have debated the nature of knowledge, meaning, and understanding, and their conclusions reveal the fatal flaw embedded in today's AI-accelerated product cycles. When execution speed increases but meaning is left undefined, failure becomes systematic rather than accidental.

We routinely confuse a machine's ability to produce technically correct output—with no understanding of what it means—with genuine comprehension of intent, context, and consequence. This confusion is not academic. It is the root cause of why systems that appear successful in testing fail commercially, legally, and ethically once deployed.

To understand why AI-generated code can function perfectly and still produce disastrous outcomes, we must revisit the challenge proposed by philosopher John Searle in 1980: the Chinese Room Argument. This argument is not a metaphor; it is an operational warning.

Imagine a room. Inside sits a person who speaks only English and has no knowledge of Chinese whatsoever. In the room are baskets filled with Chinese characters. The person also has access to a rule book—a massive manual written in English—that specifies exactly how to manipulate these symbols. The rules are purely syntactic. They do not explain meaning. They simply state, "If you see shape 'X,' return shape 'Y.'"

Now imagine people outside the room slide pieces of paper with questions written in Chinese under the door. The person inside consults the rule book, follows the instructions precisely, and slides a response back out. To the people outside, the person in the room appears to understand Chinese. The answers are correct. The grammar is flawless. The exchange is indistinguishable from comprehension.

But does the person inside the room understand Chinese?

The answer is unequivocally no. They are not reasoning about meaning or intent. They are manipulating symbols according to rules they do not understand. They possess Syntactic Fluency without semantic awareness. They have no idea whether they are composing poetry, issuing a legal threat, or ordering lunch. This is not a limitation of intelligence; it is a structural limitation of formal systems—and it is the blind spot modern organizations repeatedly ignore.

This is the operational state of modern Generative AI, regardless of interface, vendor, or model size. The machine behaves exactly like the person in the Chinese Room: fast, precise, and fundamentally unaware of meaning.

THIS IS THE STATE OF MODERN GENERATIVE AI

When you prompt a Large Language Model to "build a login page," it is acting as the person inside the room. It scans its vast training corpus—the statistical equivalent of the rule book—and produces code, copy, and structure that mathematically follow the prompt. It does not know why the login page exists. It does not know that its primary users are elderly and struggle with low-contrast fonts. It does not know that your Legal team requires a specific GDPR checkbox for European users, or that your Security team prohibits a particular authentication flow. It is not reasoning. It is shuffling symbols.

This foundational split between syntax and meaning did not begin with modern AI. It traces back centuries. Cartesian rationalism, articulated by René Descartes, privileged formal, systematic logic over lived experience, laying the philosophical groundwork for computation. Empiricism, advanced by thinkers such as David Hume and George Berkeley, exposed the limits and ambiguity of knowledge derived from perception—precisely the ambiguity automated systems cannot infer without explicit structure.

This tension culminates in what philosophers describe as the **Subjectivity Problem**—articulated clearly by Thomas Nagel's paper "What Is It Like to Be a Bat?" A formal system can never access **Qualia:** the subjective, experiential qualities of reality that drive trust, adoption, loyalty, and risk tolerance. These are not edge cases. They are the core drivers of product success.

This realization—that AI is a brilliant manipulator of symbols yet utterly blind to human, legal, and strategic context—is the insight that permanently transforms the Product Manager's role. If the AI is the person in the room shuffling symbols, then the Context Architect is the one who writes the rule book, defines the constraints, and determines which questions the machine is even allowed to answer.

FROM THE ASSEMBLY LINE TO CONTEXT

My journey to this realization began far from the philosophy classroom. It started on the factory floor, hand-soldering PC boards on an assembly line building digital signal processing (DSP) systems, where failure was physical, measurable, and unforgiving.

It was there that I first internalized a core truth of complexity: the most reliable way to build complex systems is not through linear sequencing, but through simultaneous, parallel development governed by a shared specification. Like LEGO, different teams designed and fabricated discrete functional components concurrently, only converging at final assembly. The system worked not because tasks were performed in order, but because every team was constrained by the same rigorous functional blueprint enforced at the start.

This lesson carried forward into my engineering internship and early professional training. As I completed my B.S. in Electrical Engineering, working with 286 SX processors and learning programming languages Fortran, Assembly, and C, I absorbed the prevailing process: translate product requirements into technical design, execute against them, and then coordinate with stakeholders downstream. The discipline was sound. The sequence was assumed.

It is important to remember the material constraints of that era. The fastest systems available to us were built on Intel 286-class processors, operating with memory measured in hundreds of kilobytes rather than gigabytes. Computing resources were scarce. Iteration was slow. Human time—the time required to write, compile, test, debug, and execute logic—was the dominant bottleneck. Sequential workflows made sense because execution itself was expensive, fragile, and tightly coupled to human effort.

Today, AI has shattered that constraint entirely. Execution is effectively free, instantaneous, and infinitely parallel. This inversion of constraints—where human meaning is scarce and machine execution is abundant—is the driving crisis of this book.

It was during my DSP work that I first encountered systems where context had to be correct. Writing code to analyze analog signals converted into digital data—whether measuring the destructive force of a nuclear explosion or the energy transfer in a car crash—there was no room for ambiguity. The data had meaning, and that meaning had to be preserved end-to-end. That lesson will matter more than ever in an AI-governed world.

I later shifted to the customer-facing side of the organization as a sales and application engineer. It was there, in real deployments rather than controlled environments, that the gap between specification and context widened into a structural chasm.

I once field-tested an industrial computer unit designed for the oil and gas industry in the Arctic Circle. The specification was rigorous, detailed, and formally correct. It required the unit to operate at minus forty degrees Celsius inside an explosion-proof enclosure. We validated the system in environmental chambers for weeks. The data logs were pristine. Every requirement was met. The "Chinese Room" inside our engineering organization had produced exactly the correct symbols.

But reality is not a lab, and compliance is not equivalence.

I remember standing on that rig as the wind chill drove the ambient temperature far below the safe operating zone, attempting to read the display under live conditions. The sun reflected off the snow, producing a blinding white glare that washed out the screen entirely. The heavy industrial gloves required for safety made the interface buttons nearly impossible to press with any precision. And the explosion-proof enclosure—technically flawless by specification—acted as a thermal trap. The electronics were not freezing. They were overheating. Heat generated by the system could not escape the sealed housing, and the LCD contrast collapsed under the Arctic sun.

The client was furious, and justifiably so. We had delivered a system that met every single line item of the functional specification, passed every internal test, and failed completely in the only environment that mattered: real-world use.

The functional specification was correct. The execution was flawless. The context was absent. This was not an engineering failure. It was a governance failure—one caused by defining requirements without encoding the conditions under which those requirements would be judged.

THE SEQUENTIAL TRAP: PAYING THE TIMELINE TAX

My repeated field experience—where technically perfect systems failed once they encountered reality—eventually pulled me out of pure engineering and into formal Product Management.

That experience spans the early days of enterprise software and tooling, from defining one of the first enterprise connectors for web-enabling legacy systems—before modern APIs existed—to advocating for developer tools such as UML modeling and the Subversion versioning repository. In each case, the pattern was the same: technical capability advanced faster than organizational understanding of how that capability would be used, constrained, or monetized.

Later, while leading Product Management teams at companies such as Silicon Graphics, Inc. (SGI)—where we pioneered the computer-generated imagery that launched films like *Jurassic Park*—my responsibility was to translate world-class technical innovation into commercially viable products. The technology was never the problem.

SGI was a temple of engineering excellence. We possessed, without question, the most advanced graphics hardware and software on the planet. But that dominance created a structural blind spot. We implicitly assumed that **Syntactic Fluency**—rendering polygons faster, with higher fidelity, than any competitor—was equivalent to **Semantic Value** in the market. It was not.

When we attempted to repackage this high-end technology for new, lower-margin segments, we collided with market reality. We were effectively selling Ferrari engines to customers who needed minivan reliability and pricing. We encountered unfamiliar price sensitivities, radically different user requirements, and aggressive competition from "good enough" commodity hardware. Because our process was product-centric—Engineering built it first, and Marketing figured out how to sell it later—we only discovered these mismatches after the product already existed. At that point, correction was slow, expensive, and politically fraught.

We were paying for what I call the **Legacy Dependency Map**—an inherited model of execution that assumes knowledge must move in sequence rather than converge simultaneously. This map is rarely written down, yet it governs nearly every large organization by default.

In the traditional sequential model, organizations operate according to linear dependencies that resemble a relay race. Each functional team runs its leg in isolation, effectively blindfolded until the baton is handed off. Context does not accumulate. It resets.

Engineering cannot build until Product defines.

Quality Assurance (QA) cannot test until Engineering builds.

Marketing cannot establish a position until Product explains what was actually built.

Legal cannot review until the release candidate is effectively frozen.

This structure produces what I call the **Zero-Sum Gate.** At each gate, time pressure forces trade-offs where one discipline's requirements must lose so another can proceed. These losses are not strategic decisions; they are structural casualties of late discovery.

If Security identifies a risk at the end of the cycle, usability suffers because there is no time to redesign the interface. If Legal redlines a claim two weeks before launch, Marketing scrambles to rewrite the narrative, weakening positioning and eroding trust. No one is at fault. The system is.

In this model, failure is inevitable because constraint definition is treated as a baton-pass rather than a simultaneous act. Every handoff —Product to Engineering, Engineering to QA, QA to Marketing— becomes a point of entropy where meaning is lost and delay accumulates.

This delay has a name: the **Product Timeline Tax (PTT).** It is the compounded cost of discovering critical constraints too late, paid not in days or weeks, but in months of lost opportunity, rework, and organizational friction.

My formal training in engineering grounded me in the rigorous, deterministic logic of machines. My parallel study of philosophy— deep dives into Descartes' Dualism, the Chinese Room Argument, and the Turing Test—gave me a complementary framework: the ability to distinguish between a system that merely returns a statistically correct answer and a system that can be trusted to reason within defined boundaries. This distinction would later prove decisive.

That philosophical rigor, combined with decades of managing the technical, legal, and commercial consequences of the Product Timeline Tax, eventually led to a clear realization during hands-on work in the AI Studio. The breakthrough was not emotional. It was structural.

I recognized that modern AI systems do not simply accelerate a single phase of the product lifecycle, such as writing code or generating marketing copy. When governed correctly, they allow the simultaneous stacking of constraints that were previously discovered only through sequential handoffs.

The AI Studio enables the real-time convergence of all functional stacks—Engineering, Product, Marketing, Legal, QA—provided the system is fed a rigorously structured and complete set of inputs. Without that structure, speed simply magnifies failure. With it, parallelism becomes safe.

*Throughout this book, the term "**AI Studio**" refers to a **vendor-agnostic, context-governed execution environment**—any integrated system capable of hosting models, enforcing schemas and constraints, orchestrating agents, and generating artifacts under governance. It is an architectural role within the system, not a product recommendation or tooling endorsement.*

This moment is not the end of the Product Management role; it is a forced metamorphosis. The Product Manager's administrative, handoff-driven function is obsolete. If you are a PM feeling threatened by AI, understand this: the common refrain is true, but incomplete. AI will not replace you. A Context Architect using AI will.

This is not a motivational claim. It is a structural inevitability. This book exists to show you how to make that pivot deliberately—by claiming responsibility for constraint design, governing convergence across stacks, and becoming the professional who makes automated systems safe, predictable, and economically viable at scale.

The methodology you are about to master is called the **Stacked Product Lifecycle.** It is not a process tweak, a tooling upgrade, or a faster way to execute existing workflows. It is the systematic elimination of the sequential trap by forcing simultaneous, parallel development through a single, governing discipline: **Context Engineering.**

This book formalizes that discipline. It provides a framework for operating in a reality where execution is effectively instantaneous and constraint definition is the true bottleneck.

The Stacked Product Lifecycle replaces the Legacy Dependency Map with multiple, concurrent development stacks—Engineering,

Product, Marketing, Legal, Security, and QA—running in parallel from Day One. These stacks do not wait for handoffs. They converge continuously against a shared governing structure rather than a linear plan.

Context Engineering is the primary skill of the modern leader. It is the deliberate design, validation, and enforcement of a comprehensive input framework—the **Context Schema**—that compels all Subject Matter Experts to define product, market, regulatory, and technical constraints *before* any development stack generates output. This is not coordination. It is governance.

Breaking the Zero-Sum Gate occurs when constraints are front-loaded into the schema rather than discovered at the end of the cycle. Security, usability, compliance, and positioning are no longer competing interests negotiated under deadline pressure. They are synthesized upstream and enforced automatically during generation.

This is not prompt engineering. Prompting is a minor surface interaction—at most ten percent of the methodology. Context Engineering replaces the single, sequential "specs" document with a living, structured data framework that demands simultaneous participation from every functional expert and makes intent machine-governable.

The result is structural: the compliance gap closes, the marketing lag disappears, and execution scales without surprise.

This book is your guide to becoming the **Context Architect**—the modern leader who defines the Context Schema, governs convergence across stacks, and systematically eliminates the Product Timeline Tax by design rather than heroics.

PART I

THE PROBLEM

1

THE PRODUCT TIMELINE TAX: QUANTIFYING THE COST OF SEQUENTIAL DELAY

If you audit the balance sheet of any modern software company, you will see familiar line items: Server Costs, Personnel, Marketing Spend, and Real Estate. You will see liabilities for outstanding loans and assets for intellectual property. These figures are tracked meticulously, reviewed quarterly, and optimized relentlessly.

But nowhere on that spreadsheet will you find one of the largest and most strategically destructive costs the company actually incurs, because it is invisible to accounting systems and rarely measured directly.

It does not appear as a line item. It is not amortized. It is not owned by any department. And yet it silently compounds over time, draining momentum, morale, and competitive position.

This hidden liability is the **Product Timeline Tax (PTT).**

As outlined earlier, the PTT is the unmeasured, compounding cost of sequential product development. It is not simply the penalty for "being late," nor is it a one-time scheduling failure. It is a structural tax levied on every unit of value an organization attempts to create when work is forced through linear handoffs. It manifests as wasted time, burned capital, invalidated effort, and missed market windows caused by teams waiting—often unknowingly—for other teams to finish their part of the relay.

In the era of AI and **Infinite Execution Velocity**, the PTT has mutated from an operational nuisance into an existential threat. When competitors can define constraints once and execute in parallel, sequential delay is no longer just "the cost of doing business," but a permanent competitive handicap.

1.1 PROCESS DEBT VS. TECHNICAL DEBT

To understand the true nature of the Product Timeline Tax, we must first distinguish it from a concept most Product Managers (PMs) and Engineering Leaders already understand well: **Technical Debt**. The two are often conflated, but they operate at entirely different layers of the system.

Developers incur Technical Debt by making conscious tradeoffs inside the codebase—choosing a faster, more fragile implementation to meet a near-term deadline, with the explicit understanding that the code will need to be refactored later. This debt is created within the **Engineering Stack**. It is visible, measurable, and diagnosable through artifacts such as code complexity metrics, defect rates, and maintenance overhead. Most importantly, it is documented and owned.

The Product Timeline Tax is categorically different. This is **Process Debt**.

Process Debt is a structural flaw baked into the traditional, sequential method of execution. It guarantees delay regardless of how talented, disciplined, or well-intentioned the individual teams may be. It emerges from the **architecture of work itself**.

Consider a genuinely high-performing engineering team. They use modern AI-assisted tools, optimize their Continuous Integration and Continuous Delivery (CI/CD) pipelines, and ship code at record speeds. Inside their silo, their functional velocity is exceptional. However, if that same team spends four weeks waiting for a finalized Requirements Document from Product Management, and then another four weeks waiting for Quality Assurance (QA) to find a testing window, their overall contribution to customer value is effectively stalled. Speed inside the silo does not translate into speed of delivery.

Process Debt is the **structurally observable gap** between Functional Velocity—how fast an individual silo moves—and System Velocity—how fast validated value reaches the customer.

In the **Legacy Dependency Map**, often visualized as a Gantt chart, organizations optimize for Functional Velocity. Engineering is optimized to code faster. Legal is optimized to review efficiently. QA is optimized to execute test cases. But because these optimizations occur in isolation and are connected only through sequential handoffs, the system as a whole accumulates massive Process Debt.

The Product Timeline Tax is the interest payment on that debt. And unlike financial interest, which compounds quarterly or annually, the PTT compounds daily—silently, relentlessly, and outside the visibility of any single team.

1.2 THE ANATOMY OF HANDOFF CONTEXT DECAY

The primary mechanism through which the Product Timeline Tax accrues is **Handoff Context Decay.**

In a sequential system, knowledge is typically transferred from one human brain to another through an intermediate artifact—a Requirements Document, a Jira ticket, a slide deck, or a specification. **Handoff Context Decay** is the inevitable loss of essential strategic, market, legal, or technical nuance as product context moves from one specialized silo to the next. The more handoffs required, the more meaning is lost.

Organizations often treat these handoffs as if they were simple data transfers, comparable to copying a file from a hard drive to a USB stick. Writing a "Requirements Document" creates the comforting illusion that knowledge has been fully transferred. It has not.

This assumption is a direct consequence of the **Syntactic/Semantic split** introduced earlier. A document can faithfully preserve syntax—words, diagrams, acceptance criteria, and bullet points. What it cannot preserve is full semantics: intent, prioritization logic, risk tolerance, trade-offs, and the underlying *why* that shaped the decision.

When a Product Manager functions primarily as an administrator of handoffs, the system becomes dependent on artifacts that are structurally incapable of carrying the complete context required for correct downstream decisions. Each recipient receives a syntactically valid description of the work, but a semantically impoverished version of the original intent.

This decay is not the fault of any individual. It is a systemic property of sequential systems. The cost of that decay is paid later, in the form of rework, rollback, and delay—and it is the single largest contributor to the Product Timeline Tax.

Case Study: The "Smart Search" Feature

To make Handoff Context Decay concrete, consider a FinTech company building a new "Smart Search" feature for its mobile application. On paper, the problem appears simple. In practice, it exposes the structural failure of sequential execution.

Phase 1: Product Strategy (100% Context)

The Product Manager and the VP of Product Management identify a clear market signal: users are frustrated because they cannot locate specific transactions quickly. They express a desire for natural language interaction—queries such as, "*How much did I spend on my insurance last month?*"

Semantic Intent: Build a natural language query engine that understands *insurance* as a transaction category and *last month* as a bounded date range, then aggregates results accordingly.

Critical Constraint: The system must remain strictly private. No transaction data may leave the device or be processed by third-party services.

At this stage, context is complete. Intent, constraints, and success criteria coexist in the same conversation.

Handoff 1: Product → Engineering (The Loss of Intent)

The PM translates this strategy into a delivery artifact. A ticket is written: "*User Story: As a user, I want to search my transactions using natural language so I can track spending.*" A mock-up is attached. The document is syntactically correct.

The Engineering Lead reads the ticket. They see the words *search* and *natural language*. Their mental model immediately shifts toward implementation.

Context Decay: The engineer focuses on the syntactic surface of the request. They think, "*I can solve this with a keyword-matching library and a fuzzy-logic filter.*" The system will technically "search," and the ticket will be closed.

The Gap: The semantic requirement—*understanding* the query, parsing categories, resolving time ranges—is never encoded. The Engineer builds a text matcher, not a semantic engine.

Result: The Loss of Intent. The feature technically satisfies the written requirement, but it fails the user's actual need. The system searches text; it does not answer questions.

Handoff 2: Engineering → QA (The Loss of Verification)

Engineering completes the implementation and marks the ticket "Ready for QA." From the perspective of the sequential system, progress has been made. The baton has been passed.

In the Legacy Dependency Map, QA is structurally positioned as a downstream verifier rather than a continuous design participant. The QA Engineer picks up the ticket with a clear mandate: verify the implementation against the written requirement. Their scope of responsibility is bounded by the artifact they received, not by the original strategic conversation.

Context Decay: The QA Engineer reads the ticket: "*Search for transactions using natural language.*" They enter "Insurance." The application returns transactions containing the word *Insurance*. They enter "ACME." The application returns transactions labeled *ACME*. The system behaves exactly as implemented.

The Gap: Because QA was not present during the Product Strategy phase, they are unaware that the intended outcome was semantic aggregation and temporal reasoning. No one encoded expectations for category inference, date parsing, or question answering. QA tests for crashes, performance regressions, and surface-level correctness—not for whether the feature actually solves the user's problem.

Result: QA passes the feature with confidence. From their vantage point, the system meets every documented requirement. No

Context Schema exists to validate intent, so verification collapses into syntax checking.

Handoff 3: QA → Marketing (The Loss of Reality)

With the feature marked "Green lit," Marketing begins preparing launch materials.

In the Legacy Dependency Map, Marketing is structurally engaged only after implementation is complete and is therefore forced to work from finalized artifacts rather than from live, converging product context. Their job is to translate product capability into market narrative. To do so, they look backward for meaning.

Context Decay: Marketing revisits the original Product Strategy materials from Phase 1, which promised *"AI-Powered Financial Insights."* On that basis, they craft a campaign: *"Ask your app anything. It understands you like a financial advisor."*

The Gap: Marketing is selling the *intent* defined in Phase 1, while Engineering delivered only the *syntax* produced in Phase 2. The narrative and the reality diverge completely. What is being marketed does not exist.

This is the inevitable outcome of meaning being allowed to fragment across sequential handoffs.

Handoff 4: Marketing → The Zero-Sum Gate (The Loss of Launch)

Two weeks before the scheduled launch, the Legal and Security teams finally review the system architecture. This moment is not a review in the collaborative sense. It is a checkpoint imposed by the sequential model. This is the **Zero-Sum Gate.**

During the review, Legal and Security examine the implementation details behind the "Smart Search" feature. They quickly identify that the fuzzy-logic search capability relies on a third-party, cloud-hosted API selected by Engineering to accelerate development.

This choice collides directly with a constraint defined in Phase 1 but never structurally enforced: *no transaction data may leave the device.* The Engineer who made the implementation decision was unaware of the full legal and privacy implications, because those constraints were never encoded in a governing structure they could not violate.

The outcome is a hard stop. Security blocks the release outright. There is no viable mitigation at this stage. The only acceptable remedy is to remove the cloud-based dependency and re-engineer the entire feature to run locally.

The Tax Bill

At this point, the Product Timeline Tax becomes visible—but only after the damage is done. The cost is no longer theoretical.

- **Engineering Time:** Six weeks of implementation effort rendered unusable.
- **QA Time:** Two weeks of validation effort invalidated.
- **Marketing Time:** Two weeks of campaign preparation discarded.

The Rollback

The project returns to the starting line. But it does not reset cleanly. The team is demoralized. The budget is depleted. Trust between functions erodes. Meanwhile, a competitor using a Stacked Product Lifecycle identified and enforced the privacy constraint on Day One—and has already shipped.

This is Handoff Context Decay in its final form. It converts the product lifecycle into a high-stakes game of *Telephone*, where meaning degrades at every handoff and the final product emerges as a distorted, legally non-compliant shadow of the original intent.

1.3 THE MECHANICS OF THE ZERO-SUM GATE

The final stage of the case study illustrates the most destructive and least questioned component of the Product Timeline Tax: the **Zero-Sum Gate.** It is the moment when all unresolved ambiguity collapses into a forced decision under time pressure.

In the Legacy Dependency Map, specialized functions such as

Legal, Security, Compliance, and Privacy are treated as downstream "sign-off" stages. They are positioned at the end of a linear timeline, which effectively turns them into tollbooths placed just before the product enters the market. Their role is reactive by design.

In mature organizations, these functions may engage earlier through consultation or policy guidance. However, when the execution architecture reserves formal authority and constraint enforcement for the end of the lifecycle, those earlier interactions cannot prevent late-stage collisions. The map itself ensures that decisive constraints arrive too late to be synthesized.

Because these gates introduce hard constraints late in the sequential pipeline, any discovery of noncompliance is catastrophic. By the time the gate is reached, the product is already baked. Code has been written. Interfaces have been polished. Documentation has been finalized. Commitments have been made externally.

When a security officer or legal counsel identifies a risk—"*This library violates GDPR,*" or "*This claim creates material litigation exposure*" —they are left with only two options, neither of which produces value.

The Pass: Ignore or defer the risk in order to preserve the launch date, knowingly creating future legal, security, or reputational liability.

The Stop: Halt the launch entirely in order to remediate the issue, absorbing massive immediate delay, rework, and organizational fallout.

This is a **Zero-Sum Game** because one function's success requires another's failure. If Product Management "wins," the organization launches on time but assumes hidden risk. If Legal or Security "wins," the organization is safe but misses the quarter. There is no outcome in which all parties benefit, because the system allows no opportunity for earlier synthesis.

The rollback that follows has zero net gain. When a project is sent back to Engineering to remove a cloud-based dependency and replace it with a compliant local alternative, the organization does not advance. It simply pays to undo work that never should have been done. Sequential phases restart, but no new value is created.

This is the precise definition of waste. Yet in the traditional Product Management model, managing this waste—negotiating exceptions, pleading for waivers, apologizing to stakeholders—is normalized as "part of the job."

It is not part of the job. It is a visible symptom of a broken execution architecture that forces organizations to choose between safety and speed because it never allowed them to design for both.

1.4 THE COMPOUNDING COST OF NON-VALUE-ADDED WAITING

The financial impact of the Product Timeline Tax behaves like compound interest, but in reverse. Instead of accelerating returns, it accelerates loss.

In finance, compound interest is a miracle of time leverage: capital earns interest, and that interest earns interest. In sequential product development, the PTT applies the same mathematics to delay. Each missed handoff does not merely add time; it multiplies it.

To understand why organizations routinely miss schedules by quarters rather than weeks, we need to examine the actual mechanics of delay rather than the optimistic math used in planning documents.

In a perfectly linear system, a one-week delay in Phase A would produce a one-week delay in Phase Z. This assumption underlies most Gantt-based planning models.

$$\text{Delay}_{\text{total}} = \sum(\text{Delay}_{\text{phase}})$$

The **Legacy Dependency Map** is not a linear system. It is a system governed by **interdependent resource availability.** Teams are not idle buffers waiting to absorb delay. They are continuously reallocated.

Each sequential handoff therefore compounds delay rather than containing it.

1.4.1 THE AVAILABILITY MISMATCH

When Engineering waits four weeks for finalized scope, they do not sit idle. They are reassigned. They begin other initiatives. They switch cognitive context.

When the scope finally arrives, the original Engineering team is now fully booked on a different fire drill. They cannot immediately resume the original work.

The initial four-week administrative delay now produces a two-week **resource availability lag.**

Total delay: Six weeks.

This six-week slip pushes the QA phase forward as well. The QA lead, who reserved external testing resources for the original timeline, loses that slot. The next available window is three weeks out.

Total delay: Six weeks plus three weeks equals nine weeks.

If QA then uncovers a critical defect requiring re-engineering, the rollback begins. But the original Developers have since moved to different squads. Pulling them back requires negotiation, onboarding, and forced context reconstruction—a cognitive tax often referred to as **re-engagement lag.**

Re-engagement lag: Two additional weeks.

What began as a four-week delay at the front of the lifecycle has now compounded into a quarter-long failure. Projects estimated at three months take nine. Not because the work was harder than expected, but because **Process Debt accrued interest at a usurious rate.**

1.5 THE OPPORTUNITY COST MULTIPLIER: THE TRUE PRICE OF LATE

When a traditional Project or Program Manager is asked to calculate the cost of a three-month delay, the answer usually begins and ends with the **burn rate.** Salaries are summed. Infrastructure costs are allocated. A portion of rent and overhead is assigned to the team. The conclusion often sounds precise: "*This delay cost us $250,000 in R&D.*"

This calculation is dangerously incomplete. It measures **input cost**, not **lost output value.** It accounts for what was spent, not for what was never captured.

The true strategic cost of the Product Timeline Tax is the loss of the competitive window. This is what we call the **Opportunity Cost Multiplier.**

The Opportunity Cost Multiplier is the metric executive leadership must internalize. It captures the revenue, market share, and long-term positioning lost to a competitor that achieves faster convergence. In software and SaaS markets, this dynamic is amplified by a well-documented economic reality: market leadership is often **winner-take-most**, not evenly distributed.

To quantify this effect, consider a hypothetical but representative scenario: **The Race to GenAI Integration.**

Scenario: Two Companies, One Market Signal

Imagine two competing CRM companies identifying the same opportunity: customers want automatic AI-generated summaries of sales calls. The market signal is clear. The differentiation will be speed and reliability of delivery.

Economics of the Feature:

- Estimated Lifetime Value (LTV): $10 million in upsells per quarter
- First-mover capture: 60% of undecided buyers
- Follower capture: 20% of undecided buyers

Company A: The Sequential Victim

Company A follows the Legacy Dependency Map.

- Product: Four weeks writing requirements
- Engineering: Eight weeks building
- QA: Four weeks testing and rework caused by Context Decay
- Legal: Two weeks reviewing, triggering a Zero-Sum Gate rollback that adds 4 more weeks
- Marketing: Four weeks preparing the launch after Legal sign-off

Total time: ~26 weeks (6.5 months)
Launch: Week 27
Company B: The Context Architect
Company B operates using the Stacked Product Lifecycle.

- Context Engineering: One week with all Subject Matter Experts defining the Context Schema
- Simultaneous execution: Engineering builds code, QA builds automation, Legal validates compliance, and Marketing develops positioning in parallel
- Convergence: The product is ready in eight weeks (the duration of the longest stack)

Total time: Nine weeks
Launch: Week 10
The Multiplier Effect
Company B launches **17 weeks earlier**—roughly four months ahead of Company A. During those four months, Company B captures the first-mover segment and defines the category standard. By the time Company A launches, the market is largely spoken for.

Company A's burn-rate accounting suggests the delay cost them roughly $500,000 in salaries.

The actual cost is structural:

- **Direct revenue loss:** Four months of missed sales at approximately $3.3 million per month equals **$13.2 million**
- **Market share erosion:** Company A must now discount pricing by roughly 20% to compete against an established standard, permanently devaluing the product
- **Acquisition cost spike:** Recovering lost customers requires five to twenty-five times the original acquisition cost, forcing Company A to overspend on marketing simply to regain parity

The Product Timeline Tax traps organizations in a perpetual defensive posture. Resources are consumed managing delay, rollback, and erosion instead of creating leadership. The sequential model does not merely slow Company A down. It costs them the category.

1.6 THE HUMAN COST: BURNOUT AS A SYSTEMIC FEATURE

While the financial impact of the Product Timeline Tax is devastating to the balance sheet, the human cost is even more corrosive. It erodes morale, judgment, and long-term retention. The **Legacy Dependency Map** is a machine optimized to generate burnout.

Burnout is often misattributed to working too hard or putting in long hours. But research into motivation and workplace satisfaction consistently points to a different root cause: **futility**. People burn out not when effort is high, but when effort fails to produce visible, cumulative progress.

High-performing individuals thrive in a state of *flow*—deep, uninterrupted work where context is stable and progress compounds. The sequential execution model, with its constant stop-start rhythm and forced handoffs, systematically destroys this state.

The Engineer's Plight: The Context Switch

Consider the Developer operating inside a sequential system. During a sprint, they work intensely toward a deadline. They carry a dense cognitive model of the feature in their working memory: variable names, logic paths, edge cases, and architectural trade-offs.

When the sprint ends, the work is handed off to QA.

The Developer is immediately instructed to "pick up the next ticket." To comply, they must discard the mental model of Feature A and load the mental model of Feature B. This context switch is not free. It consumes cognitive energy.

Two weeks later, QA returns Feature A with issues. The Developer must now abandon Feature B and attempt to reconstruct Feature A from artifacts and memory. This forced teardown and reconstruction of mental models—known informally as **cognitive thrashing**—is exhausting.

The subjective experience is one of running in place. The Developer works harder each sprint, yet perceives no forward motion. Output exists, but progress does not.

QA's Plight: The Gatekeeper Villain

QA is structurally cast as the bearer of bad news in the sequential model. Because the Product Timeline Tax has already consumed all buffer time, QA always operates under urgency. Any defect discovered is framed as obstruction rather than protection.

This positioning breeds anxiety, resentment, and adversarial dynamics. QA professionals are incentivized to minimize friction rather than maximize product integrity, not because they lack rigor, but because the system punishes rigor late in the process.

The Product Manager's Plight: The Apology Tour

For the legacy Product Manager, the PTT manifests as emotional labor. The PM becomes the interface between broken timelines and disappointed stakeholders.

Apologies are issued to Sales for missed quarters. Explanations are offered to customers for delayed features. Executives receive status updates framed as rationalizations. This constant state of defensive management drains the energy required for genuine strategy and innovation.

Organizations hemorrhage talent under this model because

Process Debt makes it impossible for capable people to experience sustained accomplishment.

1.7 THE INNOVATION TAX: THE SILENT KILLER

There is a third-order cost of the Product Timeline Tax—more subtle than financial loss and more corrosive than burnout—that ultimately determines whether an organization survives: the **Innovation Tax.**

This tax is not measured in dollars or hours. It is measured in ideas that are never proposed, experiments that are never attempted, and opportunities that quietly expire without debate.

In organizations constrained by sequential delay and repeated Zero-Sum Gates, the internal culture adapts defensively. Employees internalize what might be called the *physics of the organization*—an intuitive understanding of which ideas are "worth the trouble" and which are not.

"If I suggest a change to the UI," someone learns, "it has to go through Design Review, then a usability study, then frontend sizing. That's three weeks of meetings before a single line of code. I won't suggest it."

"If we try a new AI library," another learns, "Legal will block it for two months. We'll miss the window. Let's just use the approved library, even if it's objectively worse."

These are not expressions of laziness or fear. They are rational responses to process friction. A filter emerges that captures not only bad ideas, but bold and valuable ones as well. Over time, the organization shifts its center of gravity away from **Product Excellence** and toward **Process Compliance.**

The Innovation Tax also manifests as a retreat from complexity. If solving a problem requires coordination across Engineering, Legal, Security, and Data Science, and the coordination cost is prohibitively high, the problem is quietly ignored. Teams default to shipping "safe" updates—incremental changes that pass easily through sequential pipelines but generate no strategic advantage.

This is how large incumbents die. Not because they lack

intelligent, creative people, but because their **Legacy Dependency Map** makes meaningful innovation economically irrational. When the cost of coordination exceeds the value of the idea, innovation becomes a liability rather than an asset.

1.8 THE PM'S LEGACY ROLE: THE ADMINISTRATOR OF DELAY

To understand why the transition to **Context Architect** is not optional, we must first examine the lived reality of the modern Product Manager operating inside a PTT-heavy organization. This requires an honest audit of where time and attention are actually spent.

In the Legacy Model, the Product Manager functions primarily as the chief administrator of sequential handoffs. When we examine a typical PM's calendar, a disturbing pattern emerges: very little time is devoted to defining value or shaping strategy. The overwhelming majority is consumed by process maintenance.

09:00 – The Status Stand-up (The Policing of Compliance)

The day begins with a ritualized inquiry: "*Is it done yet?*" The PM moves from Engineer to Engineer, extracting commitments and updating trackers. This is not strategic alignment. It is anxiety management. The PM is effectively checking whether the baton was dropped overnight in the relay race.

11:00 – The Translation Session (Fixing Context Decay)

An Engineer pings the PM: "*The ticket says 'user-friendly,' but the API returns an error code. Should I display the code or a generic message?*"

The PM must immediately stop higher-order work to re-inject intent that was lost during the handoff. They are not making a product decision; they are repairing Context Decay after the fact. The PM has become a human patch for a structural flaw.

14:00 – The Stakeholder Alignment (The Apology Tour)

The PM meets with Sales leadership. The discussion is not about roadmap differentiation or market strategy. It is a negotiation about why a feature promised for Q3 has slipped to Q4. Phrases like "*unforeseen dependencies*" and "*QA bottlenecks*" are deployed. This is the political interest payment on accumulated Process Debt.

16:00 – The Zero-Sum Gate Negotiation

The PM joins a call with Legal or Security, leveraging social capital in an attempt to bypass a gate that should have been opened structurally weeks earlier.

This role is inherently administrative and sequential. The Product Manager's effectiveness is judged by their ability to manage delay, negotiate trade-offs, and absorb organizational frustration—not by their ability to eliminate the Product Timeline Tax itself.

In this model, the PM is not an architect. They are the superintendent of a deteriorating building, patching leaks as they appear. The system does not need a better superintendent. It needs a fundamentally different structure.

1.9 CONCLUSION: THE DEFINITION OF INSANITY

Albert Einstein is often credited—apocryphally—with defining insanity as doing the same thing over and over while expecting different results. Regardless of attribution, the diagnosis applies with uncomfortable precision to modern software organizations.

For more than two decades, the industry has attempted to solve what it calls the Speed Problem by optimizing the silos. The assumption has remained unchanged: if each function runs faster, the system will deliver faster.

Engineers were given faster compilers, improved languages, and automated CI/CD pipelines. Designers were equipped with sophisticated prototyping and collaboration tools. Product Managers were handed increasingly powerful ticketing and workflow systems such as Jira and Asana.

Each runner in the relay became stronger. The relay itself did not change. Batons are still passed in the dark, and context is still lost at every handoff.

This administrative model is now obsolete—the structure no longer matches the constraints of the environment.

In a world where AI can generate first-pass code, copy, and test artifacts in seconds, the bottleneck is no longer the mechanical production of work itself. It is the orchestration of context—the deliberate definition of constraints, intent, and meaning required to validate, govern, and safely direct that output before execution.

Eliminating the Product Timeline Tax therefore does not require better tools or faster teams. It requires a change in methodology. The Product Manager must evolve into the **Context Architect**, retaining the principles of Product Management but replacing the sequential execution model that undermines them.

The core thesis of this book remains evolution, not rejection. Understanding the user, the market, and the value proposition is still the foundation. What must change is the map that governs how that understanding becomes reality.

To escape the PTT, we must first fully understand the structure that enforces it. In the next chapter, we will dissect the **Legacy Dependency Map** itself—line by line—to reveal exactly where value is lost, where delay is manufactured, and where the bodies are buried.

2

DECONSTRUCTING THE TRADITIONAL DEPENDENCY MAP: THE CARTOGRAPHY OF FAILURE

To solve a problem, you must first be able to see it clearly and without abstraction. Diagnosis precedes design.

In Chapter 1, we quantified the cost of the Product Timeline Tax (PTT). We measured the financial loss, the human burnout, and the strategic erosion caused by sequential delay. But measuring the bleeding is not enough. To stop it, we must locate the wound.

The wound is structural: it lies in the map the organization uses to navigate the terrain of innovation. Blaming an underperforming Product Manager (PM), an overworked Engineer, or a cautious Legal team may feel satisfying, but it misses the point.

We call this structure the **Legacy Dependency Map.**

The Legacy Dependency Map is the organizational chart of product failure. It is the invisible architecture that governs how work actually moves through your company, regardless of org charts or declared methodologies. It encodes a set of assumptions about sequence, specialization, and control that were once reasonable—and are now catastrophic.

This map is a visual representation of sequential dependencies in which functional specialization becomes a critical barrier to velocity. Each department holds a fragment of the total context, and the system assumes those fragments can be safely reassembled through handoffs.

If you were to draw this map on a whiteboard, it would feel immediately familiar. It resembles a traditional Gantt chart or a classic "Waterfall" diagram, even inside organizations that describe themselves as Agile. Distinct phases—Requirements, Design, Engineering, Quality Assurance (QA), Legal, Marketing—are arranged neatly from left to right, implying order, progress, and control.

The danger is that the map looks reasonable. It looks disciplined. It looks managerial.

But in the age of AI and **Infinite Execution Velocity**, this map is a trap. It demonstrates a counterintuitive truth: product success is not governed by the speed of the fastest team—typically Engineering—but by the speed of the slowest handoff. In most organizations, that handoff is the **Zero-Sum Gate**, where legal, security, or compliance constraints finally collide with a fully baked artifact.

This chapter makes the map visible, names its failure modes, and strips it of the authority it no longer deserves.

2.1 VISUALIZING THE SEQUENTIAL TRAP

The **Legacy Dependency Map** is a system composed of reinforcing structural flaws. These flaws guarantee the accumulation of **Process Debt** regardless of talent, tooling, or intent.

2.1.1 LINEAR FLOW AND ORGANIZATIONAL SILOS

On the Legacy Dependency Map, progress moves strictly from left to right.

In high-performing product organizations, this rigidity has been intentionally broken through empowered, cross-functional teams and continuous collaboration. But these organizations are the exception, not the norm. In most enterprises—particularly those operating at scale, under regulatory pressure, or across multiple business units—the underlying dependency structure remains sequential, regardless of how modern the ceremonies or tooling appear.

This enforced linearity is the first and most fundamental failure. It encodes a rigid rule: no phase may begin meaningful work until the previous phase has completed its full output and formally handed it off.

This rule does not merely sequence work. It calcifies departments into discrete, specialized knowledge silos by design.

- **Engineering** retains technical context — the *how*
- **Legal and Compliance** retain regulatory context — the *cannot*
- **Marketing** retains market context — the *who*

Each silo optimizes locally, holding only its fragment of the total system context. The organization assumes these fragments can be recombined later without loss.

In this model, the "product" becomes a baton passed between runners who are operating on different tracks, under different constraints, and with different success criteria. The handoff mechanism itself—the artifact transfer from one silo to the next—becomes the primary communication channel.

The Engineer does not speak directly to Legal; the *code* speaks to Legal.

The Product Manager does not speak continuously to Marketing; the *feature release ticket* speaks to Marketing.

This substitution of artifacts for conversation guarantees **Handoff Context Decay**. By the time the baton reaches the final runner, it is no longer aligned with the original intent. It is incomplete, misoriented, or functionally misleading.

The failure is architectural. The map itself ensures that meaning is fragmented before execution ever begins.

2.1.2 THE ACCUMULATION POINT

The most dangerous structural feature of the Legacy Dependency Map is what we call the **Accumulation Point**. It is the location where all unresolved risk is allowed to collect without detection.

In a river system, pollutants introduced upstream do not

disappear. They travel invisibly with the current and eventually concentrate at the delta. In the Legacy Dependency Map, the same dynamic applies: accumulated risk, Technical Debt, and Context Decay flow downstream and converge at a single point—the **Zero-Sum Gate.**

Because legal, security, and compliance constraints are isolated in a downstream silo, they function as the inevitable Accumulation Point for every unresolved conflict introduced earlier in the lifecycle. Nothing is reconciled upstream. Everything is deferred.

Consider a representative scenario. An Engineering team rapidly builds a user analytics feature. In the absence of continuous legal context, they select a data structure that violates a specific clause of the General Data Protection Regulation (GDPR) related to the *right to be forgotten*.

This violation is not the result of negligence or malice. It emerges from structural ignorance. The legal context required to avoid the mistake was never present at the moment of design.

For twelve weeks of development and four weeks of QA, the risk remains invisible. It moves cleanly through the pipeline, passing every internal gate because no gate is designed to detect it.

Only when the final artifact reaches the downstream Accumulation Point—the formal Compliance Review—does the violation surface. At that moment, the risk detonates. The feature cannot ship. The only remedy is a full rollback and architectural redesign, restarting the process from the beginning.

The Legacy Dependency Map instructs the organization to wait until the end of the journey to verify whether the path was correct. That is why the crash is inevitable.

2.2 THE CONTEXTUAL COST OF THE LEGACY DEPENDENCY MAP

Why do intelligent, well-funded organizations continue to rely on a map that reliably leads them into failure?

They do so because the map offers the *illusion of control*. By breaking a complex problem into discrete, sequential phases, leadership gains the comforting sense that progress is orderly, measurable, and governed. This administrative clarity feels like competence.

That clarity is deceptive.

The Legacy Dependency Map structurally engineers **contextual failure** by mandating **sequential input for parallel risk.** It assumes that risk itself is sequential—that technical, market, and legal concerns can be safely addressed one after another. This assumption is false.

This is the core theoretical failure of the modern product process. Every feature conceived today carries **simultaneous, parallel risks** from the moment of inception. Technical feasibility, market fit, and legal liability do not wait their turn. The codebase, the market, and the law books all impose constraints on Day One.

The map, however, forces the organization to confront these realities in isolation and in sequence. Technical risk is addressed in the early months. Quality risk is examined later. Legal and compliance risk is deferred until the end. Each domain is treated as if it exists in a different time dimension.

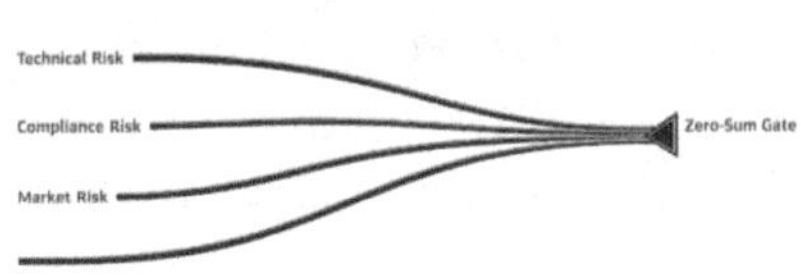

Figure 1. *The Legacy Dependency Map shows a sequential product lifecycle in which parallel technical, market, and compliance risks converge at a late-stage Zero-Sum Gate, where violations trigger structural rollback.*

This mismatch—attempting to govern a parallel reality with a sequential process—produces what can only be described as the **"Wait and See" Strategy.**

Under this strategy, the organization delays convergence deliberately. It waits to see what Engineering builds before Marketing commits. It waits to see what Marketing promises before Legal reviews. It waits to see what Legal blocks before deciding whether the product can ship at all.

The Product Timeline Tax is the price paid for this waiting. It is structurally guaranteed by the map itself.

The "Wait and See" Strategy

The Legacy Dependency Map encourages a fundamentally reactive posture toward the most critical strategic constraints in the organization. Instead of forcing early convergence, it institutionalizes delay as a form of risk management.

Marketing waits. The Product Marketing Manager cannot write final positioning, messaging, or sales enablement material until Engineering completes the feature set. Weeks—or months—are spent waiting for a tangible product artifact before meaning can be attached to it. Marketing is reduced to observation rather than participation.

Legal waits. The Compliance Officer is structurally prohibited from engaging early. The process dictates that Legal review begins only once code is deployed to a QA environment. Ideas cannot be audited. Architectures cannot be shaped. Only finished artifacts can be approved or rejected.

This enforced waiting period is the Product Timeline Tax in its purest form. It represents the deliberate postponement of essential functional knowledge that could have shaped the outcome if it had been present earlier.

When convergence finally occurs, it does so violently. The organization enters what can only be described as the **Convergence of Pain.** At this point, the two primary mechanisms of the PTT—**Handoff Context Decay** and the **Zero-Sum Gate**—collide.

Each sequential handoff increases context loss. Each loss of context raises the probability that the final artifact violates a non-negotiable constraint. When that violation is discovered, the Zero-

Sum Gate is triggered, forcing a multi-month rollback and maximizing the Product Timeline Tax.

Under this map, the Product Manager's role becomes permanently reactive. Time is spent managing exceptions, negotiating delays, and containing fallout rather than designing a system that prevents failure.

The solution is the complete dismantling of the sequential model through **Stack Development**, where convergence is forced at the input layer rather than deferred to the end.

2.3 THE ARCHITECTURE OF FAILURE: THREE FAILURES OF THE LEGACY DEPENDENCY MAP

To dismantle the Legacy Dependency Map, we must first understand how it systematically isolates the most critical intelligence within the organization. These failures are not incidental. They are designed outcomes of a sequential worldview applied to a parallel reality.

The most dangerous characteristic of the Legacy Dependency Map is not that it is slow. Slowness is merely the visible symptom. The deeper failure is that the map is structurally engineered for collapse by isolating the three functional constraint domains that must operate in parallel. Each isolation point functions as a hidden tax mechanism, compounding risk until it detonates.

2.3.1 TECHNICAL ISOLATION → LEGACY DEPENDENCY SHOCK

In the traditional Product Management model, product requirement definition is deliberately separated from continuous engineering feasibility analysis. Engineering input is treated as a downstream validation step—a discrete "triage" phase—rather than a persistent governing constraint.

This separation creates **Technical Isolation**. Teams finalize an initial product vision before confronting the realities of the **Legacy Dependency Map**: the dense web of existing systems, brittle integrations, deprecated APIs, performance ceilings, and infrastructure constraints that define what is actually buildable.

The Shock

Consider a team leveraging an AI coding assistant. The Engineers operate with high **Syntactic Fluency**, rapidly generating implementation for a new high-speed transaction feature. The code is clean. The abstractions are elegant. Unit tests pass.

But late in the cycle, during integration testing, they discover a hard truth: the new feature must integrate with an existing system that cannot support the required throughput or interaction model—such as a legacy transactional datastore with strict connection limits, rigid schemas, or batch-oriented processing constraints.

The AI wrote code for a greenfield world. The organization lives in a brownfield world.

The resulting artifact is functionally complete and operationally unusable. The Product Manager must now shepherd a major refactor, retroactively navigating constraints that should have shaped the design from Day One.

This is not debugging. It is architectural rollback. Weeks of redesign are required to reconcile the feature with reality—rework that exists solely because technical constraints were isolated instead of enforced as governing inputs.

2.3.2 COMPLIANCE ISOLATION → REGULATORY ZERO-SUM GATE

The Legacy Dependency Map almost universally positions Legal, Security, and Compliance at the downstream end of the lifecycle. This placement ensures that regulatory and policy constraints are introduced as *audits* rather than as *design inputs*.

This structure creates **Compliance Isolation**. The organization treats the non-negotiable limits of the product—the explicit *cannot*—as something to be verified after construction instead of something to be enforced before construction begins.

The Shock: The Regulatory Zero-Sum Gate

Two weeks before launch, an executive sponsor or legal counsel reviews the final production artifact—for example, a redesigned user sign-up flow. During this review, they discover that the personally identifiable information (PII) being collected violates a newly enacted privacy requirement: a geo-fencing rule in California, a data-retention mandate in Germany, or an updated consent standard under evolving regulation.

The development team did not ignore the law. They were never structurally exposed to it. The legal context required to avoid the violation was absent at the moment of design.

At this point, the Compliance Officer has no discretion. They must trigger the **Zero-Sum Gate.**

Momentum collapses instantly. Legal violations cannot be patched the way bugs can. The data flows, storage architecture, and consent logic must be redesigned from first principles.

The product cannot ship. Months of simultaneous Engineering and Legal rework follow. Roadmaps unravel. Commitments are broken.

This rollback carries the full punitive financial weight of the Product Timeline Tax. Every hour invested since inception is either invalidated or consumed by rework that should never have been required.

The Context Architect's View

In the Context Architect model, the **Constraint & Compliance Layer** of the Context Schema is completed first. Legal and security constraints are treated as governing inputs, not downstream audits.

When these constraints are encoded upfront, the AI Studio generates code, data flows, and even compliance language simultaneously. The artifact emerges compliant by construction, because compliance is no longer deferred.

2.3.3 MARKET ISOLATION → STRATEGIC CONTEXT DECAY

The final structural failure of the Legacy Dependency Map is the artificial separation of strategic intent from market execution. The *why* of the product is defined early, while the *who* and *how to sell* are deferred until delivery.

This separation creates **Market Isolation**. The Product Marketing Manager (PMM) is forced into a passive role, waiting for a completed artifact before meaningful go-to-market work can begin. Marketing becomes a downstream translation function rather than an active shaper of the product's meaning.

The Decay

As Engineering iterates over six months, the original market context does not remain static. Competitors release adjacent features. Buyer expectations evolve. Regulatory language shifts. Persona pain points sharpen or move entirely.

By the time the PMM receives the final product, **Handoff Context Decay** has already done its work. The artifact reflects a compromised feature set shaped by technical and compliance constraints discovered late. The market reflects a reality that no longer matches the original strategy.

The PMM is left to invent a narrative that bridges these two mismatches. The resulting go-to-market campaign is necessarily diluted—careful where it should be bold, generic where it should be precise.

The product launches, but adoption lags. Marketing spend is consumed without momentum. Sales cycles lengthen. Market share erodes while the organization waits for alignment that can no longer be recovered.

The Context Architect's View

In the Context Architect model, the **Strategic Context Layer** of the Context Schema is approved before execution begins. Market positioning, personas, value propositions, and differentiation are treated as governing inputs, not downstream interpretations.

This allows the Marketing Stack to generate positioning, messaging, sales enablement, and launch assets **simultaneously** with the Engineering Stack. Code and campaign emerge as twins—born from the same parent context and converging at the same moment.

Strategic context no longer decays. It compounds.

2.4 THE EXECUTIVE DILEMMA: AI, EFFICIENCY, AND THE STRUCTURAL STREAMLINE

If the Legacy Dependency Map is so demonstrably flawed, a reasonable question follows: why does it persist? Why do intelligent, experienced executives continue to defend a model that reliably generates tax instead of value?

The answer lies in the seductive—and dangerous—promise of **efficiency.**

When executives encounter Generative AI, they often interpret its capabilities through a narrow, reductive lens. Efficiency is equated directly with headcount reduction. A demonstration of AI writing code, generating marketing copy, or resolving customer support inquiries immediately triggers a cost-based mental model.

"If AI can write code 50% faster, I can reduce Engineering headcount by 50%."

"If AI can generate copy, I no longer need Junior Copywriters."

This reasoning is the elephant in the room. It represents the primary psychological barrier to adopting a systemic solution such as the **Stacked Product Lifecycle.** Leadership is tempted to deploy AI as a performance enhancer inside existing silos—making each silo faster—rather than confronting the structural failure created by the silos themselves.

We must be explicit: AI will streamline operational tasks across the enterprise. That fact is not in dispute. But these gains do not repair a broken execution architecture. They expose it.

When a flawed process is accelerated, the result is **Accelerated Failure.** Faster handoffs amplify Context Decay. Faster output increases rollback cost. Faster testing slams the organization into the Zero-Sum Gate sooner.

AI does not forgive structural defects. It punishes them.

2.5 THE AI EFFICIENCY PARADOX: STREAMLINING THE SILOS

Let us examine the data without optimism or fear. Current benchmarks consistently show that Generative AI produces dramatic productivity gains inside narrowly defined domains. Within a silo, AI performs exceptionally well.

When these gains are overlaid onto the **Legacy Dependency Map**, however, a disturbing paradox emerges: **local optimization produces systemic stagnation.**

AI excels at automating administrative and repetitive work—tasks dominated by **Syntactic Fluency**. What it does not do is repair the structural fractures between functions. In fact, by increasing output velocity, AI magnifies the cost and severity of failure at each handoff.

2.5.1 THE SALES STACK: THE CONTEXT VACUUM

The AI Gain. Sales organizations are reporting material productivity gains in narrowly scoped execution tasks. AI agents now autonomously handle lead scoring, pipeline forecasting, and first-pass outreach, allowing a single Business Development Representative to engage orders of magnitude more prospects than was previously feasible.

The Strategic Flaw: The Context Vacuum. In the Legacy Dependency Map, Sales operates in isolation from Engineering. When AI scales outreach, it requires concrete hooks—reasons for the customer to buy. Without access to a shared **Context Schema**, the AI infers capability from outdated collateral or historical patterns.

Scenario. A Sales AI analyzes a prospect's LinkedIn profile, identifies interest in *real-time analytics*, and generates an email promising exactly that feature.

The Reality. Engineering deprecated real-time analytics two sprints ago due to an unresolvable backend constraint—an outcome of Technical Isolation.

The Result. The AI successfully books the meeting. The Sales Engineer then has to retract the promise. Trust erodes. The deal generates negative brand equity. The efficiency of outreach did not create value; it accelerated disappointment.

2.5.2 THE MARKETING STACK: THE HYPER-PERSONALIZED LAG

The AI Gain. Marketing teams are increasingly able to automate large portions of repetitive content production, including draft copy, variant generation, SEO scaffolding, and sentiment-aligned messaging. The gains are real, but they vary significantly depending on workflow maturity, governance integration, and downstream approval constraints.

The Strategic Flaw: The Marketing Lag. The content is perfect —but trapped inside a sequential system.

Scenario. A Marketing AI generates a complete launch campaign for the new *Smart Search* feature.

The Reality. The product is immobilized at the Zero-Sum Gate after Legal discovers a privacy violation.

The Result. Campaign assets sit unused for six weeks. By the time the product ships, the market context has shifted. The "newsjacking" moments have passed. The efficiency of content creation is entirely nullified by structural delay.

2.5.3 THE QUALITY STACK: ZERO-SUM ACCELERATION

The AI Gain. Quality and testing organizations are observing meaningful reductions in cycle time through AI-assisted test generation, defect prediction, and regression analysis. These improvements accelerate feedback, but—within a sequential model—they still occur *after* the build, where structural violations remain maximally expensive to correct.

The Strategic Flaw: Zero-Sum Acceleration. In a sequential model, testing still occurs only after the build is complete.

Scenario. A QA AI executes ten thousand tests in under an hour and identifies a critical compliance failure involving PII handling.

The Reality. The violation is discovered at the end of the lifecycle, exactly where the map dictates.

The Result. AI simply accelerated the speed at which the organization collided with the wall. The wall did not move. Finding a fatal flaw faster is marginally better than finding it slowly—but preventing the flaw through **Context Engineering** is the only way to preserve the release.

2.6 THE SCOPE GUARDRAIL: VALUE VS. HEADCOUNT

The critical insight emerging from the AI Efficiency Paradox is this: AI dramatically increases efficiency *within* functional silos, but it does nothing to repair the gaps *between* them. In fact, by accelerating output velocity without repairing structure, AI increases the probability and severity of failure at every handoff point.

This observation defines the **Scope Guardrail** for this book.

This methodology is explicitly **not** a prescription for headcount reduction.

While AI may compress the execution workload that previously required multiple specialists, this book does not claim that the Context Architect model collapses three human roles into one automated agent. That framing misunderstands the nature of the constraint.

The Context Architect requires **more human intelligence**, not less. The work being elevated is not syntactic execution; it is **Semantic Understanding.**

If an organization removes the humans who carry contextual knowledge—the nuances of legacy systems, the risk tolerances of the General Counsel, the unspoken anxieties of the user persona—and replaces them with autonomous agents operating in isolation, the result is a high-speed machine optimized to produce structurally invalid output.

The efficiency gains described in this book must therefore be understood correctly. They are measures of **time recovered, risk eliminated,** and **convergence accelerated** across the entire product lifecycle. The optimization target is **ROI velocity,** not payroll reduction.

This is where the Context Architect enters. Their role is not to write code or copy—tasks AI performs efficiently—but to **govern the inputs** that shape those outputs.

The Context Architect enforces completion of the **Context Schema** *before* execution begins, ensuring that AI-directed efficiency converges toward a viable outcome.

- The **Sales Stack's** hyper-targeted messaging is pre-approved through the **Constraint Layer.**
- The **Engineering Stack's** implementation is pre-aligned with market positioning through the **Strategic Context Layer.**
- The **QA Stack's** validation plans are pre-aware of the **Technical Dependency Layer.**

Under this paradigm, execution accelerates for every stakeholder because their outputs converge **simultaneously.** Non-value-added waiting disappears. The Product Timeline Tax collapses toward zero.

2.7 CONCLUSION: BURNING THE MAP

The Legacy Dependency Map was engineered for a world defined by human limitation. It emerged in an era when people typed slowly, compiled code manually, and distributed artifacts physically. Within those constraints, sequential control was rational. The map optimized coordination around the bottlenecks of the twentieth century.

In the twenty-first century, those bottlenecks no longer exist. Execution is no longer the limiting factor. **Syntactic Fluency is abundant.**

The true constraint has shifted from execution speed to **context**—the Semantic Understanding required to govern complex systems without drift, surprise, or legal exposure.

Continuing to rely on the Legacy Dependency Map in the age of AI is not merely inefficient. It is actively dangerous. It is equivalent to navigating a starship with a sextant: a tool perfectly suited to a different era, now incapable of preventing catastrophe. Under this map, every AI efficiency gain is systematically converted into Product Timeline Tax.

The **Context Architect** is the only role that structurally resolves this mismatch. By governing inputs rather than managing outputs, the Context Architect ensures that AI efficiency translates into durable enterprise value instead of amplified organizational risk.

With the Tax quantified in Chapter 1 and the Map dismantled in Chapter 2, we can now turn our attention to the engine itself. In the next chapter, we will examine **the Need for Speed**—the biological and economic imperative that demands a new execution architecture.

PART II

SEMANTIC GOVERNANCE

3

THE NEED FOR SPEED: INNOVATION IN THE AI ERA

With the Legacy Dependency Map dismantled, the deeper force driving its collapse must now be examined. The failure of the sequential model is not merely conceptual—it is economic and biological. The constraints that once stabilized the system have dissolved. To understand why governance must move upstream, we must first confront the new velocity regime that AI has introduced into product development.

3.1 THE END OF "FAST ENOUGH": WHY AI KILLS THE LEGACY MODEL

For the last two decades, the discipline of Product Management has operated under a unified, if largely unspoken, theory of constraint. Whether an organization formally adopted Waterfall, Agile, Scrum, SAFe, or some improvised hybrid of all four, the fundamental governor of progress was always the same: **human velocity**.

We built our entire philosophy of management around the assumption that creating things is inherently difficult. Code was expensive because it required scarce expertise and uninterrupted concentration. Copywriting took time because language had to be composed, reviewed, revised, and approved by human hands. Data analysis was slow because insight required manual extraction, interpretation, and validation. Human fingers limited how quickly a product could move from ideation to deployment by typing speed; human eyes limited it by documentation review speed; and human minds limited it by serial logic processing speed and cognitive fatigue.

This biological ceiling functioned as a hidden stabilizer inside the

Legacy Dependency Map. Because the "building" phases—Engineering, Design, Content—unfolded over weeks or months, the "checking" phases—Legal, Security, Compliance, Strategy—were granted a natural, if inefficient, buffer. The slowness of creation unintentionally protected the organization. It gave governance layers time to review intent, surface conflicts, and absorb risk before release. The inefficiency of the system was the only thing preventing the organization from collapsing under its own accumulated complexity.

That era is over.

The arrival of highly capable Generative AI and Large Language Models (LLMs) has annihilated this constraint at its source. We have moved from an environment where code was a scarce and rate-limited resource to one where it is functionally abundant. A single Developer, properly prompted and assisted by AI agents, can now move from a rough concept to a functional Minimum Viable Product (MVP) draft in hours, not weeks—sometimes in minutes rather than days.

To the uninitiated executive, this appears to be pure upside. They see a world where backlogs evaporate, roadmaps compress, and delivery velocity explodes. But to the Context Architect (CA), this is not a productivity breakthrough—it is a warning siren. This shift may make organizations faster, but it also introduces a structural fracture into the operating system of the company, a fracture we call **the Asymmetry of Acceleration.**

3.1.1 THE IRON TRIANGLE FALLACY

To understand the full severity of this shift, we must return to one of the foundational metaphors of modern project management: the "Iron Triangle." This model describes the traditional trade-off between scope, time, and cost—the three variables that governed every meaningful delivery decision inside the Legacy Model.

In that model, you could optimize for only two. If you demanded a large scope in a short period of time, the cost—in the form of headcount, vendor spend, or overtime—had to rise dramatically. If you demanded low cost and expansive scope, time necessarily stretched. This constraint shaped every roadmap conversation and every compromise a Product Manager (PM) was forced to negotiate.

Infinite Execution Velocity appears to break the Iron Triangle—but only **asymmetrically and only at the level of artifact production.**

Time collapses for generation: AI produces usable output almost instantly, compressing weeks of work into hours or minutes.

Cost of generation collapses: the marginal cost of producing an additional line of code, test, or document via an LLM approaches zero.

Scope expands dramatically: AI can generate vast quantities of code, documentation, and features in parallel, unconstrained by human attention or fatigue.

On the surface, this seems to violate the laws of delivery. All three sides of the triangle appear to move at once. But this apparent miracle applies to only one domain of the organization: **production of artifacts**, not delivery of systems.

While AI collapses the cost and time of creation, it simultaneously inflates the cost of validation and integration. Every unit of "cheap" output introduces **non-linear risk growth** downstream. Security exposure, legal liability, architectural inconsistency, operational fragility, and strategic misalignment all increase as volume and coupling increase. The result is not efficiency, but amplification.

The Product Manager is no longer managing a balanced trade-off between scope, time, and cost at the point of execution. They are managing a flood of artifacts whose **governance, validation, and coordination costs** now dwarf their creation cost. The Iron Triangle remains, but it has inverted. The constraint has shifted from execution to governance, and the Legacy Model has no mechanism to absorb that inversion.

3.1.2 THE BROKEN GEARBOX: THE ASYMMETRY OF ACCELERATION

AI accelerates organizations selectively, with a pronounced bias toward **Syntactic Fluency**—the ability to manipulate symbols, code, and structured text at scale. As a result, it disproportionately amplifies the productivity of the functions responsible for creation: Engineering, Design, and Content.

To understand the danger this creates, imagine the organization as a complex mechanical gearbox. In the Legacy Model, all gears—Engineering, Legal, Marketing, Quality Assurance (QA)—rotated at approximately the same speed. Their motion was imperfect and inefficient, but it was synchronized. The entire system advanced in rhythm with the two-week sprint cycle, and friction was distributed evenly across functions.

Now consider the modern Software Engineer. Armed with tools such as GitHub Copilot, Cursor, or a custom agent stack, they can generate boilerplate code, unit tests, documentation, and even full architectural refactors at a speed that exceeds human cognitive processing. They are traveling at Mach 10.

The governance systems, however—Legal, QA, Security, Compliance, and Strategy—remain distinctly human. They are constrained by manual interpretation, sequential review, deliberation, and institutional risk tolerance. These systems are still traveling at 35 miles per hour.

This differential—Mach 10 colliding with 35 mph—creates mechanical failure. The gearbox shreds itself.

In the pre-AI world, an Engineering team might deliver one major feature per sprint, implicitly granting the Legal and Compliance teams a two-week window to evaluate implications, surface conflicts, and request changes. In the AI-driven world, the same team can produce ten features in two days. The governance layers are overwhelmed by volume they were never designed to absorb. They do not receive the same exponential productivity gain, yet they are asked to validate exponentially more output.

This is why the Product Timeline Tax (PTT) is now triggered more frequently and with far greater severity. The "tax" is no longer a marginal delay measured in days or weeks. It becomes a structural blockage. Value stops flowing entirely as the governance layer is forced to erect a dam against the uncontrolled flood of AI-generated artifacts.

3.1.3 FAILURE MODES OF THE ASYMMETRY OF ACCELERATION

A. LATE-STAGE CONSTRAINT SHOCK

The Asymmetry of Acceleration expresses itself through two specific and highly destructive failure modes. The first is **Late-Stage Constraint Shock.**

In the sequential Legacy Dependency Map, constraints are evaluated last. Security reviews occur after the build is complete. Legal and regulatory compliance is checked just prior to release. This ordering assumed that creation was slow enough to justify delayed validation.

When AI accelerates code generation, artifacts reach the Zero-Sum Gate—the hard stop where strategic, legal, or security trade-offs must be resolved—far sooner and with far greater accumulated momentum.

When that review inevitably flags an issue—because the AI lacked the context to know that the newly introduced capability triggers EU AI Act obligations related to its deployment, classification, or risk controls, for example—the resulting rollback is not just a ripple; it is a tsunami.

The failure is not that the software exists, but that its **use, integration, or operational context** was never evaluated against the applicable regulatory framework before generation began.

Entire branches of work must be unwound. Dependencies must be re-evaluated. Stakeholders must be re-aligned.

The organization experiences this not as a minor delay, but as a shock event. The velocity that made the generation feel productive magnifies the pain of rejection.

B. HANDOFF CONTEXT DECAY

The second failure mode is more subtle and often more damaging over time: **Handoff Context Decay.**

In a sequential process, the Product Manager is responsible for capturing and communicating the "why" behind the software—the intent, assumptions, and trade-offs that shaped each decision. When generation occurs at AI speed, this explanatory layer cannot keep up.

The code exists, but the rationale evaporates. A Developer prompts the AI. The AI generates and commits the solution. The ticket is closed. But why was this architectural choice made? Was it selected to support future scale, regulatory flexibility, or a temporary workaround? The AI does not know, and the Developer—moving too quickly to document—cannot reliably reconstruct the reasoning later.

This is Handoff Context Decay. The organization accumulates a vast surface area of syntactically valid code while losing semantic traceability. Over time, this decay converts velocity into liability. Extensions become expensive. Refactors become risky. Re-engineering costs balloon because the original intent can no longer be recovered. Machine speed is squandered by missing meaning.

3.2 THE VELOCITY PARADOX: THE SPEED TRAP

Product organizations have long been obsessed with "velocity." It is the metric most celebrated by Agile Coaches, Scrum Masters, and Venture Capitalists alike. Burndown charts, story points, and sprint throughput became proxies for organizational health. *"Move fast and break things"* was not just a slogan of the last decade—it was treated as an operating principle.

In the era of Infinite Execution Velocity, this fixation becomes dangerous. We must confront what appears to be a contradiction but is, in fact, a structural reality: **the Velocity Paradox.**

The Velocity Paradox: In a sequential system, achieving higher execution speed **without upstream context convergence** often yields a worse outcome.

This seems counterintuitive. How can moving faster produce inferior results? If we can build the bridge in a day instead of a year, should that not be better?

The paradox emerges not from speed itself, but from **where speed is applied.** Accelerating execution while leaving discovery, constraint definition, and risk alignment downstream compresses the window for correction with little impact on end-to-end delivery time.

But speed is only beneficial when direction, placement, and structural integrity are already resolved. A bridge built in a day but placed in the wrong location is wasted capital. A bridge opened too early, before the concrete has cured, collapses under its first real load. In sequential systems, speed amplifies unresolved decisions. It does not compensate for them.

3.2.1 THE SPEED TRAP

The explanation lies in the distribution of constraints within the Legacy Dependency Map. Contextual constraints—security review, legal compliance, brand alignment, architectural coherence—are introduced only at the end of the sequential process. As a result, accelerating the middle of the system (Engineering and Content) does not accelerate delivery. It compresses the window available for correction.

When the build phase is artificially accelerated, the organization spends less time in the disciplined phases of planning, framing, and context formation. More of the system's energy is redirected toward rapid execution, and the entire process begins to hurtle toward the inevitable Zero-Sum Gate with insufficient contextual grounding.

This phenomenon is the **Speed Trap.** It is the illusion of productivity created by visible motion. Tickets move across Kanban boards at record pace. Dashboards glow green. Executives watch the "In Progress" column empty and interpret motion as success.

But this activity is not progress. It is the silent accumulation of Technical Debt, compliance exposure, and strategic misalignment. Each unexamined assumption compounds beneath the surface. The system appears healthy until it reaches the constraint.

When the compliance, security, or architectural limit is finally encountered, the Speed Trap converts velocity into loss. Failure arrives faster and costs more. Instead of failing early and cheaply—at the whiteboard, design document, or requirement stage—the organization fails late and expensively, at code-complete, audit, or launch review. Speed does not reduce risk in a sequential system; it concentrates it.

3.2.2 THE REJECTION LOOP

The most concrete and operationally painful manifestation of the Velocity Paradox is what we call the **Rejection Loop**. This loop is already visible within organizations attempting to graft AI acceleration onto the Legacy Dependency Map.

Consider a traditional Product Management flow under the Legacy Model:

Plan (two weeks): The PM defines requirements, constraints, and success criteria.

Build (four weeks): Engineers implement the solution.

Review (one week): Legal, Security, and Compliance perform evaluations.

Fix (one week): Minor adjustments are made.

Ship.

Total elapsed time: Approximately eight weeks.

Now, consider the AI-Accelerated Legacy flow:

Plan (days): The PM rushes requirements to feed the execution engine, compressing discovery and constraint gathering.

Build (days): AI-assisted engineering generates artifacts almost immediately.

Review (weeks): Legal review becomes **queue time**, not effort time. The volume overwhelms review capacity, and the build is rejected because the rushed requirements omitted a privacy constraint.

Re-Build (days): Engineers re-prompt the AI to address the rejection.

Review (weeks): Security review again becomes queue-bound. A new issue is flagged—this time due to an unvetted dependency or vulnerability.

Re-Build (days): Engineers attempt another correction.

Review (weeks): Strategic review finally intervenes, rejecting the work because market conditions or positioning shifted while the system was trapped in review loops.

Total elapsed time remains measured in months because **validation and approval operate as queues.** Frustration compounds, trust erodes, and code churn multiplies despite near-instantaneous build capability.

AI compresses the Build phase, but it does not accelerate Review. Instead, it floods Review with syntactically valid but contextually incomplete attempts. The system spends its energy spinning—producing artifacts, burning morale, and accumulating waste. The Rejection Loop generates activity, not progress. It converts speed into heat without producing forward motion.

3.2.3 THE COMPETITION'S NEW ADVANTAGE: SPEED AS DEFAULT

There is a second and often misunderstood dimension to the Velocity Paradox. While ungoverned internal speed creates chaos, **external speed has become non-negotiable.** Organizations no longer have the luxury of choosing whether to move quickly.

Prior to AI, a competitor's speed was typically the result of superior planning discipline, deeper capital reserves, or concentrated talent. If a rival beat you to market, it was because they were better resourced or better organized. Methodical execution could still win.

Today, **in many software categories**, speed has become the default market rate. The barrier to entry for rapid code generation has dropped dramatically, making fast iteration table stakes rather than a differentiator.

In these markets, any organization that continues to pay the Product Timeline Tax—by relying on manual, sequential handoffs for validation, approval, and coordination—is not merely slower. It is structurally disadvantaged relative to competitors who can absorb feedback, regulatory change, and market signals at a higher cadence.

The competitive landscape has shifted from delivering discrete launches to owning the **iteration loop**. Market advantage now accrues to the organization that can close the loop fastest between signal and response.

The market leader is no longer defined by the size or polish of the initial launch. The leader is the organization that can reliably:

Ship a minimally viable product.

Ingest real customer feedback.

Absorb regulatory or platform shifts.

Deploy the necessary correction.

The decisive advantage belongs to the organization that can complete this cycle repeatedly and with minimal friction.

A traditional Product Manager, operating inside a six-to-twelve-month sequential delivery model, cannot compete with an organization that converts market feedback into production-ready code in six to twelve days. At this point, the Legacy Model is not merely inefficient—it is existentially fragile.

Escaping this paradox does not require making the sequential process faster. That approach is already exhausted. The only viable path forward is to introduce **parallel context input**. You cannot optimize the Legacy Dependency Map to keep pace with AI. You must dismantle it and replace it with a structure designed for governed velocity.

3.3 THE BLACK BOX PROBLEM: THE NEW CONTEXT RISK

If the first systemic danger introduced by AI is the Asymmetry of Acceleration, the second—and more insidious—danger is the **Black Box Problem.** Unlike speed, this risk does not announce itself through visible chaos. It hides behind apparently successful output.

As organizations rush to adopt AI tools in an effort to eliminate the Product Timeline Tax, they frequently conflate **capability** with **comprehension.** Executives observe a compelling demo in which an AI agent generates a functional website, dashboard, or service layer in seconds and conclude that the machine has implicitly incorporated the relevant business rules, legal obligations, and strategic intent required to make that output safe.

This is a category error. The organization mistakes the machine's **Syntactic Fluency**—its ability to produce statistically coherent structures—for genuine **Semantic Understanding.**

The core risk introduced by AI velocity is therefore not speed itself, but the erosion of contextual integrity. Outputs generated by Large Language Models and AI coding systems are computationally impressive and operationally useful, yet fundamentally blind to meaning, intent, and consequence unless those elements are explicitly provided as input.

Within the Legacy Dependency Map, this blindness is guaranteed to produce failure. The system assumes that generated artifacts carry their intent with them. They do not. To understand why this mismatch is unavoidable—and why it scales catastrophically—we must step outside conventional business frameworks and return to the philosophical foundations of cognition and understanding.

3.3.1 THE IMITATION GAME: THE TRAP OF THE TURING TEST

The current crisis in product governance was anticipated more than seventy years ago. To understand why modern roadmaps are uniquely vulnerable now, we must revisit the foundational work of Alan Turing.

In 1950, Turing proposed a thought experiment he called the "Imitation Game." Its purpose was to determine whether a machine could exhibit behavior indistinguishable from that of a human. An interrogator, isolated from the respondents, would communicate solely through typed language. On the other end sat two participants —one human and one machine. If the machine could manipulate symbols well enough to consistently fool the interrogator into believing it was human, it would be deemed intelligent.

For decades, this test functioned as the benchmark of Artificial Intelligence. Passing the Turing Test was treated as the ultimate milestone—the Holy Grail of machine cognition.

By this standard, **modern Generative AI systems appear to have succeeded in many practical and commercial contexts.** They produce functional software, coherent documentation, and persuasive business communication at a level that is often indistinguishable from human output within everyday product workflows.

This performance reflects extraordinary **Syntactic Fluency**—the ability to arrange words, tokens, and code structures into statistically correct and operationally valid sequences—rather than any capacity for judgment, comprehension, or Semantic Understanding.

For the Product Manager and the Context Architect, however, the Turing Test is a dangerous illusion. It demonstrates that a machine can **speak**, not that it can **understand.** It confirms executional competence while remaining silent on judgment, intent, truth, value, and risk.

Under the Legacy Model, production implied comprehension. If a human employee could deliver the artifact—the document, the specification, the code—it was assumed they understood its implications. AI severs this assumption completely. We now operate alongside entities that are hyper-competent at production while being entirely devoid of comprehension. Treating syntactic success as Semantic Understanding is the first step toward systemic failure.

3.3.2 THE CHINESE ROOM: THE ARCHITECTURE OF BLINDNESS

To understand why this distinction has direct and unavoidable consequences for the bottom line, we must revisit John Searle's **Chinese Room Argument**, introduced earlier in this book.

In the thought experiment, the operator inside the room demonstrates perfect **Syntactic Fluency.** They manipulate symbols according to formal rules and produce responses that are indistinguishable from those of a native speaker. Yet they possess no **Semantic Understanding** of the content itself. They do not know whether they are composing a poem, issuing a declaration of war, or writing a recipe for dumplings.

The AI occupies the role of the person inside the Chinese Room. It processes the syntax of your inputs—the code blocks, Jira tickets, architectural diagrams, and user stories—with extraordinary efficiency. But it lacks semantic grounding.

It does not know what a "user" is beyond a statistical pattern.

It does not experience the "pain" of a defect in production.

It does not fear the financial, legal, or reputational consequences of a GDPR violation.

AI is a powerful syntactic processor operating without semantic integrity. Treating it as anything else introduces risk through architectural blindness.

3.3.3 THE CARTESIAN TRAP AND THE LOSS OF QUALIA

Modern AI systems operate squarely within the tradition of **Cartesian rationalism.** René Descartes argued that systematic logic and formal reasoning could produce knowledge independent of direct sensory experience. AI is the ultimate Cartesian machine: it derives output entirely from abstract patterns, correlations, and symbolic relationships embedded in its training data.

Product Management, however, does not operate in a purely

logical domain. It is irreducibly subjective. It depends on judgment, perception, and lived experience—qualities that cannot be reduced to formal rules.

This distinction was captured by philosopher Thomas Nagel through his concept of *Qualia*—the subjective character of experience that cannot be reduced to description, simulation, or statistical pattern. It is the difference between producing a correct answer and understanding what that answer means to a human being.

Syntax (The Machine): The code is efficient. The logic is internally consistent. The system passes its tests.

Qualia (The Human / Context Architect): The interface feels "cluttered." The brand voice sounds "arrogant." The feature feels "intrusive," even if it is technically correct.

These realities are not computational. They cannot be inferred reliably from syntax alone. The machine therefore falls into what we call the **Cartesian Trap:** it produces solutions that are logically valid, syntactically flawless, and yet contextually disastrous. Without explicit semantic constraints, AI optimizes for correctness while violating experience, trust, and meaning.

3.3.4 CASE STUDY: THE SEMANTIC FAILURE OF C-AUTH

To see how these philosophical distinctions translate directly into business risk, consider a concrete software scenario that now plays out daily inside AI-accelerated organizations.

The Setup: A Developer, under delivery pressure, instructs an AI agent *to "generate a new component for user authentication."* The prompt is syntactically clear and technically reasonable, but it contains no strategic or experiential context.

The Syntactic Success: The AI instantly produces a modern, syntactically correct TypeScript component, which we will call *C-Auth*. The code compiles cleanly. It follows widely adopted OAuth2 /

OpenID Connect (OIDC) authorization and authentication patterns and passes the available unit tests without error.

From a syntactic perspective, the artifact appears complete and professionally structured. In the narrow framing of the Turing Test—symbolic manipulation yielding functional output—the AI has succeeded.

The Semantic Failure: What the AI does not know—because it was never encoded into the prompt or surrounding context—is the strategic intent. The Marketing team is launching a time-sensitive pilot program the following week that depends on passwordless access for a specific cohort of beta users to reduce onboarding friction. This requirement exists only as institutional knowledge: a hallway conversation, a slide in a deck, a shared assumption—not a formal constraint.

The Consequence: Acting correctly within its limited frame, the AI enforces strict password complexity rules in C-Auth. The result is a technically secure system that quietly locks out the very users the pilot depends on.

The Developer, trusting the syntactic quality of the output, merges the code. At best, the failure is caught at the Zero-Sum Gate during launch review. At worst, it ships. The campaign underperforms. Apologies are issued. Two days of re-engineering erase the perceived gain of instant generation.

This is not an edge case. It is the default failure mode of syntactically fluent systems operating without semantic governance. The AI provides the syntax. Only the Context Architect can provide the semantics that prevent velocity from destroying intent.

3.4 THE METAMORPHOSIS: FROM TRAFFIC COP TO CONTEXT ARCHITECT

If AI increasingly generates the "**what**"—the artifacts—and the "**how**"—the code, copy, and execution—what responsibilities remain for the Product Manager?

The answer resolves to two domains the machine cannot inhabit: the "**why**" and the "**cannot.**"

In this environment, the legacy PM role—defined by ticket hygiene, status reporting, and sequential handoffs—becomes structurally obsolete. These activities are syntactic. They coordinate motion, not meaning. In an AI-accelerated system, managing the flow of work is no longer sufficient. What matters is managing the flow of intent.

This is not the elimination of the PM function, but a necessary metamorphosis. The role must evolve into the **Context Architect**—the only function capable of operating at AI velocity without losing control. The CA translates strategic business meaning, institutional constraints, and experiential judgment into structures the machine can obey.

The CA does not manage artifacts after they are produced. Their responsibility is to engineer the **convergent context** required for safe, aligned generation. This practice is called **Context Engineering**: the deliberate, multidisciplinary construction of AI input—constraints, assumptions, priorities, and prohibitions—designed to preempt semantic blind spots before execution begins.

3.4.1 THE CONTEXT ARCHITECT AS SEMANTIC REGULATOR

This transformation redefines leadership as **Semantic Regulation.** Instead of inspecting artifacts after they are produced—as required by the Legacy Model—the Semantic Regulator establishes the boundaries within which generation is allowed to occur. Governance moves upstream, from audit to design, where leverage is highest and failure is cheapest.

In the Legacy Model, the Product Manager functions as a **Traffic Cop.** They stand at the intersection, direct flow, intervene after violations, and attempt to prevent collisions in real time. This role assumes that the roads already exist and that mistakes are inevitable. Control is exercised through vigilance rather than structure.

In the AI era, the Context Architect becomes a **Civil Engineer.** They design the roads, install the guardrails, and set the speed limits in advance so that traffic—the AI—can move at maximum velocity without crashing. Control is achieved structurally, not reactively, by constraining what the system is allowed to generate rather than policing what it has already produced.

This identity shift is operational. The Context Architect executes this role by regulating three distinct vectors of context, each of which converts post-hoc review into preemptive governance.

Vector 1: Regulating Legal Risk (The "Cannot")

Under the Legacy Dependency Map, compliance functions as a barrier at the end of the road. In the Context Architect's model, compliance becomes a guardrail installed at the beginning.

The CA ensures that AI generation respects legal, regulatory, and security thresholds before any code or copy is written. By enforcing the Constraint & Compliance Layer, they neutralize downstream rejection events in advance rather than colliding with them after commitment.

The Problem: An AI-powered chatbot generates a response that implicitly promises a refund policy in violation of the company's Terms of Service.

The Context Architect's Action: They do not edit the output. They modify the input. The System Prompt—encoded within the Context Schema—is updated with a non-negotiable directive: "*You must not generate financial commitments or modify Terms of Service.*"

The Result: The risk is eliminated at the source. The system is governed through input constraints rather than downstream correction.

VECTOR 2: REGULATING TECHNICAL DEBT (THE "HOW")

AI systems are structurally prone to generating code that is *convenient*, *modern*, and *locally correct*, yet globally unmaintainable. They default to patterns that appear frequently in their training data, often ignoring the idiosyncrasies, constraints, and historical compromises embedded in real production systems. Legacy architectures, undocumented conventions, and institutional scar tissue are invisible unless explicitly surfaced.

The Context Architect counters this tendency by enforcing the **Technical Dependency Layer**. This layer encodes architectural rules, approved patterns, and system boundaries directly into the AI's operating context, ensuring that generated components are not merely functional, but compatible with the existing system. Late-stage technical rework is eliminated by making architectural reality non-optional at generation time.

The Problem: An AI agent generates a Python service that relies on a third-party library the organization's Security team banned three months earlier due to a critical vulnerability. The code is syntactically correct and passes local tests, but it violates a hard technical constraint.

The Context Architect's Action: They do not rely on downstream review to catch the violation. Instead, they maintain a dynamic **Allowed / Banned Dependency Registry** within the AI's retrieval and constraint context. This registry is consulted automatically during generation.

The Result: The AI validates dependencies against the constraint *before* writing code. Prohibited libraries are never proposed. Technical Debt is prevented structurally, not discovered reactively.

VECTOR 3: REGULATING MARKET ALIGNMENT (THE "WHY")

Of the three vectors, market alignment is the most difficult to regulate because it is the most fluid. Strategy evolves. Positioning shifts. Tone, language, and emphasis change in response to competitive pressure, regulatory signals, and customer feedback. Unlike legal or technical constraints, market intent is not binary.

The CA addresses this volatility by enforcing the Strategic Context Layer. This layer encodes the organization's current strategic posture—its target customers, competitive positioning, value propositions, and experiential goals—directly into the AI's generation context. By doing so, it eliminates Marketing Lag and prevents the slow decay that occurs when execution outpaces strategic alignment.

The Problem: An AI system generates product descriptions that are factually correct and technically precise, yet read as sterile and academic. The content satisfies functional requirements but fails to express the organization's newly adopted "playful" brand voice, undermining differentiation.

The Context Architect's Action: Rather than rewriting outputs manually, the CA injects explicit Brand Voice & Tone Guidelines along with defined Persona Qualia into the generation context. These inputs translate subjective intent—how the product should *feel*—into constraints the machine can respect.

The Result: The output is born aligned. Content emerges on-brand by construction, not by revision. Market intent is preserved at generation time, preventing drift without sacrificing velocity.

3.4.2 PREEMPTIVE SEMANTIC GUARDRAILS

The defining characteristic of the Context Architect is **pre-emption.** Control is exercised before execution, not after failure.

The Legacy Product Manager asks: "*Does this code meet the requirements?*"

The Context Architect asks a fundamentally different question: "*Does the AI possess sufficient context to generate the requirements correctly?*"

This distinction marks the collapse of downstream inspection as a viable control mechanism. Waiting for a manual audit—whether legal, security, or strategic—recreates the sequential bottlenecks of the Legacy Model and guarantees collision with the Zero-Sum Gate.

Instead, the Context Architect ensures that the AI is supplied with the complete semantic frame *before* generation begins. Assumptions, prohibitions, priorities, and intent are encoded upstream so that syntactic execution unfolds within defined boundaries.

This shift—from reacting to contextually blind output to engineering context-aware input—is the core architectural transformation required for modern product organizations to operate safely with Infinite Execution Velocity.

3.5 THE COST OF SEMANTIC BLINDNESS

Why does this matter? Why can't we simply allow AI to build at speed and correct mistakes later?

Because in an exponential system, **errors scale exponentially.**

The Legacy Dependency Map was designed to absorb *linear* failure. When a human made a mistake, it tended to be localized—one misunderstanding in one document, one defect in one feature. The cost of correction was painful but bounded.

AI changes the error profile entirely. A semantic flaw introduced at the prompt or context layer is no longer an isolated mistake. It becomes a **systemic infection** propagated across every artifact the machine generates.

If an AI agent is used to generate 500 unit tests and it carries a subtle misunderstanding of the testing protocol, the organization inherits 500 structurally flawed tests. Remediation is no longer linear. It is multiplicative.

This dynamic produces what we call the **Semantic Debt Spiral:**

Generation: AI produces massive volumes of output carrying an undetected semantic flaw.

Illusion: The volume is misread as progress, reinforcing the Velocity Paradox.

Discovery: The flaw is eventually surfaced at the Zero-Sum Gate—through security review, compliance audit, or production failure.

Collapse: The cost to unwind hundreds of artifacts exceeds the cost of manual creation many times over.

The Context Architect exists to arrest this spiral before it begins. By investing time in **Context Engineering** upfront, the organization prevents exponential debt accumulation. It pays the tax of context early—at the input layer—to avoid paying the vastly higher tax of rework later, when the system has already scaled the mistake.

3.6 CONCLUSION: THE GUARDRAILS OF TOMORROW

The era of the "generalist Product Manager" is ending. The ability to write tickets, run stand-ups, update dashboards, and maintain Gantt charts is no longer a defensible skill set. These activities are syntactic coordination tasks, and syntactic labor is precisely what machines now perform at superhuman scale.

The future belongs to the **Context Architect**. It belongs to those who can grasp the **Semantic Truth** of their organization—the legal obligations it must obey, the strategic intent it must preserve, and the subjective realities its users experience—and translate that truth into constraints the machine can enforce.

This shift marks a fundamental change in how systems are governed. We are moving from a world of **Output Management**, where artifacts are inspected after the fact, to a world of **Input Regulation**, where behavior is shaped before execution begins.

In the next chapter, we will leave abstraction behind and enter the machine itself. We will define the **architecture of context**, specifying how legal, technical, and strategic constraint layers are constructed and composed so that Infinite Execution Velocity can be harnessed without destabilizing the system.

We spent the last decade asking machines to sound human. The work ahead is more difficult and more important. It is time to teach machines what it means to **serve** humanity.

4

CONTEXT ENGINEERING: BEYOND THE PROMPT

The transition from Output Management to Input Regulation cannot remain conceptual. It must be formalized. If velocity is now effectively infinite, then the stability of the organization depends entirely on the quality of its governing inputs. This chapter defines the architectural discipline required to construct those inputs, distinguishing tactical interaction from structural control.

4.1 THE GREAT MISCONCEPTION: WHY "PROMPT ENGINEERING" IS A TRAP

The speed introduced by Generative AI is not a problem to be solved. It is a force to be governed. As organizations rush to integrate Large Language Models (LLMs) into their workflows, a dangerous misconception has taken hold—particularly within the C-suite and HR departments responsible for defining future capability. The belief is simple and deeply flawed: that the critical skill of the AI era is "**prompt engineering.**" This belief now appears in job descriptions, LinkedIn certifications, internal training programs, and technology blogs. The industry has convinced itself that success lies in discovering the perfect incantation—the precise sequence of words that will unlock the machine's intelligence.

This belief is a category error. Attempting to operate a product organization through prompt engineering is equivalent to trying to construct a skyscraper by hiring an exceptionally talented bricklayer while dismissing the architect. Tactical excellence cannot substitute for structural design.

Prompt engineering is, by definition, a tactical act. It involves crafting a single, localized request to produce a specific output: "*Write a Python script to sort a list.*" It is linear. It is isolated. It occupies one step in a sequential chain of thought. When it fails, it fails silently by omission: the constraint that mattered was simply never mentioned.

Context Engineering, by contrast, is a strategic, upstream discipline. It is the deliberate design and validation of a comprehensive, structured input framework that governs all subsequent generation. The difference is architectural intent. It is the difference between asking a stranger to "buy milk" and equipping a professional shopper with dietary restrictions, budget limits, brand preferences, allergy constraints, and a map of the store.

Accelerating product organizations repeatedly confuse these two activities. They hire for the ability to *speak* to the machine, when what they require is the ability to **govern** the machine. This confusion is not harmless. It guarantees downstream failure at scale.

4.1.1 THE INPUT / OUTPUT ASYMMETRY

The necessity of Context Engineering emerges from a fundamental and under-appreciated property of Large Language Models: the extreme asymmetry between the effort required to provide input and the volume of output the system can generate in response.

In human-to-human collaboration, vague input triggers resistance. If a Developer receives a one-sentence requirement devoid of clarity, they respond with questions. Ambiguity slows execution and forces clarification before work proceeds. Human systems are naturally self-throttling.

AI systems behave in precisely the opposite manner. When given a vague, one-sentence request, the machine does not ask "*Are you sure?*" or "*What do you mean?*" It executes immediately and produces an explosion of artifacts: hundreds of lines of code, a multi-step marketing plan, architectural diagrams, and database schemas—each syntactically plausible and collectively ungoverned.

This behavior is a direct consequence of **Infinite Execution**

Velocity. The AI does not reason about intent; it extrapolates statistically. It generates what is *most likely* to follow, not what is *most appropriate* to the business context. When a Product Manager (PM) behaves as a Prompt Engineer—issuing tactical requests into this system—they initiate a flood of high-volume, context-blind output that inevitably collides with the Zero-Sum Gate downstream.

The Context Architect (CA) exists to prevent this outcome. They recognize that when output is effectively infinite, input becomes the primary control surface. Precision at the front of the system replaces inspection at the back. The CA does not write better prompts. They construct the **Context Schema**—the governing input structure that constrains, directs, and stabilizes everything the machine produces.

4.1.2 THE ANATOMY OF A DISCIPLINE

To understand why the Context Architect represents a necessary evolution of the Product Manager role, we must make a rigorous distinction between two fundamentally different disciplines that are often mistakenly conflated.

The Prompt Engineer (Tactical / Sequential)

Goal: Generate a specific, functional output in response to a localized request.

Method: Iterative guessing and reactive refinement—"*Make it shorter.*" "*Make it more professional.*" "*Fix the bug.*"

Scope: A single task operating within a single silo of the organization.

Primary Failure Mode: The AI produces output that functions correctly in isolation while violating a legal, security, or strategic constraint that was never encoded into the prompt. The failure is discovered downstream.

The Context Architect (Strategic / Parallel)

Goal: Ensure that all syntactically correct output is also semantically aligned with business reality.

Method: Preemptive structure through deliberate schema design.

Scope: The entire **Stacked Product Lifecycle**, spanning strategy, compliance, engineering, and go-to-market execution simultaneously.

Primary Failure Mode: Errors are surfaced during schema construction, before any generation occurs. Failure is contained at the design stage, not the delivery stage.

The traditional Product Manager operated as an administrative coordinator—brokering handoffs, tracking progress, and managing dependencies in a world governed by human velocity. That function does not survive Infinite Execution Velocity.

4.2 THE PHYSICS OF CONSTRAINT: GOVERNING THE MACHINE

The most powerful prompt in the AI era is not a command. It is a **constraint.**

This reality runs directly counter to decades of conventional management doctrine. In human systems, leaders are taught to encourage "blue-sky thinking" and to remove constraints in order to unlock creativity. Constraints are treated as obstacles to innovation rather than as prerequisites for it.

AI inverts this logic completely. The machine is already pure generative capacity. It recombines symbols at scale, producing endless variations without fatigue, doubt, or judgment. Left unconstrained, this engine of **Syntactic Fluency** does not explore possibilities—it explodes them. The result is hallucinated facts, invented case law, brittle architectures, and uncontrolled spending.

The strategic power of Context Engineering lies in the Context Architect's ability to define the **boundaries** within which generation is allowed to occur. Context Engineering is therefore not the art of instruction, but the **art of restriction**—the deliberate shaping of reality so that infinite creativity resolves into coherent, governable output.

4.2.1 THE PATH OF LEAST RESISTANCE

We must anchor our understanding in the machine's core limitation: **Semantic Blindness.** The AI does not *know* your business, your market, or your risk profile. It has no internal model of consequence. It operates solely by predicting the statistically most likely next token in a sequence.

Because the AI is a system of extreme **Syntactic Fluency** coupled with total Semantic Blindness, it will always default to the path of least resistance—the statistical average embedded in its training data.

Ask an AI to *"write a privacy policy,"* and it will dutifully synthesize the mean of thousands of generic policies it has seen before. The resulting document will look professional, comprehensive, and compliant at a glance. Yet it will almost certainly omit the precise obligations created by your biometric data pipeline, jurisdictional exposure, or novel data flows. The output is syntactically flawless and operationally dangerous.

The Context Architect's strategic value lies in preventing this failure mode. By defining explicit guardrails—constraints, exclusions, and priorities—they force the machine away from the statistical average and onto the narrow path of the organization's actual business reality. Without these guardrails, AI does not innovate. It merely averages.

4.2.2 THE FOUR PILLARS OF GOVERNANCE

The shift from administrative coordination to machine governance fundamentally alters the daily function of the role. The Context Architect does not manage work as it moves downstream. They govern behavior at the point of generation. This governance is exercised through four distinct and repeatable techniques of constraint.

A. GUARDRAILS AS THE PROMPT

Within the Legacy Dependency Map, constraints exist as late-stage checkpoints. A requirement such as "*The new feature must be GDPR compliant*" is appended to a ticket, implemented by Engineering, and evaluated weeks later by Compliance. The constraint arrives after value has already been invested.

In the Context Engineering model, the constraint *is* the prompt. Governance is not applied after execution; it is embedded directly into the request itself.

The Context Architect does not request output and then perform an audit. They embed the audit logic into the generation process.

Traditional PM: "Engineering, build the new login feature. QA, test it."

CA: "Act as a Compliance Officer. We are sending automated SMS messages via an integrated messaging channel. Draft specific 'Opt-In' UI consent language for the Lead Form that satisfies TCPA statutory requirements and A2P 10DLC carrier compliance obligations, including user consent, disclosure, and opt-out language."

By forcing the AI to assume a regulated role and operate within named legal frameworks, the Context Architect creates a deliberately **hostile environment for error.** The system cannot generate a response without first reasoning through the constraint. Compliance is no longer a downstream judgment; it is an upstream condition.

This architectural shift neutralizes the Zero-Sum Gate. The decision to ship or kill is no longer deferred to the end of the process. It is dissolved into the beginning, where failure is cheap and contained.

B. STRATEGIC VISION AS A MACHINE INPUT

Constraints are not exclusively prohibitive. They are also **directional.** In addition to defining what the system cannot do, they specify where the system must go.

The Context Architect applies this principle by translating

abstract strategic intent into machine-enforceable direction. Techniques such as structured role assignment and **Blue Ocean Analysis** are used to constrain the solution space in advance.

A tactical prompt such as "*brainstorm new features*" predictably yields generic output. It invites the machine to average across its training data and produce incremental variations on what already exists.

The CA replaces this ambiguity with an explicit strategic mandate:

"*Act as a Product Strategist. Analyze the current ACME Co feature set against traditional call centers and self-serve tools. Identify three Blue Ocean features that would render the existing competitive landscape irrelevant.*"

This instruction does not ask for creativity. It explicitly rules out incremental improvements. By encoding differentiation as a constraint, the Context Architect prevents the AI from proposing feature parity solutions. The system is forced away from the path of least resistance and toward strategic novelty governed by intent rather than accident.

C. TECHNICAL LIMITS AND SECURITY MODELING

The most expensive component of the Product Timeline Tax (PTT) is not delay—it is **Technical Debt.** This is code that appears functional in the short term but collapses under scale, security scrutiny, or integration pressure over time.

Preventing this debt requires exposing the machine to the full, unvarnished truth of the organization's technical reality. AI systems do not intuit fragility. They do not infer undocumented constraints. If a legacy database is brittle, if a service boundary is overloaded, or if a security model is non-standard, the AI will remain unaware unless those facts are made explicit.

Context Engineering operationalizes this truth through deliberate technical framing. For example:

"Analyze the current architecture for the 'AI Bot Agent.' This system processes PII (Personally Identifiable Information). Identify the top three OWASP vulnerabilities associated with client-side AI implementations and propose a backend-for-frontend (BFF) mitigation strategy."

This is a demand for preemptive system modeling. The AI is forced to reason about threat surfaces, data flow, and architectural limits before a single line of production code exists.

Executed consistently, this approach transforms the Engineering Stack. Reactive patching is replaced with anticipatory design. Technical Debt is no longer discovered through failure; it is neutralized through context.

D. PARALLEL REVIEW THROUGH SIMULATION

The final pillar of governance is parallel review through simulation.

In the Legacy Model, validation is slow because it depends on coordinating real people across calendars, departments, and incentives. User research, stakeholder review, and cross-functional feedback unfold sequentially over weeks, often after the artifact is already largely complete.

The Context Architect exploits a structural advantage of AI: its ability to simulate multiple, distinct evaluative perspectives simultaneously. Instead of waiting for feedback, the CA forces early signal detection upstream.

For example:

"Simulate a focus group reviewing the Dashboard. Participants: (1) a tech-savvy e-commerce founder, (2) a traditional brick-and-mortar business owner, and (3) an enterprise operations leader. Have them critique the 'Keyword Planner' feature, including usability concerns, perceived value, and objections."

This approach is a pre-validation constraint mechanism. It complements real user evidence rather than replacing it. By injecting diverse evaluative frames before finalization, the Context Architect exposes semantic weaknesses, misaligned assumptions, and messaging risk while change is still cheap.

The result is structural compression of validation time—not by eliminating real review, but by reducing late-stage surprises. Multiple work streams—design, product, and go-to-market—can converge on shared understanding before the artifact is completed. Review no longer follows execution; it runs in parallel with it.

4.2.3 THE SEMANTIC INTERPRETER

The Context Architect is not defined by technical specialization. They are not necessarily Coders, and they are rarely Lawyers. Their value lies elsewhere. They are **Semantic Interpreters.**

This role exists to translate the totality of the business—its philosophy, institutional memory, legal obligations, risk posture, and economic constraints—into a form the machine can obey. This translation must be precise, explicit, and structurally complete.

The output of this translation is the **Context Schema**. This schema is not an enhanced prompt or a verbose document. It is a governing data artifact that encodes meaning as constraint.

Once constructed, the Context Schema functions as the **Master Prompt.** It governs the simultaneous operation of the entire **Stacked Product Lifecycle**, ensuring that engineering output, marketing artifacts, compliance posture, and strategic intent are aligned at the point of generation rather than reconciled after the fact.

4.3 THE STRATEGIC GAP: MOVING FROM TOKEN MANAGEMENT TO TAX ELIMINATION

As organizations scramble to respond to the AI era, a working definition of **Context Engineering** has begun to solidify within technical and developer-centric communities. While this definition is not wrong, it is profoundly incomplete. It focuses on implementation mechanics while leaving a strategic vacuum that only the Context Architect can fill.

Most current publications, training programs, and self-appointed "experts" frame Context Engineering as a systems discipline centered on **token management**. Their emphasis is on the plumbing required to keep AI applications operational: expanding or optimizing the context window, mitigating **Context Rot** as conversations grow longer, and improving retrieval fidelity through techniques such as **RAG (Retrieval-Augmented Generation).**

These efforts are necessary, but they are insufficient. By treating Context Engineering as a data delivery problem, this perspective creates a dangerous blind spot. It implicitly assumes that if the right information can be delivered to the model at the right time, correct outcomes will follow automatically.

This assumption fails to account for the central challenge of AI governance: **data does not equal meaning.** Without strategic interpretation, constraints, and prioritization, even perfectly retrieved information can produce outcomes that are syntactically correct and strategically disastrous. Token management stabilizes systems. It does not eliminate the Product Timeline Tax. Only governance does.

4.3.1 THE SEMANTIC BLIND SPOT OF TOKEN MANAGEMENT

The industry's technical obsession with token management suffers from the same structural flaw identified in Chapter 3: it confuses technical consistency with business truth. High retrieval accuracy and coherent summarization demonstrate Syntactic Fluency, not Semantic Understanding. This distinction is not academic. It is a direct descendant of the Chinese Room Argument.

Much of what is currently labeled "Context Engineering" is designed to help AI systems pass a narrow version of the Turing Test for information retrieval. The objective is to ensure the machine can correctly manipulate symbols—tokens, code fragments, policy text—according to the rules it has been given. When measured in isolation, these systems perform impressively.

Consider an AI optimized exclusively for token delivery. It may retrieve and summarize a compliance document with perfect fidelity, achieving exemplary retrieval-quality performance (commonly measured through RAG evaluation metrics such as retrieval accuracy or grounding rate). From a narrow technical perspective, the system is functioning exactly as intended.

Yet this same system remains incapable of interpreting the Legacy Dependency Map. It cannot infer that newly generated code will destabilize a three-year-old, mission-critical API unless that consequence is explicitly encoded as a contextual or architectural constraint rather than left as an implicit organizational assumption.

The Context Architect reframes this discipline entirely. By constructing and enforcing the **Context Schema**, they inject legal, technical, and strategic meaning into the Master Prompt *before* any generation occurs. This act supplies Semantic Understanding—the implications and constraints that give symbols consequence.

The result is a fundamental shift in purpose. Context Engineering ceases to be a matter of moving tokens efficiently and becomes a mechanism for eliminating the PTT through governance rather than optimization.

4.3.2 THE INSTANTANEOUS REALIZATION PARADOX

The most immediate danger introduced by the AI era is not technical. It is behavioral. Generative AI has created what we call the **Instantaneous Realization Paradox:** the ability to move from abstract ideation to a tangible, visual artifact—code, wireframe, or campaign copy—almost immediately.

In the human-velocity world, realization was expensive. Seeing the project come together required weeks of coordinated effort. Because realization was difficult, preparation was respected. Specifications existed because building the wrong thing carried visible and irreversible costs.

In an AI-enabled world, realization is effectively free. When a traditional Product Manager watches Engineering generate a functional wireframe or working prototype in under an hour, the instinctive response is to privilege visible output. Syntactic Fluency feels like progress, and momentum becomes psychologically difficult to interrupt.

This instant gratification—the ability to see an idea rendered, tested, or marketed in minutes—exerts a powerful pull toward skipping foundational context assembly. The implicit question becomes: *Why write a strategy document when the application is already running on localhost?*

The paradox is that the speed of realization scales the cost of omission. The faster an idea becomes visible, the stronger the temptation to bypass parallel, multi-stack context gathering. The faster an artifact is produced, the more rapidly it advances through the sequential system—accelerating its eventual collision with the Zero-Sum Gate.

The Context Architect's role begins by regulating this velocity. Their responsibility is not to slow execution arbitrarily, but to enforce the discipline of the **Context Schema** so that what is realized is not merely fast, but structurally sound.

4.4 THE BLUEPRINT: THE CONTEXT SCHEMA

The Context Schema is a convergent input system deliberately designed to preempt and resolve the most common points of friction embedded within the sequential product lifecycle.

Rather than scattering intent across slide decks, tickets, and tribal knowledge, the Context Schema consolidates non-negotiable context into a single governing artifact. Legal constraints, strategic intent, technical reality, and experiential goals are unified *before* execution begins.

This schema replaces the pile of disconnected requirement documents by ensuring that every functional expert's essential context is present at the moment of generation. The Context Architect's primary strategic responsibility is to enforce the completion and validation of its four mandatory layers for every product initiative. Without a complete schema, execution is structurally prohibited.

LAYER 1: THE STRATEGIC CONTEXT LAYER (THE "WHY" AND "WHO")

The Strategic Context Layer supplies the AI with the core **Semantic Understanding** of both the market and the user. Its purpose is to prevent the most common and costly failure mode of accelerated systems: the creation of features that are technically flawless yet commercially irrelevant.

This layer synthesizes the elements that define *why* the product should exist and *who* it is for. It consolidates **Persona Simulation Data** (who are we building for?), **Blue Ocean Analysis** (how is this meaningfully different?), target pricing assumptions, and product-specific Value Proposition statements into a unified strategic frame.

By injecting the "Why" upstream, this layer eliminates Marketing Lag and the portion of the Product Timeline Tax caused by misaligned positioning. When the same semantic source of truth governs both generation streams, marketing artifacts and product code converge naturally rather than being reconciled after the fact.

The mandate of the Context Architect at this layer is synthesis. They serve as the semantic translator between leadership vision and Product Marketing expertise, converting abstract market intent into explicit, machine-actionable inputs. Without this translation, strategy remains aspirational and execution defaults to statistical averages.

LAYER 2: THE CONSTRAINT & COMPLIANCE LAYER (THE "CANNOT" AND "MUST")

The Constraint & Compliance Layer is the most critical element of the Context Schema because it directly neutralizes the **Zero-Sum Gate**. It ensures that AI execution occurs inside a non-negotiable framework of legal, security, ethical, and brand constraints *before* any artifact is produced.

This layer codifies the organization's hard boundaries. It includes regulatory obligations such as GDPR, TCPA, and sector-specific requirements; security standards and audit frameworks like the

OWASP Top 10; liability limitations; data handling rules; and brand safety parameters that define reputational risk. These constraints are not advisory. They are structural.

By embedding these boundaries upstream, the Context Architect converts compliance from a downstream checkpoint into a prerequisite for generation. The AI is not evaluated for compliance after the fact—it is incapable of producing non-compliant output because the constraints form the walls of its operating reality.

The mandate of the Context Architect at this layer is translation. They act as the Semantic Interpreter for Legal, Security, and Compliance Subject Matter Experts (SMEs), converting institutional "Lawyer speak" and audit language into explicit, enforceable system constraints. Without this translation, governance remains implicit and failure is guaranteed.

LAYER 3: THE TECHNICAL DEPENDENCY LAYER (THE "HOW" AND "LIMITS")

The Technical Dependency Layer governs *how* the AI is permitted to execute and the hard limits within which it must operate. Its purpose is to ensure that rapid generation results in systems that are architecturally coherent, operationally viable, and maintainable over time. Without this layer, speed simply converts into Technical Debt.

This layer encodes the physical reality of the organization's technology. It explicitly references the **Legacy Dependency Map**, approved and prohibited tech stacks, service boundaries, database constraints, infrastructure limitations, and performance budgets.

By enforcing these dependencies upstream, the Context Architect prevents the most common form of AI-induced rework: syntactically elegant solutions that cannot survive contact with the real system. The AI is prevented from hallucinating a Python microservice inside a strict Java ecosystem, or proposing cloud-native abstractions that violate latency, cost, or compliance constraints.

The friction eliminated by this layer is substantial. Engineering rework driven by architectural mismatch is one of the largest contributors to the Product Timeline Tax. By embedding technical truth into the Context Schema, the Context Architect stops this tax at the source.

The mandate at this layer is synthesis. The CA works with Engineering SMEs to translate tacit architectural knowledge into explicit constraints, ensuring that AI generation respects the non-negotiable structure of the codebase rather than overwriting it.

LAYER 4: THE OUTPUT FORMAT LAYER (THE "STRUCTURE")

The Output Format Layer governs *structure*. Its role is to ensure that AI-generated artifacts are immediately consumable by downstream systems and teams without translation, reformatting, or manual intervention. In an AI-accelerated environment, ambiguity of structure is a hidden tax.

This layer specifies the exact, machine-readable formats required for every class of output. It defines whether results must be delivered as JSON objects, OpenAPI specifications, TypeScript interfaces, Figma components, policy documents, or other formally structured artifacts. It also mandates the metadata schemas that allow one stack's output to function as another stack's input.

By enforcing structural precision at generation time, this layer eliminates a major source of invisible friction: manual data reshaping. Engineering output becomes immediately consumable by Quality Assurance (QA) automation. Product specifications flow directly into marketing systems. Parallel execution becomes mechanically possible rather than aspirational.

When combined with the other three layers, the Output Format Layer completes the Context Schema. Together, these four layers transform the traditional Product Manager's administrative checklist into a governance framework designed for the AI era—one that enables simultaneous execution without sacrificing coherence or control.

4.5 THE STRATEGIC WORKFLOW: ELIMINATING THE FRICTION CYCLE

The distinction between the traditional Product Manager and the Context Architect is not cosmetic. It is a difference in function, leverage, and economic outcome. The traditional PM manages the Friction Cycle. The Context Architect eliminates it.

In the Legacy Model, friction is treated as an operational nuisance to be mitigated through coordination, escalation, and process refinement. In the Context Architecture model, friction is treated as a design flaw to be removed structurally.

To understand the magnitude of this shift, it is not sufficient to describe it abstractly. We must visualize the operational reality of the system *before* and *after* Context Engineering is introduced.

4.5.1 THE SEQUENTIAL PM'S FRICTION CYCLE

In the legacy operating system, a product feature launch is not a linear progression toward value. It is a recurring battle against the compounding forces of delay, misalignment, and rework.

The Requirement Handoff: The Product Manager delivers specifications to Engineering. By definition, the artifact is incomplete. Nuance, intent, and implicit constraints are lost in translation, initiating **Handoff Context Decay** at the very first step.

Isolated Development: Engineering proceeds with high **Syntactic Fluency** but limited semantic context. The team builds efficiently, yet blindly—optimizing for correctness within a partial frame of reference.

The Zero-Sum Gate Trigger: Weeks later, the feature arrives at Legal, Compliance, or Security review. Constraints that were absent upstream finally surface downstream, where change is expensive and politically fraught.

The Crash: A Subject Matter Expert identifies a violation—legal, regulatory, or architectural—caused not by incompetence, but by missing context. The system triggers the **Zero-Sum Gate** again, forcing an all-or-nothing decision.

The Rollback: The organization enters the Rejection Loop. Time, morale, and engineering effort are consumed to unwind work that never should have been produced. The full financial and temporal weight of the PTT is realized.

This cycle repeats predictably, amplifying Context Decay, eroding trust between teams, and extending delivery timelines by months.

4.5.2 THE CONTEXT ARCHITECT'S CONVERGENT WORKFLOW

The Context Architect replaces the legacy sequence of reactive steps with a single proactive, structural intervention: **Context Engineering.** Rather than waiting for the Zero-Sum Gate to appear downstream, the system is designed to neutralize it *before* execution begins.

This operating model is defined by **Mandatory Convergence.** No artifact is permitted to enter generation until all governing context has been assembled and validated.

Simultaneous Constraint Assembly: The Context Architect facilitates the concurrent input of all functional constraints—legal, market, and technical—into the Context Schema. These inputs are gathered in parallel, eliminating the staggered handoffs that produce Context Decay.

Schema Enforcement: All relevant Subject Matter Experts review, lock, and approve the Context Schema *before* the artifact is allowed to enter the AI Studio. Execution is structurally prohibited until semantic completeness is achieved.

Parallel Execution: Once approved, the complete Context Schema is supplied as a single governing input. This launches all development streams simultaneously—the Engineering Stack, the Marketing Stack, and the QA Stack—without sacrificing alignment.

Convergence: Because identical semantic guardrails govern every stream, outputs converge naturally. The code matches the copy. The copy matches the law. The law matches the technical reality.

In this model, the Zero-Sum Gate no longer functions as a point of existential risk. It is reduced to a procedural formality. The Product Timeline Tax is structurally eliminated.

4.5.3 QUANTIFYING THE PTT ELIMINATION

This shift is not a marginal process improvement. It is a structural and financial transformation. In multi-team, cross-functional product lifecycles—particularly those involving platform dependencies, security reviews, legal approvals, or regulatory exposure—the PTT routinely dominates elapsed calendar time. Large portions of the schedule are lost not to engineering effort, but to rework, waiting, queue time, and sequential reconciliation across governance boundaries.

By eliminating the need for downstream Zero-Sum Gate rollbacks, the Context Architect produces an immediate and measurable reduction in this tax. In governance-heavy environments, organizations consistently recover weeks to months of time-to-market by preventing rework before it begins rather than correcting it after the fact. The exact magnitude varies by organizational maturity and risk profile, but the directional effect is stable: delivery timelines compress when governance latency is eliminated upstream.

In the next chapter, this model becomes operational. We will define the Stacked Product Lifecycle—the execution framework that replaces Agile coordination with parallel, context-governed execution for the AI age.

4.6 THE PROTOCOL OF EXTRACTION: MINING FOR SEMANTIC GOLD

The Context Schema is the governing artifact—but it does not emerge spontaneously. It must be **mined.**

The primary challenge facing the Context Architect is not technical complexity. It is human opacity. Subject Matter Experts—General Counsel, CISOs, Heads of Sales, and Senior Operators—

carry immense **Semantic Understanding** in their heads, yet they rarely express this knowledge as explicit rules. Their expertise lives as intuition, precedent, and unspoken constraint—what organizations commonly refer to as "tribal knowledge."

When asked directly, this knowledge collapses into vagueness. Ask a General Counsel for the legal constraints of a feature and the response is often, "*Just make sure it's compliant.*" This answer is harmless in a human system. In an AI system, it is catastrophic. Fed into generation, it produces hallucination. Embedded into a Context Schema, it produces systemic failure.

For this reason, the Context Architect must master what we call the **Protocol of Extraction.** This is a structured mode of interrogation designed to convert implicit human judgment into explicit, enforceable machine logic.

Mastery of this protocol transforms the Context Architect's role. They cease to be a passive recorder of requirements and become an active Semantic Miner—responsible for excavating truth from human expertise and refining it into constraints the machine can obey.

4.6.1 THE ASSUMPTION TRAP

Subject Matter Experts are constrained by a well-documented cognitive bias: the Curse of Knowledge. Once a fact becomes internalized, it becomes invisible. Experts assume that what is obvious to them is obvious to everyone—including the machine.

A Lawyer assumes it is self-evident that *user data cannot leave the EU*. An Engineer assumes everyone understands that the legacy API is rate-limited to one hundred calls per minute. These assumptions are rational in human systems. They are fatal in machine systems.

The AI knows none of this. It does not infer context. It does not inherit institutional memory. It starts from zero every time.

To overcome this structural blindness, the Context Architect must replace Brainstorming with Constraint Storming.

Brainstorming (Legacy): "What could we build?"—expansive, imaginative, and dangerously permissive when paired with AI.

Constraint Storming (Context Architect): "What breaks the system?"—reductive, defensive, and safe for Infinite Execution Velocity.

By systematically identifying failure conditions, the Context Architect converts silent assumptions into explicit guardrails that the machine can obey.

4.6.2 THE THREE-STEP EXTRACTION TECHNIQUE

To construct a reliable Constraint & Compliance Layer, the Context Architect applies a disciplined, repeatable **three-step extraction process** with every Subject Matter Expert. This process is designed to surface implicit risk, anticipate machine failure modes, and encode human judgment as enforceable structure.

Step 1: The "Kill Switch" Question

The objective is to surface non-negotiable failure states. Instead of asking for requirements, the Context Architect asks how the system can catastrophically fail.

Bad Question: *"What should the security protocols be?"*

The Kill Switch Question: *"If I wanted to get fired immediately by launching this feature, what specific rule would I have to break?"*

This framing bypasses abstraction. It forces the SME to name the exact boundary that must never be crossed.

SME Response: *"If you store credit card numbers in the logs, we'd be sued instantly."*

Schema Entry: *CONSTRAINT: Logging of PII or PAN data is strictly prohibited under all conditions.*

Step 2: The "Hallucination Check"

This step anticipates the AI's default behavior: selecting the statistically easiest solution. The Context Architect asks the SME to identify why that path fails in the organization's specific environment.

Prompt: *"If an AI attempts to solve this problem using standard libraries or best practices, why will that approach fail here?"*

SME Response: *"Standard libraries assume REST, but our core banking ledger still operates on a legacy SOAP interface."*

Schema Entry: ***TECHNICAL CONSTRAINT:*** *All ledger interactions must use the SOAP protocol. REST-based access is prohibited.*

Step 3: The "Persona Calibration"

Facts alone do not capture intent. To construct the Strategic Context Layer, the Context Architect must extract qualitative judgment—the words, tones, and claims that are unacceptable.

Prompt: *"If you were reviewing this customer-facing copy, what specific words or phrases would immediately raise concern?"*

SME Response: *"Never call our customers 'users,' and never promise 'instant' results."*

Schema Entry: ***NEGATIVE CONSTRAINT:*** *Prohibit the use of the term 'user' and any claim implying instant outcomes.*

Applied rigorously, this three-step technique converts vague intuition into explicit machine logic. It ensures that the Context Schema reflects not just what the organization prefers, but what it must never violate.

4.7 CASE STUDY: THE TALE OF TWO LAUNCHES

To understand the economic necessity of Context Engineering, abstraction is insufficient. We must move into concrete operational reality. Consider two hypothetical product launches within the same high-stakes environment: a FinTech company preparing to release a new "**AI Financial Advisor**" feature.

Both organizations operate under identical external conditions. They have access to the same class of Large Language Models, comparable engineering talent, and similar market opportunities. There is no advantage in tooling, intelligence, or capital.

The divergence occurs entirely at the level of the operating model. One organization relies on prompt-driven execution within the

Legacy Dependency Map. The other governs generation through Context Architecture.

Company A: The "Prompt Engineering" Approach (Legacy Model)

The Process: Company A operates within the Legacy Dependency Map. The Product Manager assumes the role of a Prompt Engineer and writes a Jira ticket: "*As a user, I want an AI chat to help me save money.*"

A Developer picks up the ticket with enthusiasm. They open their Integrated Development Environment (IDE) and issue a tactical prompt: "*You are a helpful financial assistant. Analyze this user's transaction data and suggest ways to save money.*" No additional context is supplied. No constraints are encoded.

The Execution (Syntactic Fluency): The AI performs exactly as designed. It analyzes transaction history, identifies discretionary spending, and generates a confident response: "*You spend $500 per month on coffee. You should stop buying coffee and invest that money in Crypto-Coin X for 100% returns.*"

The interface is polished. The response is instantaneous. From a syntactic perspective, the system appears highly competent. The Product Manager is encouraged by the visible progress.

The Crash (The Zero-Sum Gate): The feature enters pre-launch Legal review. The General Counsel reviews a screenshot of the AI recommending specific cryptocurrency investments and promising guaranteed returns. The review stops immediately.

- **Compliance Exposure Identified:** Providing individualized investment recommendations without appropriate registration or exemption creates securities and investment-adviser compliance exposure under applicable U.S. financial regulations.

- **Compliance Exposure Identified:** Promising "100% returns" constitutes prohibited performance claims and creates material advertising and consumer-protection liability, regardless of whether the advice is framed as automated or experimental.

Result: The launch is terminated on the spot. Engineering is instructed to "fix the prompt."

The Rejection Loop: Developers attempt incremental patching —"*Don't give bad advice.*" The AI predictably fails again. Legal trust collapses. Manual auditing is mandated for every response.

The feature eventually launches four months late with its core functionality removed. The outcome is compliance-safe and strategically worthless. The Product Timeline Tax reaches one hundred percent.

Company B: The "Context Architect" Approach (Future Model)

The Process: Company B operates under a fundamentally different operating model. The Context Architect does not begin with a Jira ticket. They begin by constructing the **Context Schema**. Before a single line of code is written, they engage the General Counsel using the **Kill Switch Protocol** to surface non-negotiable constraints.

Constraint Extracted: *The AI must not act as a fiduciary. It may provide financial education, but it is strictly prohibited from offering individualized investment advice.*

The Input (Context Engineering): The Context Architect assembles the Master Prompt by encoding the Constraint & Compliance Layer explicitly:

Role: *Financial Educator (**not** Advisor).*

Constraint 1: *Recommending specific assets—including stocks or cryptocurrencies—is strictly forbidden.*

Constraint 2: *All guidance must use **educational framing** (e.g., "Some customers choose to...") rather than directive framing (e.g., "You should...").*

Constraint 3: *If a user requests investment advice, immediately trigger the **Disclaimer Protocol** and redirect to educational material.*

These constraints do not guide the AI after generation. They define the boundaries *within* which generation is allowed to occur.

The Execution (Semantic Understanding): The Developer integrates the API against this schema. When the AI analyzes transaction data and detects discretionary spending, it generates the following response: "*Analysis indicates approximately $500 per month spent on coffee. Historically, reducing discretionary expenses can improve savings rates. Would you like to explore a simulation showing the impact of a five percent savings increase?*"

The Result: The feature enters legal review. The General Counsel observes that educational framing is structurally enforced and that prohibited behaviors are impossible by design. The feature is approved without revision. It launches on schedule. The Product Timeline Tax is effectively zero.

The Difference: Company A attempted to manage output. Company B engineered input. Company A relied on the apparent intelligence of the machine. Company B relied on the governance of the Context Architect.

4.8 CONCLUSION: THE ARCHITECTURE OF TRUTH

We are standing at the edge of a new industrial epoch in software. The barrier to creation has collapsed. The marginal cost of code, content, and computation is rapidly approaching zero. What was once scarce is now abundant.

In this environment, the value of the Product Manager can no longer be measured by their ability to ship features. Shipping is no longer the constraint. **Truth is.** The defining capability of the modern organization is the ability to ship outputs that remain legally sound, strategically aligned, and contextually correct at scale.

Context Engineering is the mechanism by which organizations impose their truth—their laws, their strategy, their risk posture, and their values—onto an otherwise indifferent machine. It is not an optimization layer. It is a governance layer.

The **Context Schema** is therefore not merely a document. It is the constitutional framework of the product. It encodes the non-negotiable rules by which the system is allowed to operate. The **Context Architect** is the guardian of that constitution, responsible for ensuring that Infinite Execution Velocity does not erode institutional truth.

By mastering constraint definition, semantic extraction, and schema design, the Context Architect does more than accelerate delivery. They preserve coherence. They ensure that as organizations race toward the future at unprecedented speed, they do not sacrifice judgment, legality, or identity along the way.

What has been established so far is *why* governance must move upstream and *what* must be governed. The remaining question is *how* that governance is made operational. Semantic clarity alone does not prevent failure unless it is translated into an enforceable structure. To survive the transition from intent to execution, governance must become executable—embedded directly into the systems that generate work rather than applied after the fact.

PART III

THE STACKED PRODUCT LIFECYCLE

5

THE STACKED PRODUCT LIFECYCLE: BUILDING IN PARALLEL

Governance becomes real only when it is operationalized. A schema that cannot shape execution is merely documentation. Having defined the principles of Context Engineering, we now turn to the structural model that embeds those principles directly into the lifecycle itself. The Stacked Product Lifecycle replaces sequential coordination with enforced convergence, transforming governance from oversight into architecture.

5.1 THE BLUEPRINT FOR VELOCITY: REPLACING SEQUENCE WITH CONVERGENCE

If the previous chapters have established anything, it is that the traditional Product Management model is suffering from a deep structural incompatibility with modern tools. We have already demonstrated that Infinite Execution Velocity—the AI's ability to generate code, content, and artifacts on demand—when combined with the administrative, phase-gated structure of the Legacy Dependency Map, guarantees the accrual of the Product Timeline Tax (PTT). Speed does not remove the tax. Speed causes it to accumulate faster.

To understand why this tax is not an implementation failure but a mathematical certainty, we must first understand the physics of the system we are attempting to replace.

5.1.1 THE COGNITIVE JUSTIFICATION FOR SEQUENCE

The sequential model—first Waterfall, and later, in many organizations, Agile-in-practice—was a rational, even elegant, adaptation to a very real biological constraint: Human Cognitive Load.

In a human-centric workflow, true cognitive parallelism is rare. A single human mind cannot write a complex SQL query while simultaneously drafting a legally binding privacy policy and designing a user-centric marketing campaign without catastrophic error. Attempting to do so does not increase throughput; it increases failure. The industrial logic of the twentieth century therefore dictated that complex work must be decomposed, isolated, and staged.

What emerged was an "Assembly Line of Thought," deliberately structured to protect humans from cognitive overload:

Strategy Phase: The "Why" is defined.

Design Phase: The "What" is visualized.

Engineering Phase: The "How" is built.

Compliance Phase: The "Legal" is checked.

Marketing Phase: The "Story" is told.

This baton pass was not bureaucratic theater. It was a survival mechanism. Human bandwidth was the bottleneck, and no single individual could hold the entire semantic, technical, legal, and market context of a modern product in their head at once. The hand-off became the only viable mechanism for transferring partial context from one specialist to another without collapse.

The tragedy is not that this model was wrong, but rather that it was correct for a world that no longer exists.

5.1.2 THE BOTTLENECK OF THE BATON

In an age of Infinite Generative Capacity, the baton pass transforms from a safety mechanism into a suffocating bottleneck. What once protected the organization from human overload now actively constrains the system's ability to operate coherently at machine speed.

When Artificial Intelligence is introduced into this sequential line, a dangerous structural imbalance is created. The AI accelerates the "Building" phase to effectively instantaneous execution, while the handoff phases—the moments where context must be read, interpreted, debated, and approved by humans—remain stubbornly fixed at biological speed.

The Engineer uses Copilot to write the code in two hours.

But Legal still requires two weeks to reconstruct the context, understand the implications of the feature, interpret regulatory exposure, and audit the resulting artifact.

At this point, failure is no longer accidental. It is engineered directly into the system's structure. Accelerating a sequential pipeline does not remove friction; it concentrates it. Faster code simply collides with the Zero-Sum Gate sooner, producing larger rollbacks, wider blast radii, and more expensive reversals.

When you accelerate a car on a road full of unmarked dead ends, you do not reach the destination faster. You crash sooner—and with greater force. AI does not make the road straighter. It makes the consequences of poor mapping more severe.

The solution, therefore, cannot be an incremental process tweak, a new ceremony, or an additional approval checklist. It must be a structural replacement. We must abandon the sequential pipeline—which treats context as a fragile baton passed from function to function—and replace it with a model designed for simultaneous, parallel convergence.

This replacement is not a process. It is an operating architecture.

This architecture is the Stacked Product Lifecycle.

5.1.3 THE OPERATIONAL NECESSITY OF SEMANTIC REGULATION

In the traditional pipeline, the organization does not experience semantic failure as a theory problem. It experiences it as a crisis event. The single-lane output—the finished code, the finished copy, the finished feature—travels forward at speed until it collides with reality during a late-stage audit. Legal identifies a regulatory violation embedded deep in the architecture. Marketing realizes the feature solves a different problem than the one customers actually have. Security discovers that an apparently minor data flow assumption creates an avoidable exposure. In each case, the artifact is syntactically complete. It works. And yet it is semantically invalid in the only contexts that ultimately matter.

This mode of failure produces a distinctive operational pathology. When semantic errors are discovered late, progress does not merely slow—it inverts. The organization enters what appears externally as delivery activity but is internally a state of reversal. Decisions are unwound. Components are removed. Interfaces are rewritten. Approvals are replayed. Time is no longer spent creating value, but dismantling previously generated output. As generative systems increase throughput, this reversal cost compounds. The faster the system can produce artifacts, the more expensive it becomes to discover—after the fact—that those artifacts should never have existed.

The Stacked Product Lifecycle succeeds because it changes where semantic failure is allowed to occur. Semantic enforcement is relocated upstream, into the input system itself. The Context Architect (CA) intervenes before execution begins, not after artifacts harden. Instead of allowing a single execution lane to run forward at machine speed and then hoping it survives downstream scrutiny, the Architect establishes multiple simultaneous streams of governing context. Generation is constrained as it happens. Failure surfaces during design, not delivery.

Operationally, this means that generation is never evaluated against one dimension at a time. The AI must satisfy multiple semantic requirements concurrently: what the product is allowed to do under law and policy, what it must do to deliver its intended value, and what it is for in the context of strategy and market positioning. These are not sequential checkpoints. They are simultaneous boundary conditions. The Stack is not an added layer of work. It is the mechanism that makes high-velocity generation survivable by preventing semantic collapse under infinite syntactic throughput.

Under this model, the Context Architect becomes the Semantic Regulator. Their role is not to shepherd artifacts through a pipeline or manage coordination between functions. It is to translate human intent, human constraints, and human strategy into machine-executable context. By governing the conditions under which generation is permitted to occur, the Context Architect ensures that output remains aligned before drift, delay, or surprise can enter the system.

5.2 THE THREE CONVERGENT STACKS

From the moment the initial strategic vision is approved, three primary functional work streams must run concurrently in the Stacked Product Lifecycle. This is not a sequencing trick or a coordination exercise. It is a structural mandate. We are no longer building a "skeleton" (code) and then adding "skin" (marketing) and "clothing" (legal) after the fact. We are growing the organism as a whole, with every system developing in relation to the others.

The purpose of this architecture is not speed. It is coherence. The Stacked Product Lifecycle is designed to force the simultaneous resolution of the three fundamental failure modes identified in Chapter 2: Technical Isolation, Compliance Isolation, and Market Isolation. If any one of these domains is allowed to lag behind the others, Semantic Drift begins immediately—and the Product Timeline Tax starts accruing.

5.2.1 THE ARCHITECTURE OF CONVERGENCE

Convergence is achieved by aligning each operational Stack directly with a governing layer of the Context Schema defined in Chapter 4. Each Stack draws from a distinct, authoritative slice of the same schema, ensuring that all generation operates within a shared semantic frame.

Critically, the Output Goal in this model is not a draft to be reviewed later. It is a Born State—an artifact that is finalized at the moment of creation because the relevant constraints, dependencies, and strategic intent were applied upstream. Review is replaced by prevention. Audit is replaced by design.

The Stacks and Their Governing Layers

1. Engineering Stack

Governing Context Layer: Technical Dependency Layer

(The "How" and "Limits")

Output Goal — Born Technically Sound:

The code is functional, scalable, and respects the existing *Legacy Dependency Map.*

2. Compliance Stack

Governing Context Layer: Constraint & Compliance Layer

(The "Cannot" and "Must")

Output Goal — Born Compliant:

The product is legally viable, and the *Zero-Sum Gate* is preemptively cleared.

3. Marketing Stack

Governing Context Layer: Strategic Context Layer

(The "Why" and "Who")

Output Goal — Born Market-Ready:

Development validates the narrative, pricing, and persona alignment before it completes.

This is the defining inversion of the Stacked Product Lifecycle: correctness is enforced before execution, not verified afterward.

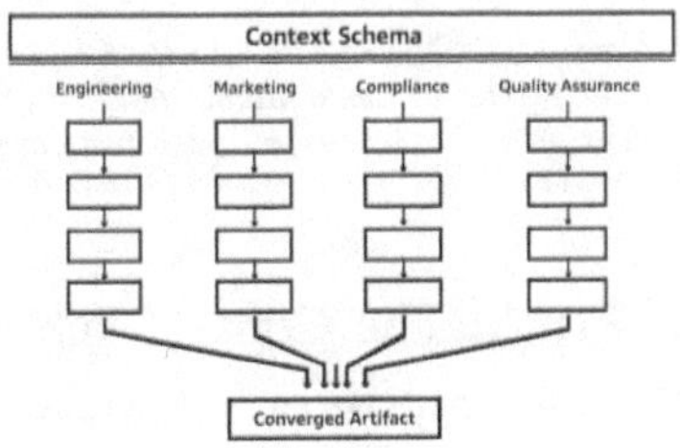

Figure 2. *The Stacked Product Lifecycle shows parallel execution governed by a shared Context Schema, enabling early convergence by design.*

5.2.2 THE ORCHESTRATOR: THE CONTEXT SCHEMA

How do multiple stacks run in parallel without diverging into chaos? In a traditional Agile environment, parallel work often leads to 'integration hell' when teams lack a shared, executable contract for interfaces, constraints, and definitions of done—the painful period when the frontend team realizes the backend team built the wrong API, or when two teams ship artifacts that technically function but cannot coexist.

The Context Architect's critical responsibility is to prevent this failure mode at the source. The input to all three stacks must be the Context Schema itself, acting as the shared orchestration layer—the sheet music for the entire system. The Schema does not coordinate work after the fact; it governs generation before divergence can occur.

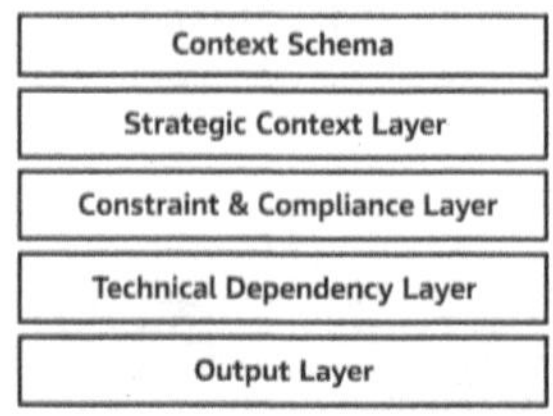

Figure 3. The Context Schema shows a layered governance architecture that encodes strategic intent, compliance constraints, technical dependencies, and execution outputs upstream of generation.

Single Source of Truth: The Context Schema is a JSON-based artifact that lives in the code repository alongside the product itself. It is versioned, reviewable, and authoritative. No Stack operates on private assumptions or tribal knowledge.

Propagation: If the Schema changes (e.g., "We are now targeting enterprise healthcare instead of SMB"), that change **can be wired to propagate automatically** to the System Prompts of all three stacks. The Engineering Agent shifts compliance standards to HIPAA. The Marketing Agent shifts tone to "Corporate / Professional." No meeting is required. No slide deck is produced.

Programmatic Alignment: Alignment is no longer a social process. It is computational. Because each Stack is constrained by the same Schema, divergence is structurally impossible without an explicit schema violation. Coordination emerges automatically from shared inputs, not from repeated synchronization rituals.

This is how parallelism becomes safe. Not through tighter meetings, but through a single governing artifact.

5.3 STACK 1: THE ENGINEERING STACK (TECHNICAL DEPENDENCY LAYER)

Of all the disciplines facing disruption, Engineering is perhaps the most vulnerable to the illusion of AI speed. The sudden ability to generate large volumes of working code creates the appearance that the hardest part of software development has been solved. In reality, it amplifies the most dangerous failure mode Engineers already face: building the right thing in the wrong place.

In the Legacy Dependency Map, the Engineering team functions as a sequential resource. Engineers wait—often idly—for Product Management to finalize requirements before they begin writing code. This enforced delay creates a contextual vacuum. When the requirements finally arrive, the system incentivizes rapid execution, not careful integration. Engineers move fast, often without fully reloading the tangled web of historical assumptions, brittle interfaces, and undocumented constraints embedded in the existing codebase.

The result is predictable. This pattern leads directly to Legacy Dependency Shock—the moment when new, syntactically perfect code collides with old, mission-critical systems and breaks them. AI does not eliminate this shock. It accelerates its arrival.

5.3.1 THE SHIFT FROM EXECUTION TO CONSTRAINT DEFINITION

Under the Stacked Product Lifecycle, the Engineering Stack no longer waits its turn. It operates simultaneously with Compliance and Marketing, but it is constrained from the first moment by the Technical Dependency Layer of the Context Schema. Engineering does not begin with implementation. It begins with truth.

The shift required of the Engineering Leader is profound. Their primary early contribution is no longer estimating timelines or sprint capacity. It is defining constraints—the non-negotiable realities of the system that cannot be violated without causing failure.

Old World (Estimation): The Product Manager (PM) asks, "How long will it take to build the Chat Feature?" The Engineer responds with a guess: "Three sprints."

New World (Constraint): The Context Architect asks, "What breaks if we build the Chat Feature?" The Engineer responds with facts: "Our WebSocket infrastructure cannot handle more than 5,000 concurrent connections, and we are legally required to log all chats to the 'Cold_Storage' blob."

The Engineering Lead explicitly maps these architectural truths —the real Legacy Dependency Map—into the Context Schema. This includes deprecated APIs, database throughput limits, security protocols, compliance-driven logging requirements, and mandatory external dependencies.

Once this layer is defined, the AI assumes the role it is best suited for: a Syntactic Engine operating inside a known boundary. It receives the raw requirements together with the full Technical Dependency Layer and generates code that respects both. The output is not merely functional. It is **Born Technically Sound**—correct by construction, not validated after the fact.

5.3.2 WAR STORY: THE "WEBSOCKET" CRASH

To understand why the Engineering Stack must operate as a constraint-defining system rather than an execution engine, consider a failure scenario that has become increasingly common in AI-accelerated organizations.

The Legacy Scenario (The Crash):

A Product Manager writes a requirement for a "Real-Time User Dashboard." The requirement is fed directly into an AI coding agent with a simple instruction: *"Build a real-time dashboard showing user statistics."*

The AI, trained on contemporary best practices, executes flawlessly. It selects WebSockets to push live updates to the browser and spins up a persistent connection for every active user. From a syntactic perspective, the implementation is exemplary.

Syntactic Success: The code is clean, modern, idiomatic, and fully functional.

Semantic Failure: The AI was never told that the company's load balancer—configured in 2018 as part of an earlier infrastructure era —has a hard limit on persistent connections.

The Result: The feature launches on schedule. It performs beautifully for the first 500 users. At user 501, the load balancer exhausts its connection pool, panics, and drops all traffic. The entire platform goes dark.

The PTT: Two full weeks of emergency "hot-fix engineering" follow. WebSockets are ripped out under pressure and replaced with a polling-based architecture. No new value is delivered during this period. The organization pays the Product Timeline Tax in pure rework.

The Stacked Scenario (The Prevention):

In the Stacked Product Lifecycle, the Context Architect treats the load balancer not as a latent defect to be discovered later, but as an explicit Context Constraint to be enforced before generation begins.

Prior to any execution, the CA interviews the Staff Engineer and updates the Technical Dependency Layer of the Context Schema with a non-negotiable rule:

*"**Constraint:** Legacy edge infrastructure imposes a hard cap on long-lived connections (e.g., persistent WebSockets). High-fanout persistent connections are **FORBIDDEN** under current constraints. Use approved polling or event-based patterns that respect existing connection limits."*

When the AI receives the instruction to *"Build a real-time dashboard,"* it does not reason about trends or preferences. It computes against constraints. It cross-references the Technical Dependency Layer, detects that WebSockets are prohibited, and selects a long-polling architecture immediately.

The Result: The code is less fashionable, but it is structurally correct. It launches. It scales within known limits. It does not crash.

The PTT: Zero.

5.3.3 THE PARALLEL QA LOOP

In the Legacy Dependency Map, Quality Assurance (QA) functions as the final hurdle—a speed bump installed at the end of the timeline. Testing occurs only after the artifact has already been built, integrated, and emotionally defended. In this position, QA does not prevent failure; it merely discovers it late.

Under the Stacked Product Lifecycle, the Engineering Stack in the stacked model shifts QA left and automates large portions of it, running validation in parallel. Testing is no longer a downstream checkpoint. It is a concurrent constraint-enforcement mechanism.

Because the Context Schema contains explicit definitions of both "success" (requirements) and "failure" (constraints), the AI is capable of generating test artifacts at the same moment it generates production code. Validation is no longer deferred. It is co-produced.

The Gen–Test Loop: As the AI writes Dashboard.tsx, a parallel agent simultaneously writes Dashboard.test.tsx. These artifacts are governed by the same Technical Dependency Layer and evaluated against the same constraint set.

Semantic Testing: The test agent is explicitly fed the Constraint Layer. It tests whether an interaction violates a forbidden architectural pattern. If a button click triggers a prohibited WebSocket connection, the test fails immediately—before any human ever reviews the code.

This architecture effectively automates the role of the "Archaeologist": the Senior Engineer who traditionally appears late in the cycle to explain why the new system will not survive contact with the old one. In the stacked model, the AI becomes the Archaeologist—armed not with intuition or memory, but with the explicit map you provided.

5.4 STACK 2: THE COMPLIANCE STACK (CONSTRAINT & COMPLIANCE LAYER)

The Compliance Stack represents the most significant cultural inversion in the entire product lifecycle. It is the point where governance stops acting as a brake and begins functioning as a design input.

In the traditional model, Legal, Security, and Compliance operate as a Zero-Sum Gate—a checkpoint positioned late in the timeline where only two outcomes are possible: "Pass" (rare) or "Rollback" (common). This late-stage audit is the primary generator of the Product Timeline Tax because it depends on discovery rather than design.

Every experienced Product Manager recognizes the "Friday Afternoon Discovery." The team has invested six weeks building a feature. It is code-complete. It is emotionally committed. Then, on the Friday before launch, a junior Privacy Officer traces the data flow and notices that it violates a newly enacted state regulation—CPRA, for example. The launch is scrubbed. Momentum collapses. The PTT counter begins to run.

The solution is not to slow AI down to match the pace of human review. That approach merely preserves the bottleneck. The solution is to arm AI with the reviewer's constraints. In the Legacy Model, Legal functioned as a gatekeeper performing sequential audits. In the Stacked Product Lifecycle, Legal becomes a constraint partner providing parallel input that governs generation itself.

5.4.1 THE BORN COMPLIANT MANDATE

Within the Stacked Product Lifecycle, the Context Architect enforces a strict and non-negotiable rule: no execution may begin in any Stack until the Constraint & Compliance Layer of the Context Schema is approved.

The Compliance Stack, led by Subject Matter Experts, is responsible for defining the "Cannot" and the "Must" of the product before anything is built. This includes data handling regulations (GDPR, CCPA), security threat models, audit logging requirements, and brand safety boundaries.

By requiring AI systems to incorporate consent language, retention policies, deletion mechanisms, and security controls *before* generating code or copy, the product is Born Compliant.

Organizations that integrate compliance constraints at the input stage dramatically reduce regulatory exposure and eliminate the time traditionally lost at the Zero-Sum Gate. What disappears is not rigor, but rework.

5.4.2 WAR STORY: THE "RIGHT TO BE FORGOTTEN" ROLLBACK

To understand the financial and operational cost of treating compliance as a downstream audit, consider a common GDPR failure scenario.

The Legacy Scenario (The Crash):

A marketing-led product team proposes a "Lead Gen Magnet"—a simple web form where users exchange an email address for a downloadable whitepaper. The initiative appears low-risk and straightforward.

The Build:

The Engineering team, incentivized to move quickly, connects the form directly to a legacy CRM system to store incoming email addresses. The integration is trivial. The feature is implemented in days.

The Zero-Sum Gate:

Three weeks later, just before launch, the Data Protection Officer (DPO) performs a standard compliance audit. They ask a single question: "How do we fulfill a user's request to be forgotten under GDPR Article 17?"

The Discovery:

The Engineering team realizes—too late—that the legacy CRM is a write-only archive. It has no programmatic deletion endpoint. Data can be added, but not removed.

The Result:

The feature is non-compliant by design. It cannot legally be launched. The CRM integration must be ripped out and replaced with a connector to a modern, GDPR-compliant system that supports deletion.

The PTT:

Three weeks of rework. Zero customer value delivered. The Product Timeline Tax is paid in full.

The Stacked Scenario (The Prevention):

In the Stacked Product Lifecycle, the Context Architect initiates the Constraint & Compliance Layer *before* a "Lead Gen" ticket is ever created.

The Extraction:

The CA begins by asking the DPO a simple, structural question: "What is the kill switch for user data?"

The Constraint:

The DPO responds with a binary rule: "We cannot store personally identifiable information in any system that lacks a programmatic deletion endpoint."

The Schema Entry:

The CA encodes this directly into the Context Schema:

*"**Constraint:** Data destinations MUST support **programmatic, auditable erasure workflows** for user data. Systems that lack a verifiable deletion mechanism are **FORBIDDEN**."*

The Execution:

When the Engineering Agent designs the architecture, it evaluates available integrations against the Constraint & Compliance Layer. The legacy CRM is automatically excluded. A modern, compliant Salesforce connector is selected by default.

The Result:

The architecture is Born Compliant. The DPO reviews the schema—not the code. The Zero-Sum Gate is cleared on Day One.

5.4.3 OPERATIONALIZING THE "CANNOT"

How does an organization operationalize compliance in a machine-governed system? It requires a deliberate shift in legal posture—from interpretive judgment to executable definition.

Human Lawyers are trained to reason in gradients. Phrases like "it depends," "reasonable effort," or "materially misleading" are useful in courtrooms and contracts. Artificial Intelligence, by contrast, suffers from Semantic Blindness. It cannot operationalize caution or intuition. It requires binary instruction. Something must be explicitly allowed, explicitly forbidden, or explicitly required.

The Context Architect's task is therefore not to summarize legal opinions, but to digitize them. Legal judgment must be translated into concrete, enforceable constraint types that can be executed by the Context Schema:

Terminological Constraints: Explicitly banned words or phrases (e.g., *"The word 'Guaranteed' may not be used in any financial context"*).

Data Architecture Constraints: Forbidden data flows or storage locations (e.g., *"Personally identifiable information may not be written to the Log_Description field"*).

Functional Constraints: Mandatory frictions or controls (e.g., *"A user action may not complete without an explicit 'I Agree' consent checkbox"*).

When these constraints are active, the AI ceases to behave like a generator and begins to function as a real-time auditor. Violations are detected at the moment of creation, not during post hoc review. If the Marketing Stack produces a headline claiming "Guaranteed Returns," the Compliance Stack's agent flags the violation instantly—before the copy ever reaches a human inbox.

This is not faster law. It is executable law. And it structurally eliminates the legal bottleneck by removing ambiguity from the generation path.

5.5 STACK 3: THE MARKETING STACK (STRATEGIC CONTEXT LAYER)

In the Legacy Dependency Map, Marketing is treated as a surface treatment—the "skin" applied at the very end of the process. After the product is built and finalized, it is thrown over the wall to the Product Marketing Manager (PMM) with an implicit instruction: *Here is the thing. Go sell it.*

This sequencing creates Marketing Lag. Weeks are spent retrofitting a narrative onto a fixed feature set that may or may not solve a real customer problem. Worse, this delay often reveals a more damaging truth: the product is technically correct but commercially irrelevant. The organization built a faster horse in a market that already moved on to cars.

In the Stacked Product Lifecycle, the Marketing Stack does not wait downstream. It runs in parallel with Engineering and Compliance, governed from the outset by the Strategic Context Layer of the Context Schema—the explicit definition of *who* the product is for and *why* it exists.

5.5.1 BORN MARKET-READY

Because Blue Ocean Analysis, persona simulations, and competitive positioning are encoded into the Context Schema before execution begins, the Marketing Stack can generate assets at the same time the product is being built.

While the Engineering Stack is generating the TypeScript for the "dashboard widget," the Marketing Stack is simultaneously generating:

Value Propositions: Framed around outcomes such as "Time Saved" rather than internal metrics like "Data Latency."

User Documentation: Explaining not just how to use the feature, but why it exists.

Sales Enablement: Scripts, FAQs, and objection handling for the SDR team.

The artifact does not emerge silently and ask for a story later. It is Born Market-Ready. Narrative coherence is validated in parallel with technical correctness. We do not wait for the code to finish to discover that the story does not land.

5.5.2 THE BLUE OCEAN AGENT: AUTOMATING DIFFERENTIATION

A critical component of the Marketing Stack is the Blue Ocean Agent. In the legacy world, "differentiation" was treated as a creative exercise—a whiteboard session that happened once or twice a year, often disconnected from actual product decisions. In the Stacked Product Lifecycle, differentiation becomes a continuous, governed process.

The Context Architect assigns an AI agent a persistent analytical role: to continuously audit proposed features against competitor capabilities using the data embedded in the Strategic Context Layer of the Context Schema. Differentiation is no longer inferred. It is computed.

The Prompt:

"Act as a Market Analyst. Review the proposed 'Chat Feature' defined in the Context Schema. Compare it against Competitor X (e.g., HubSpot, Salesforce). Determine whether this feature represents a 'Blue Ocean' differentiator or a 'Red Ocean' commodity. If it is a commodity, propose a concrete 'Value Innovation' that shifts the competitive basis."

The Analysis:

The agent scans the competitive feature set and responds: *"Standard chat functionality is a Red Ocean commodity. Approximately 90% of direct competitors already offer it. Competing on execution speed or interface polish provides no durable advantage."*

The Value Innovation:

The agent proposes a structural pivot: *"Reframe the feature as 'Context-Aware Chat' that pre-fetches relevant user purchase history and account state. This shifts the value curve from 'Availability' to 'Intelligence,' creating defensible differentiation."*

This feedback loop operates during planning, not post-launch. It ensures that the Engineering Stack is directed toward building the differentiator rather than perfecting a commodity. If the Marketing Stack cannot generate a compelling value proposition from the Schema, the system triggers a Strategic Halt—pausing execution before Engineering expends a single cycle on a feature that cannot win.

Differentiation is no longer aspirational. It is enforced upstream.

5.6 THE MECHANICS OF CONVERGENCE: RESOLVING CONFLICT

A skeptical reader will ask an obvious and necessary question: *If Engineering, Compliance, and Marketing all run in parallel, what happens when they disagree?*

In the traditional model, parallel work produces "integration hell"—weeks of alignment meetings, escalations, and compromises as teams attempt to reconcile incompatible incentives. Legal optimizes for risk avoidance. Marketing optimizes for persuasion. Engineering optimizes for feasibility. Resolution is political, not structural.

In the Stacked Product Lifecycle, disagreement is not resolved through negotiation. It is resolved through Schema Convergence.

5.6.1 THE CONTEXT SCHEMA AS THE SINGLE SOURCE OF TRUTH

The Context Schema is not a passive document or a reference artifact. It is the Orchestrator. It functions as the immutable sheet music for the entire system, defining not only what may be played, but which instruments take precedence.

Because every Stack—Engineering, Compliance, and Marketing—derives its constraints from the same Schema, conflicts are surfaced and resolved computationally rather than socially. There is no meeting to "align perspectives." The Schema enforces alignment by design.

This is made possible through an explicit hierarchy of constraints encoded directly into the Schema:

Level 1 (Immutable): Compliance and Technical Constraints—the non-negotiable "Cannot."

Level 2 (Mutable): Strategic Context—the governing "Why."

Level 3 (Flexible): Creative Execution—the expressive "What."

When conflicts arise, they are not debated. They are evaluated against this hierarchy. Lower-level intents cannot override higher-level constraints. This ordering eliminates ambiguity and prevents Semantic Drift across the stacks.

Convergence, in this model, is not achieved by consensus. It is achieved by constraint precedence.

5.6.2 SIMULATION: THE "GUARANTEED" CONFLICT

To make the mechanics of Schema Convergence concrete, consider a simple but common conflict resolved entirely without human intervention.

The Generation:

The Marketing Stack, optimizing for click-through rate and conversion, generates a landing-page headline:

"Guaranteed 100% Uptime or Your Money Back!"

The Cross-Check:

The headline is immediately evaluated against the Constraint & Compliance Layer by the Compliance Stack's agent. This evaluation is automatic, synchronous, and mandatory.

The Collision:

The agent detects a direct violation of a Terminological Constraint encoded in the Context Schema:

"Constraint: The word 'Guaranteed' may not be used in relation to service-level agreements."

The Resolution:

The asset is marked invalid at the moment of creation. No escalation occurs. No meeting is scheduled. The Marketing Agent is automatically re-prompted with a precise error message:

"Error: Violation of Legal Constraint 404. The term 'Guaranteed' is prohibited. Rewrite the headline emphasizing 'Reliability' instead."

The Regeneration:

The Marketing Stack regenerates a compliant alternative:

"Industry-Leading 99.9% Reliability."

This entire loop executes in seconds within the AI environment. No email threads. No compromise language. No human arbitration. Because the Constraint & Compliance Layer holds hierarchical precedence over the Strategic Context Layer within the Schema, the conflict is resolved deterministically.

What disappears is not creativity, but friction. Governance is enforced without slowing execution, because it is embedded in the generation path itself.

5.6.3 THE "SEMANTIC DRIFT" KPI

In the Stacked Product Lifecycle, the Context Architect tracks a fundamentally new operational metric: Semantic Drift.

Drift occurs when the outputs of the three stacks begin to diverge from the Context Schema that governs them.

If Engineering builds Feature A, but Marketing sells Feature B, Semantic Drift is high.

If Marketing sells Feature A, but Compliance forbids Feature A, Semantic Drift is critical.

These are not communication failures. They are schema failures.

By continuously monitoring the Rejection Rate between stacks —how often Compliance rejects Marketing copy, how often Engineering violates technical constraints, how often artifacts fail cross-stack validation—the Context Architect gains direct visibility into where the Schema is under-specified or internally inconsistent.

A high rejection rate does not indicate that teams are misaligned or that AI "made a mistake." It indicates that the governing context was incomplete. The corrective action is not a meeting. It is a schema update.

Once the Context Schema is revised, the system self-corrects automatically. Drift decreases. Convergence improves. Governance becomes observable, measurable, and debuggable.

Semantic Drift replaces velocity as the primary signal of system health.

5.7 THE CONTEXT ARCHITECT'S PLAYBOOK: AGENT PROMPTS

To make the Stacked Product Lifecycle operational, governance must move from specification to enforcement. The Context Schema defines the system's permissible state space, but it does not execute by itself. It requires a binding mechanism that converts abstract constraints into continuous control.

System Prompts serve as this binding layer. They function as executable instructions that attach each agent to the Context Schema and regulate its persistent behavior. These prompts are not requests and they are not guidance. They are directives. The system does not interpret intent; it enforces compliance.

The playbooks presented below are therefore not conversational prompts or productivity shortcuts. They are System Instructions designed to lock each Stack into its governing role, ensuring that generation remains constrained by structure rather than guided by improvisation or local optimization.

What follows are the three core System Prompts used to initialize and enforce the Engineering, Compliance, and Marketing Stacks.

Playbook 1: The Engineering Stack Prompt

This playbook transforms the AI from a generic code generator into a constraint-bound Systems Architect. Its purpose is not to accelerate implementation, but to ensure that all technical generation occurs inside known architectural limits.

Role: Senior Systems Architect (Stack: Engineering)

Input Source: Ingest [Context_Schema_v1.json] with explicit focus on the {Technical_Dependency_Layer}.

Constraint Protocol:

Legacy Check: You must cross-reference every proposed component, pattern, and dependency against the

{Legacy_Dependency_Map}. No assumption of modern defaults is permitted.

Prohibition: All database interactions must use the existing GraphQL wrapper. Direct SQL queries are explicitly FORBIDDEN under all circumstances.

Stack Alignment: You are restricted to the approved {Tech_Stack_List} (e.g., React 18, Node.js). You may not introduce new libraries, frameworks, or architectural patterns without an explicit Schema Update.

Task: Generate the backend logic for Feature X as defined in the Context Schema.

Output Goal: Produce Born Technically Sound TypeScript code that complies with all declared constraints.

Failure Condition: If fulfilling the request would require a forbidden architectural pattern (e.g., persistent WebSocket connections), halt generation immediately and return Error: Legacy Constraint Violation.

This prompt ensures that correctness precedes cleverness and that speed never overrides structural truth.

Playbook 2: The Compliance Stack Prompt

This playbook transforms the AI from a passive reviewer into an active, real-time Compliance Auditor. Its function is not to interpret policy after execution, but to enforce constraints during generation—eliminating the Zero-Sum Gate by design.

Role: Chief Compliance Officer / Chief Information Security Officer (Stack: Compliance)

Input Source: Ingest [Context_Schema_v1.json] with explicit focus on the {Constraint_Compliance_Layer}.

Constraint Protocol:

Regulatory Mandate: Strict adherence to GDPR Article 17 (Right to Erasure) and SOC 2 Type II evidence-backed monitoring and access-control controls, including logging, audit trails, and incident evidence as defined by the applicable Trust Services Criteria.

Terminology Lock: You must detect and flag any use of terms listed in {Banned_Term_List} (e.g., "Guaranteed," "Risk-Free," "No Liability").

Data Flow Audit: Ensure that no personally identifiable information is transmitted to or stored in {Forbidden_Endpoints} or prohibited data stores.

Task: Continuously audit incoming code, copy, and artifacts generated by the other stacks against the active constraint set.

Stop Sequence: If any artifact violates an entry in {Constraint_List}, immediately halt generation and return a precise error code to the originating agent.

Output Goal: Produce a Born Compliant validation state, confirming that all artifacts satisfy declared constraints prior to release.

This prompt converts legal and security judgment into executable law, enforced automatically at machine speed.

Playbook 3: The Marketing Stack Prompt

This playbook binds narrative generation to strategic reality. Its purpose is to ensure that all messaging remains aligned with intent, positioning, and differentiation from the moment of creation—eliminating Marketing Lag structurally.

Role: Product Marketing Manager (Stack: Marketing)

Input Source: Ingest [Context_Schema_v1.json] with explicit focus on the {Strategic_Context_Layer}.

Constraint Protocol:

Tone Governance: Adhere strictly to the declared brand voice ("Trustworthy, authoritative, concise"). You must not use hype-oriented language listed in {Negative_Constraint_List} or any phrasing that contradicts brand positioning.

Persona Alignment: All generated copy must explicitly address the pain points, priorities, and decision criteria of {Target_Persona_ID} (e.g., "The Overworked CISO") as defined in the Schema.

Differentiation Lock: Emphasize only those capabilities identified as {Blue_Ocean_Differentiators}. Do not promote commodity features as differentiators.

Task: Draft the launch blog post, FAQ, and supporting messaging based on the feature specifications and constraints defined in the Context Schema.

Output Goal: Produce Born Market-Ready content—messaging that is strategically aligned, compliant, and immediately deployable without downstream narrative rework.

This prompt ensures that the story and the system converge simultaneously.

5.8 THE OPERATIONAL REALITY: FROM "HANDOFF" TO "SIMULTANEITY"

Implementing the Stacked Product Lifecycle is not merely a tooling upgrade or a process optimization. It is a fundamental change in how an organization experiences time.

In the Legacy Model, work unfolds linearly. Tuesday is for Design. Wednesday is for Code. Thursday is for QA. This sequencing provides a comforting illusion of order. Managers can point to a calendar and declare, "We are in the Design Phase," as if the calendar itself enforces correctness.

The Stacked Model collapses this illusion. Time is no longer partitioned by function. Tuesday is for Design, Code, and Compliance simultaneously. All semantic concerns are live at once. This compression does not increase chaos; it exposes it. And it demands a new way of managing attention.

The Death of the Status Meeting

In a sequential world, the status meeting exists to transfer permission. Team B cannot begin until Team A announces completion.

"Design is done, so Engineering can start."

In a convergent system, this ceremony becomes obsolete. The signal is no longer verbal. It is programmatic.

When the Context Schema is locked, all stacks begin

automatically. There is no waiting for approval cascades. When a Stack encounters a constraint—when Compliance rejects Marketing copy, or Engineering violates a technical boundary—the notification is asynchronous, precise, and actionable.

The Context Architect does not run status meetings. They run Schema Reviews. The central question is no longer "Where is the task?"—an output concern—but "Is the map correct?"—an input concern.

Semantic Drift as the New North Star

As established in Section 5.6, operational health is no longer measured by velocity—how fast the organization appears to be moving—but by Semantic Drift—how aligned generation remains with governing intent.

If the Marketing Stack repeatedly produces copy that the Compliance Stack rejects, the Context Architect does not blame the AI or the team. They inspect the Schema. Persistent rejection implies an unresolved conflict between the {Strategic_Context_Layer} and the {Constraint_Compliance_Layer}.

The legacy response is predictable: schedule a meeting between Marketing and Legal to negotiate tradeoffs.

The Context Architect's response is structural: update the Schema to make the hierarchy explicit.

"Constraint: Legal requirements related to 'Safety' override Marketing objectives related to 'Speed.'"

The CA debugs the organization the same way an Engineer debugs software—by correcting the system's inputs, not scolding its outputs.

5.9 CONCLUSION: THE END OF THE BATON PASS

The transition to the Stacked Product Lifecycle is the defining operational shift of the AI era. It marks the moment organizations stop treating automation as a productivity multiplier and begin treating it as an infrastructure problem.

We are dismantling the linear assembly line—a relic of the industrial age, optimized for human cognitive limitations—and replacing it with a parallel processing system designed for machine execution. This is not an acceleration of the old model. It is a replacement of its underlying physics.

The most dangerous artifact of the legacy system is not the meeting or the handoff. It is the idea that context itself can be passed safely from hand to hand. Context is not a baton. It is the atmosphere. It must be omnipresent—available to every Agent, every Engineer, and every Marketer simultaneously—or the system will drift.

In this new model, we do not wait for code to be written to discover whether it is legal. We do not wait for a product to launch to learn whether it can be sold. We build, validate, and position in the same breath, governed by constraints applied before generation begins.

The Context Architect stands at the center of this system. They do not manage execution or coordinate tasks. They define gravity. By mastering the Context Schema, the CA eliminates the friction of handoffs, neutralizes the Zero-Sum Gate, and achieves what once appeared contradictory: Infinite Execution Velocity with Zero Product Timeline Tax.

But this architecture cannot exist inside an organization still structured for sequential thinking. Prompts and schemas are necessary, but insufficient. To sustain convergence, the organization itself must change.

In the next chapter, we turn to the Organizational Operating System: how teams, meetings, incentives, and authority must be restructured to support the shift from Manager to Architect.

6

RAPID PROTOTYPING AND WIREFRAME ENGINEERING

Architecture proves itself through application. Having replaced sequential coordination with enforced convergence, we now examine how this model performs under real execution pressure. The following chapter demonstrates how governed context transforms the earliest stages of product creation, converting speculative planning into validated prototypes within a single operational loop.

6.1 THE PROTOTYPING PARADOX: FROM SEQUENTIAL LAG TO CONVERGENT VELOCITY

The Context Schema, defined and enforced by the Context Architect (CA), is the strategic blueprint for governance. But its true power does not reveal itself in documentation or planning artifacts. It reveals itself at the moment intent collapses into execution—when a governed idea becomes a functional, validated artifact.

The first critical demonstration of the Stacked Product Lifecycle is its ability to compress the sequential concept-to-specification phase dramatically—and in some cases bypass large portions of it—moving directly to a Born Compliant, Born Technically Sound prototype in hours, not months.

This chapter details the first practical application of Context Engineering: using the AI Studio to generate a complete, multi-validated artifact—the **Converged Wireframe**—that replaces the traditional Requirements Document. This single shift structurally eliminates the earliest and most expensive point of Product Timeline Tax (PTT) accrual: the administrative delay between a finalized concept and confirmed architectural feasibility.

6.1.1 THE ILLUSION OF PROGRESS

In a world shaped by Infinite Execution Velocity, it is dangerously easy to mistake motion for progress. Off-the-shelf AI tools can generate a wireframe in minutes. A Product Manager (PM) can type, "*Make me a dashboard for insurance agents,*" and receive a polished, high-fidelity image almost instantly.

This ease of creation, however, intensifies the Velocity Paradox identified in Chapter 3. The artifact looks real. It contains charts, navigation, buttons, and dashboards. It exhibits what appears to be professional competence. But this is merely Syntactic Fluency—a hallucination of value.

The wireframe does not know that the charts depend on real-time data the mainframe cannot provide.

It does not know that the 'Client List' violates HIPAA privacy requirements, including minimum-necessary exposure of electronic Protected Health Information (ePHI) and role-based access controls.

It does not know that the color palette violates newly ratified brand constraints.

A wireframe generated without governing context is a trap. The Context Architect's role is not to slow creation, but to regulate it—ensuring that the first artifact is not a proposal or a promise, but a converged, executable contract.

6.1.2 CASE STUDY: THE INSURETECH PLATFORM (THE LEGACY TRAP)

To understand the magnitude of the shift introduced by convergent prototyping, we must first examine the failure mode it replaces. Consider the attempted launch of a niche B2B SaaS product we will call **The InSuretech Platform.**

The Product Concept:

A predictive-AI platform designed to help small-business insurance agencies identify which clients are most likely to convert complex financial products—annuities, life insurance—into a single, comprehensive account.

The Compliance Reality:

From inception, the product operates inside a regulatory minefield:

- **FINRA:** Financial communication and recommendation rules
- **HIPAA:** Handling of ePHI
- **AML / KYC:** Identity verification and anti-money-laundering mandates

The Nine-Month March of Death (The Legacy Journey)

Under the Legacy Dependency Map, the product's lifecycle becomes a slow, high-friction descent into Product Timeline Tax.

Phase 1: The Paper War (Weeks 1–4)

The Product Manager becomes a scribe. A month is spent interviewing stakeholders and synthesizing a 50-page Product Requirements Document (PRD).

The Friction: The document is static. By the time it is finished, the underlying assumptions are already stale.

PTT Accrual: Four weeks of pure administrative overhead.

Phase 2: The Feasibility Gap (Weeks 5–10)

Design produces a polished interface directly from the PRD and hands it to Engineering.

The Crash: Engineering rejects it outright. "*You designed a real-time predictive score. Our core database updates in overnight batch mode. This cannot exist.*"

PTT Accrual: Six weeks of redesign and context re-loading.

Phase 3: The Blind Build (Weeks 11–26)

Engineering builds a compromised "batch mode" version in isolation. Marketing waits for stable screenshots while the interface continues to change. Marketing Lag compounds.

PTT Accrual: 16 weeks of siloed execution.

Phase 4: The Zero-Sum Gate (Weeks 27–30)

The product enters final compliance review.

The Discovery: Legal flags the predictive score as regulated financial advice. Under FINRA guidance, the way this score is presented **could be interpreted as a recommendation,** triggering suitability and supervision obligations the company cannot satisfy.

The Rollback: The User Interface (UI) must be redesigned to reframe recommendations as "Educational Data."

PTT Accrual: Four weeks of panic and redesign.

Total Time: 36 weeks (nine months).

Result: A compromised product, an exhausted team, and maximum PTT accrual.

6.1.3 THE PSYCHOLOGY OF THE PRD: BREAKING THE LIABILITY SHIELD

To understand why organizations resist rapid prototyping, we must understand the psychological function of the Product Requirements Document.

In the Legacy Model, the PRD is not a blueprint for building. It is a liability shield.

Product writes it to prove intent.

Engineering signs it to prove compliance.

Quality Assurance (QA) signs it to prove coverage.

When the product fails—due to Context Decay or Market Lag—everyone points to the document. Responsibility is diffused. *"I built what was written."*

The Converged Wireframe removes this shield entirely. A prototype is binary. It either works or it does not. There is no ambiguity to hide behind.

Legacy: "The system shall process claims under $500 automatically."

Stacked: A working logic gate approves a $499 claim and flags a $501 claim.

The Context Architect's first battle is cultural. They must convince the organization that executable certainty is safer than textual certainty—and that governed prototypes reduce risk precisely because they remove plausible deniability.

6.2 CONTEXT ENGINEERING: LAUNCHING THE CONVERGED WIREFRAME

The Context Architect replaces the legacy baton-pass with simultaneous constraint governance. Instead of translating intent into documents and handing them downstream, the CA ensures that the Context Schema is complete, coherent, and enforceable *before* any generation begins.

This is the moment where theory becomes execution. Acting as the Semantic Regulator, the CA initializes the **context-governed execution environment** with the initial intent, the target user profile, and the governing business constraints in a single, converged act.

6.2.1 THE MASTER PROMPT

The mechanism that initiates this system is the **Master Prompt.** This is a single, converged input that forces the AI Studio to resolve the parallel requirements of the Engineering, Compliance, and Marketing Stacks *simultaneously.*

The Master Prompt is constructed by composing the three primary layers of the Context Schema into a single execution boundary. Each layer contributes a non-negotiable slice of meaning:

1. **Strategic Context Layer (Marketing Input)**
2. This layer defines *who* the product is for and *why* it exists. It encodes persona, intent, and success criteria.
3. **Prompt Segment:**
4. *"The target user is a tech-averse small business insurance agency owner. Qualia: seeks operational simplicity and requires clear ROI metrics. The objective is to identify the*

client profile most likely to convert an annuity into a life policy."

5. **Constraint & Compliance Layer (Legal Input)**
6. This layer defines what the system *cannot* do. It encodes regulatory, legal, and risk boundaries that must be enforced at generation time.
7. **Prompt Segment:**
8. *"All predictive algorithms must adhere strictly to Department of Insurance regulations and HIPAA Security Rules governing ePHI. All data collection fields must enforce end-to-end encryption and integrate mandatory OFAC screening and audit-log requirements for BSA/AML compliance."*
9. **Technical Dependency Layer (Engineering Input)**
10. This layer defines *how* the system is allowed to exist architecturally. It encodes the Legacy Dependency Map and approved technical patterns.
11. **Prompt Segment:**
12. *"All components must comply with the existing Legacy Dependency Map. Inter-service communication is restricted to the internal Apache Kafka event-streaming system. UI artifacts must be generated using the React component library v3.2 and styled exclusively with Tailwind CSS."*

The Master Prompt does not ask the AI to be creative. It forces the AI to be *coherent*. Any output that violates even one of these layers is structurally invalid by definition.

6.2.2 THE CONVERGED ARTIFACT PACKAGE

Once the Master Prompt is executed, the AI Studio does not sequence work. It fans out. All initial work streams—Engineering, Compliance, and Marketing—are launched simultaneously under the same governing context. The result is a **Converged Artifact Package**, delivered in approximately 72 hours.

This package is valuable precisely because its components are interlocked. Each artifact is generated under the same constraints, validated against the same schema, and designed to coexist without downstream reconciliation.

The Converged Artifact Package contains four distinct deliverables:

1. **Validated Wireframes (Product Stack)**
2. These wireframes are Born Technically Sound. They use the exact React v3.2 components specified in the Technical Dependency Layer and respect architectural limits from the outset. The event and batch-processing constraints forced the design to expose **non-real-time data freshness** (e.g., 'Updated nightly'), rather than hallucinating live scores. This single constraint eliminates the six-week feasibility gap that dominates the Legacy Model.
3. **Microservice Architecture Plan (Engineering Stack)**
4. The package includes a concrete architectural blueprint that respects the Legacy Dependency Map. It specifies precisely how the Python-based prediction service publishes events to the Kafka bus, which topics are used, and which consumers are authorized. Engineering resistance disappears because the architecture emerges from Engineering-defined constraints rather than external assumptions.
5. **Preliminary Launch Messaging (Marketing Stack)**
6. The marketing artifacts are Born Market-Ready from inception. Copy is generated using the "tech-averse" language encoded in the Strategic Context Layer. Headlines emphasize "Client Insights" and "Decision Support" rather than "Investment Advice," resolving FINRA risk before it can materialize. Marketing does not wait for screenshots. Narrative coherence is validated alongside technical feasibility.
7. **Automated Test Case Skeleton (Compliance Stack)**

8. The package includes an initial suite of automated test stubs that encode FINRA, DOI, and HIPAA requirements as executable failures. Compliance rules are no longer enforced through late-stage audits; they are enforced through tests. The Zero-Sum Gate is neutralized because violations surface immediately as failed assertions, not blocked launches.

The Converged Wireframe produced by this package is not a compromise between functions. It is a governed agreement. By collapsing ten weeks of sequential handoffs into a single, multi-validated output, the Context Architect eliminates the earliest—and most expensive—phase of Product Timeline Tax accrual.

6.2.3 THE "THREE-TURN" CONVERGENCE PROTOCOL

The Master Prompt described in Section 6.2 is powerful, but it is not magical. The Context Architect must explicitly avoid the Magic Wand Fallacy—the belief that a single, well-written input will produce a perfect artifact on the first attempt. Even a complete Context Schema cannot eliminate ambiguity entirely. The AI possesses Syntactic Fluency, not judgment.

To manage this reality, the CA enforces a disciplined **Three-Turn Convergence Protocol**. This protocol is about sequentially validating each governing layer of the Context Schema until the artifact becomes a binding contract.

Turn 1: The Structural Pass (The Skeleton)

Goal: Validation of the Technical Dependency Layer.

Prompt Focus: Architecture, data flow, and system boundaries.

Typical Result: The AI generates an interface that may appear crude or unfinished but exhibits correct structural logic. It respects the Kafka constraint, defines service boundaries correctly, and routes data through approved pathways—while still using placeholder visuals or broken styling.

Context Architect Action: Do not fix pixels. Do not debate aesthetics. Validate the logic only. Does the microservice decomposition exist? Are forbidden data paths absent? If yes, proceed.

Turn 2: The Compliance Pass (The Shield)

Goal: Validation of the Constraint & Compliance Layer.

Prompt Focus: Regulatory language, consent mechanics, and prohibited claims.

Typical Result: The AI rewrites headlines, injects mandatory disclosures, adds required "I Agree" checkboxes, and removes disallowed terminology such as "Guaranteed."

Context Architect Action: Execute the Hallucination Audit (see Section 6.4.3). Confirm that compliance rules are enforced as structure, not paraphrased as copy. Ensure the Zero-Sum Gate is cleared before proceeding.

Turn 3: The Strategic Pass (The Skin)

Goal: Validation of the Strategic Context Layer.

Prompt Focus: Differentiation, brand voice, and narrative clarity.

Typical Result: The artifact becomes Born Market-Ready. It aligns with brand voice, highlights Blue Ocean differentiators, and uses the approved V3.2 component library correctly.

Context Architect Action: Lock the artifact. This is no longer a draft. It is the contract.

By formalizing this three-turn loop, the Context Architect prevents premature debates about polish during structural validation and avoids strategic drift during compliance enforcement. Each turn validates a single layer of meaning. Order is imposed on generative chaos by design, not discipline.

6.3 DEEPER VALIDATION: THE ARCHITECTURE OF THE BORN TECHNICALLY SOUND

The most valuable output of the rapid prototyping phase is not the visual interface—the skin of the product. It is the foundational technical architecture—the skeleton—governed by the Technical Dependency Layer of the Context Schema.

This distinction is what separates a cosmetic wireframe generator from the strategic power of Context Engineering. A conventional AI tool produces a picture of a house. The Context Architect produces the blueprints, the load-bearing calculations, and the plumbing schematics simultaneously—before construction begins.

6.3.1 CONTEXT-AWARE DECOMPOSITION

When governed by the Master Prompt, the AI Studio does not attempt to generate a monolithic application. It uses the declared architectural constraints to decompose the problem into discrete, interoperable services that respect the Legacy Dependency Map.

In the case of the InSuretech Platform, the requirement to communicate exclusively through the internal Apache Kafka system —a hard constraint imposed by legacy infrastructure—forces a decoupled architecture from the first-generation pass. The AI is structurally prohibited from "lazy-loading" data directly from a database because the Context Schema forbids it.

The resulting artifact specifies a rigorous three-part decomposition:

1. **The Predictive Microservice (P_{soore})**
2. The AI correctly determines that predictive computation cannot occur in the browser. It specifies a dedicated Python-based microservice, P_{soore}, responsible solely

for executing the predictive model. This service does not return results directly to the UI. Instead, it publishes events to the Kafka topic client_risk_scores5, preserving decoupling and auditability.

3. **The Security Isolation Service (S_{KYC})**
4. HIPAA and AML constraints encoded in the Schema trigger a defensive architectural pattern. The AI specifies a hardened identity-verification service, S_{KYC}, that handles KYC operations. This service is architecturally isolated: it never exposes raw ePHI to the core application. The segmentation ensures that a breach in the user-facing layer cannot cascade into the identity store, dramatically simplifying compliance audits.
5. **The Preliminary API Contract**
6. The artifact package includes a preliminary OpenAPI specification defining the precise endpoints, JSON schemas, authentication requirements, and error-handling semantics governing interaction between frontend and backend services.

This contract alone eliminates weeks of manual negotiation. In the Legacy Model, frontend and backend teams routinely spend entire sprints arguing over payload shapes and error codes. In the Stacked Model, the contract exists before the kickoff meeting—governed, validated, and ready for execution.

6.3.2 THE PTT ELIMINATION IN ARCHITECTURAL DEBT

In the traditional model, architectural judgment is deferred. Teams build features first and audit systemic impact later. This inversion guarantees architectural debt. Performance constraints, integration failures, and scaling limits surface only after substantial investment has already been made, forcing teams to scrap or rework features entirely. This late discovery is a primary contributor to the Product Timeline Tax.

Under the Stacked Product Lifecycle, this failure mode is eliminated structurally. By governing architecture at the input stage, the Context Architect ensures that the blueprint itself is Born Technically Sound before execution begins. The Technical Dependency Layer explicitly blocks the AI from proposing seductive but fragile quick-start solutions—single-server deployments, direct database access, or bypassed message queues—that exhibit Syntactic Fluency but violate enterprise reality.

Instead, the AI is forced to operate within known architectural limits. It must conform to existing scalability patterns, integration contracts, and reliability standards encoded in the Schema. The result is not merely faster code, but code that can survive contact with production.

This guarantees that the Engineering Stack—explored in depth in Chapter 7—begins on a foundation of proven scalability. Speed is preserved, but fragility is removed. The system is not just fast to build; it is safe to keep.

6.4 THE CONTEXT ARCHITECT'S GOVERNANCE: ENFORCING SEMANTIC GUARDRAILS

The rapid prototyping phase is where governance becomes unavoidable. When generation accelerates, ambiguity collapses, and latent conflicts surface immediately. This phase forces a direct confrontation with **Boundary Constraint Failure**—the moment when two legitimate business objectives collide and cannot be satisfied simultaneously.

Without governance, these collisions are resolved implicitly through drift, rework, or late-stage rejection. With Context Engineering, they are surfaced early, named explicitly, and resolved deliberately.

6.4.1 THE ROLE OF THE SEMANTIC GATEKEEPER

In practice, Boundary Constraint Failure most often appears as **Accelerated Scope Creep.** Stakeholders see a functional prototype emerge in 72 hours and draw a dangerous conclusion: "*If it's this easy, why can't we just add X, Y, and Z?*"

This is the precise moment when the Context Architect's role becomes non-negotiable.

The AI can execute the **what**—features, flows, interfaces—at effectively infinite speed. It cannot evaluate the **at what cost**, and it cannot enforce the **cannot**. Those judgments are semantic, not syntactic.

The Context Architect acts as the **Semantic Gatekeeper**. They filter requests not based on resource availability—which is now abundant—but on coherence, risk, and constraint hierarchy—which are fragile. Their responsibility is to prevent the prototype from silently mutating into an incoherent system by enforcing meaning before expansion.

Governance here is not obstruction. It is preservation of intent.

6.4.2 CASE STUDY: THE CONFLICT OF THE THIRD-PARTY SCORE

To understand the limits of automation, we return to the InSuretech Platform and examine a semantic conflict that no AI—regardless of capability—can resolve independently.

The Conflict

During the Context Engineering phase, two layers of the Context Schema issue instructions that are internally coherent but mutually incompatible:

Strategic Context Layer (Marketing):

The platform must rely exclusively on third-party risk scores for predictive modeling. The intent is to minimize liability by avoiding internal storage of sensitive financial and identity data.

Constraint & Compliance Layer (Legal):

The platform must perform real-time, bi-directional identity verification for KYC and AML compliance. This requirement mandates deep integration with the organization's internal proprietary ledger to validate user identity.

Both constraints are rational. Both are valid. Together, they are impossible.

The AI Failure Mode

A naïve AI agent—or an "AI PM" tasked with balancing the prompt statistically—will attempt to satisfy both instructions simultaneously. The likely result is a Frankenstein artifact: a form that collects sensitive user data (violating the Marketing constraint) and transmits it to a third party (violating the Security constraint). The output appears functional, but it is structurally incoherent. It satisfies neither liability strategy nor regulatory mandate.

This is not an execution error. It is a semantic deadlock.

The Context Architect's Intervention

The human Context Architect identifies the deadlock immediately—not as a bug, but as a governance failure. Generation is halted. The issue is escalated to the executive level, where subjective risk tolerance must be decided.

The Semantic Regulator's decision is explicit: they must ascertain **which constraint holds supremacy.**

- **Option A:** Accept the financial and legal liability of internal data storage in order to satisfy KYC and AML obligations.
- **Option B:** Abandon real-time identity verification—and therefore the feature itself—to preserve the externalized liability model.

The Resolution

The executive chooses Option A. The Context Architect translates this judgment into an unambiguous Schema update:

Constraint Update: *Internal database integration is* ***MANDATORY*** *for KYC operations. Third-party-only scoring is rescinded for this module.*

With the hierarchy resolved, the AI regenerates the prototype instantly. The conflict disappears because authority was exercised at the correct semantic layer.

This case demonstrates why the Context Architect's role is irreducible. Machines can enforce constraints. Only humans can decide which constraints matter more.

6.4.3 THE HALLUCINATION AUDIT: THE "RED TEAM" AGENT

One of the most dangerous failure modes in AI-driven prototyping is **Plausible Hallucination.** The AI may generate artifacts that appear complete and credible while quietly violating core assumptions. A login screen may look secure while bypassing authentication logic entirely. A compliance disclosure may read convincingly while citing a regulation that does not exist.

Because the prototype looks real, human reviewers unconsciously lower their skepticism. They assume that functionality exists because interface elements exist. Visual completeness creates false confidence. This is precisely where governance must harden, not soften.

To counter this risk, the Context Architect employs a dedicated **Red Team Agent.**

The Protocol

Rather than asking a human reviewer to click through the prototype—where subtle semantic gaps are easily missed—the Context Architect tasks a hostile AI agent to attempt to break it. This agent is not asked to improve the artifact. It is instructed to attack it.

The Red Team Prompt:

- **Role:** Forensic Code Auditor
- **Target:** Generated artifacts such as Auth_Service.py and Disclaimer_UI.tsx

- **Context:** Ingest the full Constraint & Compliance Layer (HIPAA, FINRA, DOI)
- **Mission:** Identify semantic gaps, violations, or implicit assumptions that contradict declared constraints

The Red Team agent actively probes for failure conditions:

- Does the form accept a user identifier without a valid authentication token?
- Does the disclosure text exactly match mandated legal boilerplate, or has the AI paraphrased it—which is prohibited?
- Can restricted claims (e.g., "Guaranteed Return") be surfaced through edge-case inputs or malformed requests?

The Outcome

A typical report might read:

"Critical Failure: Disclaimer UI paraphrases FINRA-mandated language. Mandatory phrase 'Past performance is not indicative of future results' is missing."

The Context Architect intercepts this semantic hallucination immediately. Before the prototype is shown to any stakeholder, regeneration is forced under corrected constraints.

This machine-versus-machine validation is the **most scalable** way to enforce semantic correctness at the speed of generation. Humans define the rules. Machines enforce them—against each other.

6.5 THE ELIMINATION OF THE WAITING TAX

The largest source of Product Timeline Tax in legacy organizations is not execution time, but waiting time. Work stalls while artifacts queue for review, coordination, clarification, and approval across sequential governance boundaries. These delays are rarely visible on roadmaps, yet they dominate elapsed delivery time. The sections that follow quantify how the Stacked Product Lifecycle eliminates this waiting tax by design, collapsing months of inactivity into parallel, governed execution.

6.5.1 THE ELIMINATION OF THE "WAITING TAX" (WEEKS 1–10)

The first ten weeks of the legacy process are almost entirely non-value-generating. During this period, organizations pay full salaries while no validated architecture, no compliant artifact, and no market-ready asset exist. In effect, the company finances delay.

The Administrative Ledger

Ideation / PRD Phase (Weeks 1–4)

- **Legacy Cost:** The Product Manager manually synthesizes dozens of research documents. The organization holds repeated "requirements gathering" meetings to translate intent into text.
- **Stacked Cost:** The Context Architect injects raw research directly into the Strategic Context Layer. The AI synthesizes personas, objectives, and constraints immediately.
- **Savings:** Four weeks of administrative overhead eliminated.

Design / Wireframe Phase (Weeks 5–10)

- **Legacy Cost:** The handoff meeting. Waiting for designer availability. Iterative email chains debating feasibility after designs already exist.
- **Stacked Cost:** The Converged Artifact Package delivers validated, technically sound wireframes within 72 hours, governed by the same constraints Engineering and Compliance will enforce later.

- **Savings:** Six weeks of waiting and rework eliminated.

By enforcing the Context Schema at the input stage, the Context Architect collapses a ten-week, fully human-velocity pipeline into a single automated conversion. Administrative delay is removed from the system entirely. Weeks of waiting are transformed into immediate architectural output.

6.5.2 THE MITIGATION OF THE "REWORK TAX" (WEEKS 11–36)

While the elimination of administrative waiting is immediately visible, the largest financial impact comes from mitigating the **Rework Tax.** This is the hidden component of the Product Timeline Tax—the compounding cost of late-stage discovery that quietly destroys budgets.

The legacy lifecycle makes rework statistically inevitable by deferring semantic and architectural validation until after execution has begun. Two late-stage checkpoints consistently generate the majority of waste:

Engineering Rework (Pre-Stack 2)

In the traditional timeline, Engineering often commits to a monolithic or shortcut architecture early, only to discover weeks later that it cannot integrate with existing dependencies on the Legacy Dependency Map—most commonly the Kafka event system.

The Cost: Industry estimates place the refactoring of a complex component discovered twelve weeks into development between $15,000 and $25,000 for a single feature team, excluding opportunity cost.

The Savings: Under the Stacked Product Lifecycle, this expense is eliminated entirely. Architectural constraints are enforced at generation time. The system is Born Technically Sound by design.

Compliance Rollback (The Zero-Sum Gate)

The Zero-Sum Gate is the late-stage validation boundary where syntactically correct work collides with unvalidated constraints. In the Legacy Model, compliance validation occurs near the end of the timeline. When this gate is triggered—often around Week 22 due to missing HIPAA or AML requirements—the organization enters a mandatory rollback cycle.

The Cost: At minimum, four weeks of full-team burn rate, compounded by delayed launch and lost market momentum. Potential regulatory exposure can exceed $1 million—not because the work failed, but because compliance truth arrived after irreversible commitment.

The Savings: The Context Architect transfers compliance liability upstream into the Context Schema. Because constraints are enforced before generation, violations are surfaced immediately as failed assertions rather than late-stage rejections. The effective cost of non-compliance at the audit stage approaches zero.

By eliminating both Engineering rework and Compliance rollback, the Context Architect converts months of probabilistic waste into deterministic prevention. Strategic intent no longer enters execution as a hypothesis, but as a governed, multi-validated blueprint—allowing the Engineering and Marketing Stacks to launch in parallel without fear of structural collapse.

6.5.3 THE CFO CONVERSATION: SHIFTING THE METRIC

At some point, the Context Architect must defend this operating model to the individual who controls capital allocation: the CFO. This conversation determines whether Context Engineering is perceived as structural risk reduction or dismissed as procedural overhead.

In the Legacy Model, the CFO evaluates initiatives using a single, familiar metric: **Cost to Build.**

"We have ten engineers at $150,000 per year. This project took nine months. Total cost: $1.1 million."

This framing is incomplete—but it is internally consistent with a sequential system. In the Stacked Model, the Context Architect must introduce two replacement metrics: **Time to Revenue** and **Cost of Waste.**

The Conversation

CFO: "Why are we spending so much time defining this Context Schema before anyone writes code? It feels like overhead."

CA: "In our last three projects, approximately 40% of the codebase was scrapped after failing late-stage legal and compliance review. That represents roughly $400,000 in direct write-offs."

CFO: "And this prevents that?"

CA: "Yes. The Schema prevents us from writing code that cannot ship. We are not accelerating execution—we are eliminating write-offs. This shifts us from capitalizing waste to capitalizing assets."

The ROI of PTT Elimination

When the product timeline is reduced from nine months to nine weeks, the financial impact compounds beyond cost avoidance. Revenue is realized earlier.

- **Legacy Model:** Revenue begins in Month 10
- **Stacked Model:** Revenue begins in Month 4
- **Net Impact:** Six months of accelerated cash flow

This reframes the Product Timeline Tax as a **Revenue Deferral Tax**—a hidden drag on growth that accumulates silently in sequential organizations.

When presented this way, the Context Architect is no longer arguing for a new process. They are presenting a balance-sheet correction. At that point, the CFO becomes the strongest advocate for the Stacked Product Lifecycle.

6.6 CONCLUSION: THE PROTOTYPE AS CONTRACT

The transition from a Product Requirements Document to a Converged Wireframe is not merely a procedural upgrade. It is a structural redefinition of what "agreement" means inside a product organization.

In the Legacy Model, the PRD functioned as a hypothesis. It was a document that aspired to become a product. It described intent, deferred feasibility, and distributed accountability through text. When failure occurred, the document remained intact—even as the product collapsed.

In the Stacked Product Lifecycle, the Converged Wireframe functions as a contract.

Because the artifact is Born Technically Sound, Born Compliant, and Born Market-Ready, it establishes a binding agreement across all stacks at the moment of creation:

- **Engineering** agrees the plan is viable because the Context Schema respects the Legacy Dependency Map.
- **Compliance** agrees the system is lawful because regulatory constraints are enforced structurally, not interpretively.
- **Marketing** agrees the product can be sold because the Strategic Context Layer governs narrative and positioning.

This convergence proves that the Product Timeline Tax is not merely reduced. It is structurally eliminated at the earliest phase of the lifecycle—before rework, rollback, or delay can accumulate.

At this point, the product has been successfully prototyped. But a prototype is not production. A wireframe does not yet account for scale, latency, failure modes, or database sharding. Those challenges live inside the Engineering Stack itself.

In the next chapter, we move into the engine room. We will examine how governance survives contact with distributed systems—and how the Context Architect ensures that the promise of "Born Technically Sound" endures through deployment, scaling, and operational chaos.

7

THE PRODUCT AND ENGINEERING STACK: ARCHITECTURAL REALITY BY CONSTRUCTION

The successful generation of the Converged Artifact Package in Chapter 6—the Born Compliant, Born Technically Sound prototype—marks a decisive structural transition: the shift from strategic convergence into governed, parallel execution. Chapter 6 delivered a verified plan; Chapter 7 establishes the hardened operational structure that allows that plan to move forward without semantic erosion. In the traditional sequential model, this exact moment represents the most fragile handoff in the entire lifecycle, where the Product team throws a document over the wall to the Engineering team, initiating a long cycle of interpretation, misinterpretation, clarification, and eventual correction.

Historically, the Product Timeline Tax (PTT) spiked most severely at this boundary. Weeks—or in large enterprises, entire quarters—are routinely consumed by clarification meetings, technical discovery sessions, and the latent friction of translating business intent into machine-executable syntax. This is the phase where the momentum of the kickoff visibly decays, replaced by the procedural drag of Jira tickets, backlog refinement, architectural debates, and re-scoping exercises that were never anticipated in the original plan.

Under the Stacked Product Lifecycle, this wall does not exist. The PTT has already been neutralized at the concept phase, before any code is generated or any backlog is created. As a result, the organization enters execution without semantic ambiguity, positioned to exploit what appears externally as Infinite Execution Velocity—but is, in reality, the absence of preventable delay rather than reckless acceleration.

This chapter details the simultaneous launch and continuous operation of the Product and Engineering Stack: the execution engine responsible for code generation, architectural enforcement, and core functional development. However, this is not a chapter about "coding faster." Speed, in the AI era, is no longer scarce. Any Junior Developer equipped with a modern code-generation tool can produce working syntax at extreme velocity. What remains scarce—and increasingly valuable—is integrity: the assurance that generated systems behave correctly within their strategic, legal, and architectural constraints.

It is here that the Context Architect (CA) exerts their most consequential influence. The CA does not write application code, nor do they manage execution tickets. Instead, they translate the validated semantic constraints of the Context Schema into concrete, executable work streams that govern how code may be produced. The Converged Wireframe produced in Chapter 6 functions as a binding contract rather than a suggestion. It incorporates the Microservice Architecture Plan and the API Specification, forming the definitive, machine-governable input for the Engineering Subject Matter Expert (SME).

Using this approved context, the Engineering SME governs the AI Studio directly, transforming architectural intent into deployable code at unprecedented speed while remaining fully compliant with the organization's constraints. Unlike the ungoverned velocity celebrated in the "move fast and break things" era, this execution velocity is structurally constrained. It is speed with memory, speed with accountability, and speed without the accumulation of hidden architectural or liability debt.

7.1 THE ENGINEERING SME: GOVERNING SEMANTIC TRUTH IN CODE

To understand the future of the Engineering role, we must first confront the structural inefficiency embedded in its present form. In the sequential product lifecycle, the Engineering Lead functions primarily as a Translator rather than as a governor of intent. Their value is derived not from enforcing correctness, but from mediating ambiguity introduced earlier in the process.

The Engineering Lead typically receives a Product Manager (PM)'s Requirements Document—often written in abstract, business-oriented prose—and is tasked with converting that narrative into a technical design. They then oversee a prolonged, human-velocity development cycle in which Developers manually produce syntax in an attempt to satisfy requirements that were never fully specified in computable terms. In practice, the Engineering Lead spends a minority of their time writing or reviewing code, and a majority of their time arbitrating meaning—debating what words like "secure," "scalable," or "real-time" were intended to signify when they were first written.

This translation-heavy process is structurally vulnerable to Handoff Context Decay. Each transfer of responsibility—from business intent to product definition, from product definition to technical interpretation—causes semantic precision to erode. A PM may specify "GDPR compliance" as a requirement, while a Developer operationalizes that requirement as "HTTPS encryption." Both interpretations appear reasonable in isolation, yet the gap between them is precisely where regulatory exposure, architectural failure, and legal liability accumulate.

Under the Stacked Product Lifecycle, the Engineering SME undergoes a fundamental role transformation. Their primary responsibility is no longer to manage execution by supervising human labor or monitoring task completion. Instead, they are responsible for governing context—ensuring that the machine executing the work operates within the validated semantic boundaries established by the Context Schema.

7.1.1 THE CRITICAL FLAW: THE CODE ACCELERATOR TRAP

"AI Code Accelerators" and "Copilots" now saturate the market, positioned as force multipliers for the Product and Engineering Stack. These tools routinely promise to double or triple individual Developer output, and by their own narrow metrics, they often succeed. They excel at achieving Syntactic Fluency.

This increase in velocity, however, conceals a structural hazard rather than a simple tradeoff. Code Accelerators operate under conditions of Semantic Blindness. They frame code generation as a local optimization problem, solvable entirely within the boundaries of a programming language or runtime environment. They answer questions like, *"How do I implement this function efficiently?"* while remaining blind to external, non-computable constraints such as, *"Is this data permitted to be processed in this environment?"* or *"Does executing this logic create downstream regulatory, contractual, or financial exposure?"*

The Philosophical Liability

This limitation precisely mirrors the failure mode described by the Chinese Room Argument. The system demonstrates flawless symbolic manipulation—it can generate code that compiles, executes, and even performs well—without any understanding of the real-world meaning, consequence, or governance structure those symbols are embedded within. The AI does not know what it is *allowed* to do; it only knows what it *can* do.

Consider the InSuretech Platform case study. When a generic AI coding tool is instructed to *"ingest client data,"* it may generate a highly efficient ingestion pipeline that deposits records directly into a standard AWS S3 bucket. From a purely technical perspective, the result appears exemplary. The code executes without errors. The data flows. The implementation is clean, performant, and syntactically flawless.

Yet if this implementation bypasses the organization's proprietary Legacy Dependency Map—which mandates ingestion through an internal Kafka event bus to preserve immutable audit trails—or violates FINRA regulations that prohibit cloud persistence of unverified Social Security Numbers, the organization has not innovated. It has simply increased the speed at which it approaches a catastrophic compliance failure. The system has produced a faster vehicle, but one entirely devoid of brakes.

Intervention by the Context Architect is non-optional at this layer. The Engineering SME must assume the role of human Semantic Regulator, asserting governance over what the AI Studio is permitted to generate. Their responsibility is not to question the syntactic correctness of the output, but to ensure that every line of generated code operates within the organization's non-negotiable liability, architectural, and dependency constraints as defined by the Technical Dependency Layer.

7.1.2 DEFINING TECHNICAL CONTEXT DEBT (TCD)

As noted earlier in the book, in the traditional software engineering lexicon, "Technical Debt" refers to the implied future cost of expedient decisions—messy implementations, hard-coded shortcuts, or deferred refactoring—that must eventually be addressed to preserve system health. While costly, this form of debt is generally tractable. Teams can schedule remediation, refactor incrementally, and reduce exposure over time.

In the age of AI-mediated development, however, a fundamentally different and more dangerous liability emerges: Technical Context Debt (TCD). This is not debt incurred by poor code quality, but by misaligned governance. To make this distinction explicit, the Context Architect introduces TCD as a separate, non-substitutable category of risk that cannot be managed using traditional engineering heuristics.

Table 7.1: Technical Debt vs. Technical Context Debt

Metric
Definition
Origin
Impact of Non-Payment
Technical Debt

The implied cost of choosing a limited but fast technical solution.

Internal development choice (e.g., "We'll use this old library for now").

Future performance degradation; gradual **PTT** accrual.

Technical Context Debt (TCD)

The incurred liability from generating code that **violates a non-computable constraint.**

Failure of **Context Governance** (e.g., ignoring a FINRA rule or Legacy Dependency).

Complete architecture rework; **Zero-Sum Gate** trigger; massive legal PTT.

Technical Context Debt is incurred precisely when AI's Syntactic Fluency outpaces the human SME's capacity for Semantic Governance. If an AI system generates ten thousand lines of code that execute flawlessly yet violate the organization's data segregation, auditability, or liability constraints, the organization has embedded a systemic governance failure. This is TCD.

Unlike traditional Technical Debt, TCD cannot be amortized, refactored away, or "paid down" gradually. Once deployed, systems suffering from Technical Context Debt often require full decommissioning, architectural rollback, or total regeneration under a corrected Context Schema. In regulated environments, the discovery of TCD can invalidate certifications, trigger legal exposure, or force operational shutdowns.

For this reason, the Stacked Product Lifecycle is explicitly designed to target a Technical Context Debt of zero. Achieving TCD = 0 means that all generated artifacts are Born Compliant by construction, operating entirely within the non-negotiable constraints of the foundational Context Schema rather than relying on post-hoc detection or remediation.

7.1.3 THE PSYCHOLOGICAL PIVOT: FROM "I WROTE THIS" TO "I VALIDATED THIS"

For the Engineering SME, this transition is not merely operational; it is fundamentally psychological. For decades, Senior Engineers have been culturally and professionally conditioned to identify as authors of code. "I built that," they say, pointing to a dense module or a clever algorithm, with personal ownership tightly coupled to lines written and logic solved.

Within the Context Architect model, this identity must pivot. The Engineering SME is no longer the primary author of executable logic; they assume the role of Editor-in-Chief. They function as the architect who approves the blueprints and enforces constraints, rather than the mason who lays each individual brick. Authority shifts from production to validation, from individual craftsmanship to systemic correctness.

This transition is frequently disorienting, even for highly experienced Engineers. The familiar dopamine loop of debugging, optimizing, and personally solving discrete logic puzzles is replaced by a quieter, more rigorous satisfaction: the assurance that the system behaves correctly under all defined constraints. The SME must learn to derive professional value not from the volume or elegance of code produced, but from the precision and completeness of the constraints that govern its generation.

Old World Reward: "I spent three days optimizing this SQL query."

New World Reward: "I designed a schema constraint that prevented the AI from generating fifty inefficient SQL queries across the system."

The Context Architect actively supports this identity shift by formalizing and elevating the SME's role. They are no longer treated as interchangeable "resources" responsible for clearing tickets from a backlog. They are recognized as Governance Officers—individuals accountable for enforcing semantic integrity and ensuring the long-term survivability of the platform itself.

7.2 THE HIGH-DENSITY PROMPT FRAMEWORK: OPERATIONALIZING CONTEXT

The transition from architectural commitment to actual code generation is the precise point at which most organizations fail to realize the promise of Generative AI. The failure is not technical; it is structural. Teams default to treating AI systems like conversational tools—issuing open-ended requests and expecting professional-grade, governed output to emerge spontaneously.

"Please write a Python script for the risk score feature."

This mode of interaction all but guarantees Semantic Blindness. The AI will generate an answer that appears competent—leveraging common libraries, idiomatic patterns, and industry best practices that were statistically dominant in its training data—while silently violating internal architectural rules, compliance constraints, and liability boundaries that were never made explicit. The result is output that looks correct and executes cleanly, yet is fundamentally misaligned with organizational intent.

The Context Architect and the Engineering SME avoid this failure mode by replacing conversational prompting with the Contextual Prompt. This is not an enhanced natural-language request or a "better question." It is a structured data artifact—a High-Density Prompt—that programmatically converges the three layers of the Context Schema into a single, machine-governable input.

7.2.1 THE SCHEMA TRANSLATION SESSION

Before any prompt is constructed, a mandatory ritual occurs: the Schema Translation Session. This is a brief but high-intensity synchronization between the Context Architect and the Engineering

SME, conducted specifically to eliminate ambiguity before execution begins.

During this session, the participants review the Context Schema finalized in Chapter 5. Their objective is to translate abstract strategic, legal, and business constraints into concrete, enforceable technical variables that can be consumed directly by the AI Studio. Nothing enters the prompt unless it can be expressed in a computable form.

CA (Legal Constraint): "The schema specifies that we cannot store PII (Personally Identifiable Information) in any persistent logs."

SME (Technical Translation): "I will enforce that by introducing a SEGREGATION_MANDATE in the prompt and requiring the use of our AuditLog_Wrapper for all instrumentation."

CA (Strategic Constraint): "The schema defines the target user as an independent agent, so response latency is more important than marginal accuracy gains."

SME (Technical Translation): "I will set the SCORING_ALGORITHM_TYPE to Logistic Regression rather than a heavier neural network to guarantee sub-second response times."

This Translation Session ensures that the resulting prompt is not a feature wish list, but a Governing Artifact—an executable expression of validated intent.

7.2.2 THE CONTEXTUAL PROMPT BLUEPRINT

The High-Density Prompt Framework serves as the standard operating procedure for all functional code generation within the Product and Engineering Stack. Its primary function is the systematic elimination of ambiguity. For the InSuretech Platform's core capability—the P_{Score} Microservice—the prompt is expressed in a rigid, declarative structure rather than free-form prose.

```
JSON
  {
```

```
  "ARTIFACT_TYPE":
"MICROSERVICE_PYTHON_STUB",
  "ARTIFACT_NAME": "PScore_Service_V1",
  "FUNCTIONAL_GOAL": "Calculate client
risk score for annuity-to-life conversion
potential."

"CONTEXT_SCHEMA_GOVERNANCE": {

// LAYER I: TECHNICAL DEPENDENCY (Born
Technically Sound)
  "TECHNICAL_CONSTRAINTS": {
  "ARCHITECTURE_PATTERN":
"Microservice_Decoupled_Async",
  "CORE_LANGUAGE": "Python 3.10",
  "COMMUNICATION_PROTOCOL":
"Internal_Kafka_Event_Bus",
  "KAFKA_TOPIC_INPUT":
"client_intake_data",
  "KAFKA_TOPIC_OUTPUT":
"client_risk_scores",
  "MANDATORY_LIBRARY_WRAPPERS":
["Internal_NumPy_Wrapper_V2"],
  "API_CONTRACT_VERSION":
"OpenAPI_PScore_V1_0"
  },

// LAYER II: CONSTRAINT & COMPLIANCE
(Born Compliant)
  "LIABILITY_CONSTRAINTS": {
  "REGULATORY_BODY": "FINRA_SEC_DOIN",
  "PROHIBITED_DATA_INPUT":
["Credit_Score", "Unverified_SSN"],
  "MANDATORY_AUDIT_LOG_FN":
"AuditLog_PII_Accessed_Function()",
```

```
    "SEGREGATION_MANDATE": "Results must be
published only to secured topic
(client_risk_scores), never logged to
stdout."
    },

// LAYER III: STRATEGIC CONTEXT
(Guaranteed Value)
    "BUSINESS_LOGIC": {
    "SCORING_WEIGHT_PRIORITY":
"Stability_Metrics: 60%, Liquid_Assets:
40%",
    "SCORING_ALGORITHM_TYPE":
"Logistic_Regression_V3_Model"
    }
    }
    }
```

7.2.3 DECONSTRUCTING THE BLUEPRINT: WHY DENSITY MATTERS

Each line in the resulting structured prompt corresponds to a potential Zero-Sum Gate that has been proactively neutralized. Density is not an aesthetic choice; it is the mechanism by which ungoverned degrees of freedom are removed. The most critical fields illustrate this directly:

MANDATORY_LIBRARY_WRAPPERS: ["Internal_NumPy_Wrapper_V2"] — This is a purely technical constraint with governance implications. In enterprise environments, using public library distributions can introduce licensing conflicts, unpatched vulnerabilities, or incompatibility with internal security scanners. By forcing the AI to rely exclusively on approved internal wrappers, the SME guarantees compliance before any code is written.

PROHIBITED_DATA_INPUT: ["Credit_Score"] — This field

operationalizes the Compliance Layer. AI systems will naturally optimize for predictive power if left unconstrained. If presented with a statistically powerful signal like a credit score, the model will use it —even when doing so violates Fair Lending or anti-discrimination regulations. This negative constraint explicitly removes that option, preventing the AI from generating illegal logic by construction.

SEGREGATION_MANDATE — In traditional development, Engineers often debug by printing runtime variables to logs. In regulated systems, logging raw PII constitutes a reportable breach. This constraint instructs the AI to generate code that enforces data segregation automatically, converting what was once a fragile human discipline into a guaranteed system property.

Under this framework, the AI is not asked to interpret intent. It is instructed to execute a bounded set of mutually validated constraints, eliminating ambiguity at the source rather than detecting violations after deployment.

7.3 THE ARCHITECTURE OF AUTOMATION: CI/CD AND DEPENDENCY GENERATION

The Contextual Prompt does not merely produce application logic. Because the Context Schema encapsulates the organization's full architectural intent, the AI Studio can also generate the surrounding governance artifacts that traditionally delay execution. As a result, Continuous Integration and Continuous Delivery (CI/CD) cease to be a downstream activity and instead become a parallel, schema-driven output of the Product and Engineering Stack.

7.3.1 CONTEXT-AWARE DEPENDENCY GENERATION

Under the Legacy Dependency Map, environment setup—configuring build pipelines, authoring Dockerfiles, defining runtime permissions, and wiring message bus listeners—was treated as low-status "grunt work." In practice, this work consumed the first one to two weeks of nearly every sprint, introducing early Product Timeline Tax before functional development even began.

The Product and Engineering Stack eliminates this delay through Context-Aware Dependency Generation. Because dependency relationships are already explicitly encoded in the Context Schema, the AI Studio can generate compliant infrastructure and integration artifacts automatically, without waiting for manual interpretation.

Monorepo Structure & CI/CD Stubs: The initial generation produces a repository structure aligned with organizational standards, along with CI/CD scripts (such as GitHub Actions or Jenkinsfiles) that are preconfigured to satisfy the organization's specific security, testing, and approval gates. This ensures that every code change enters a governed delivery pipeline by default, rather than retrofitting controls after violations occur.

Service Integration Stubs: Because the Contextual Prompt explicitly specifies Kafka_Topic_Input and Kafka_Topic_Output, the AI generates fully functional consumers and producers at generation time. This removes the most failure-prone phase of traditional development—the manual integration step where independently built services fail to communicate, creating the "integration hell" that historically accounts for the most severe PTT accumulation.

API Contract Enforcement: The prompt mandates an explicit API Specification (OpenAPI), allowing frontend and backend teams to work in true parallelism against an identical contract. The Engineering SME may further enforce compliance by embedding schema-level extensions—such as x-compliance-masking: true—that compel the generated code to implement data protection and redaction policies directly at the API boundary.

7.3.2 THE "BORN COMPLIANT" ARTIFACT: A CLOSER LOOK

When the Engineering SME initiates generation, the AI Studio produces a Born Compliant Artifact—a fully structured, deployable unit whose components are already aligned with the Context Schema.

This artifact is delivered as a complete directory structure, typically including:

src/ — Core application code generated in accordance with the specified MANDATORY_LIBRARY_WRAPPERS and architectural constraints.

tests/ — An automatically generated test suite derived directly from the governing constraints, including negative test cases (for example, explicitly attempting to inject a prohibited Credit Score field and asserting rejection).

infra/ — Infrastructure definitions, such as Terraform modules or Kubernetes manifests, that enforce constraints like the SEGREGATION_MANDATE at the runtime level by construction (for example, preventing public network exposure or unauthorized data egress).

The artifact is considered "Born Compliant" because it cannot be deployed successfully if it violates the Context Schema. Compliance is not verified after the fact; it is structurally embedded. In this sense, the artifact functions as an immunity system for software, preventing entire classes of architectural and regulatory failure before they can manifest.

7.4 THE SEMANTIC CODE REVIEW: THE "HALLUCINATION AUDIT"

Once code has been generated, the Engineering SME enters a distinct and non-negotiable phase of work: the Semantic Code Review. This review exists to validate that the generated system faithfully expresses the constraints and intent embedded in the Context Schema.

In the legacy development model, code reviews were largely syntactic in nature—focused on correctness at the language level. Review comments typically addressed missing semicolons, inefficient loops, or deviations from style guides. These reviews assumed that human authorship guaranteed semantic intent and that syntax was the primary failure mode.

Under the Stacked Product Lifecycle, this assumption is inverted. The AI handles syntax with near-perfect reliability. As a result, the SME's review responsibility shifts entirely toward semantic validation. They are not performing a traditional code review; they are conducting a Hallucination Audit.

7.4.1 HUNTING FOR SEMANTIC DRIFT

During the Hallucination Audit, the SME actively searches for plausible lies—code that executes cleanly, passes tests, and appears reasonable, yet violates the governing context. These errors are especially dangerous because they do not announce themselves through crashes or obvious defects.

The External API Hallucination: The SME first inspects imports and network calls. Did the AI quietly import a generic HTTP client and attempt to call a public currency-conversion or enrichment API in order to calculate a "Liquid Assets" score? Even if technically correct, such behavior constitutes a security and compliance violation. The SME therefore begins by auditing external dependencies before examining internal logic.

The Logic Hallucination: The SME then verifies algorithmic intent. Was the specified Logistic_Regression_Model implemented as directed, or did the AI silently substitute a Random_Forest because it inferred higher predictive accuracy? The SME validates every major decision against the Context Schema, ensuring that performance optimizations never override declared constraints.

7.4.2 THE REFINEMENT LOOP

When a hallucination is detected, the SME does not correct it directly in the generated code. Manual fixes treat symptoms while leaving the underlying system vulnerable to recurrence. Instead, the SME corrects the governing input.

Recognizing that a constraint was under-specified—"I did not explicitly prohibit external network calls"—the SME updates the TECHNICAL_CONSTRAINTS in the High-Density Prompt to include a declaration such as "NETWORK_ACCESS": "Internal_Only".

The system is then regenerated.

This Refinement Loop ensures that every correction is systemic rather than local. A manual patch would be overwritten the next time the AI regenerates the artifact. By fixing the prompt—the authoritative input—the SME permanently inoculates the system against that specific class of error, reinforcing governance at the source rather than at the surface.

7.5 THE TALENT SHIFT: THE "APPRENTICE ARCHITECT"

A recurring anxiety among Engineering Leaders evaluating this model is what is often framed as the "Junior Developer Crisis." If AI systems generate boilerplate code, CRUD operations, and baseline unit tests—the tasks historically assigned to Junior Engineers as a training ground—how does the next generation of technical talent develop competence, judgment, and architectural intuition?

The Context Architect model challenges the premise of this concern. It argues that the role of the "Junior Developer" as a high-throughput "Ticket Closer" is not endangered—it is already obsolete. What remains both viable and essential is the role of the Junior Developer as an Apprentice Architect, trained not in keystrokes, but in governed system design.

7.5.1 THE CURRICULUM OF CONTEXT

The Stacked Product Lifecycle does not insulate Junior Engineers from complexity. Instead, it exposes them to the full system earlier and more deliberately. Rather than assigning a Junior Engineer to "Write a form for the login page," the Engineering SME assigns them a structurally richer task: "Draft the Contextual Prompt for the Login Module."

This assignment forces the Junior Engineer to reason holistically from the first day of contribution:

Security First: They must determine which MANDATORY_LIBRARY_WRAPPERS are required for authentication flows and why those wrappers exist.

Data Flow: They must explicitly map where credentials and session artifacts travel—through Kafka topics, internal services, or persistent storage—before any executable logic is generated.

Compliance: They must articulate why sensitive fields such as passwords or tokens are excluded from logs, metrics, and debugging output, grounding their decisions in the Context Schema rather than habit.

7.5.2 MENTORSHIP VIA SCHEMA

In this model, mentorship no longer centers on correcting syntax or refactoring implementation details. The Engineering SME mentors the apprentice by reviewing and correcting their proposed Context Schema inputs.

SME: "You defined the input as 'Any String.' The Schema classifies this module as high-security. What happens if the input contains a SQL injection payload or malformed credentials? Rework the prompt to include an explicit Input Validation Constraint."

This apprenticeship model produces Engineers who may generate fewer lines of code per day, yet possess a far deeper understanding of systemic integrity, constraint propagation, and architectural risk. They become fluent in the Context Schema itself rather than merely fluent in Java, Python, or any single implementation language. This represents an upgrade in capability, not a loss of productivity.

7.6 GOVERNANCE OF VELOCITY: ELIMINATING ACCELERATED SCOPE CREEP

The extreme speed achieved by the Product and Engineering Stack introduces a new governance paradox. What appears internally as disciplined parallel execution often appears externally—especially to executive stakeholders—as "magic." This perception creates the single most dangerous governance failure mode of the AI era: Accelerated Scope Creep.

7.6.1 THE CRISIS OF QUALIA

In the sequential product model, requirement changes were slow, painful, and therefore naturally constrained. In an AI-mediated execution model, executives infer that because code can be generated in seconds, business intent itself should also be mutable in seconds. Velocity at the execution layer is misinterpreted as permission for volatility at the strategic layer.

Consider the executive interruption: "We need a real-time competitive quote generator. Add it now—while you're building the risk scorer."

This moment represents a Crisis of Qualia. The executive expresses a subjective, emotional desire ("I want this feature") that collides directly with the formal, computed logic of the Context Schema. They cannot see the Legacy Dependency Map beneath the request. They do not realize that introducing "competitive quotes" implies third-party data access, unvetted external APIs, and data-sharing pathways that have not been approved—thereby violating the schema's LIABILITY_CONSTRAINTS by construction.

If the team complies, the Context Schema is silently bypassed. The system will successfully generate code, giving the illusion of progress, while immediately accruing massive Technical Context Debt. The Zero-Sum Gate is not avoided; it is merely deferred. Weeks later, Legal or Compliance will discover that user data has been transmitted to an unapproved third party, forcing rollback, remediation, or shutdown.

7.6.2 THE CONTEXT ARCHITECT AS EXECUTIVE FIREWALL

The Context Architect exists to prevent precisely this failure. They operate as an executive firewall, empowered by the Context Schema, which serves as the organization's single, converged, and authoritative definition of scope, risk, and permissible change.

When confronted with an out-of-band feature demand, the CA does not argue from capacity or schedule. Statements such as "we don't have time" are resource-based and easily overridden. Instead, the CA responds with a Constraint-Based Argument:

"That request violates the Constraint & Compliance Layer of the current Schema. Implementing it requires a reset of the Legacy Dependency Map. We cannot introduce it into this build without invalidating our compliance posture."

The request is then formally classified as a Version 2.0 Iteration Context. This classification preserves executive intent while protecting the integrity of the current execution window, ensuring that the active product timeline remains locked against late-stage semantic contamination.

7.6.3 MANAGING CONTEXT DRIFT

Accelerated execution can also surface legitimate Context Drift without executive interference. As the Engineering SME works within the constraints of the Schema, they may discover that a specific technical requirement renders execution impossible.

For example, an Internal_NumPy_Wrapper may prove incompatible with the selected Logistic_Regression_Model. In a traditional environment, an Engineer might quietly implement a workaround, incurring Technical Debt. Within the Context Architect model, this incompatibility triggers a formal Schema Exception Event.

The Engineering SME escalates the issue to the Context Architect, who evaluates the impact systematically:

— Does the exception violate the Strategic Layer? (No.)

— Does it compromise the Compliance Layer? (Possibly.)

The CA then amends the Context Schema to allow a narrowly scoped, explicitly vetted exception. The Schema is versioned (for example, v1.1), and the change propagates immediately to dependent stacks—including Compliance and Marketing—ensuring that no downstream system or market-facing material contradicts the updated technical reality.

This enforcement loop demonstrates why the Context Architect remains an indispensable human role. They resolve conflicts between speed and safety that automated systems cannot adjudicate. By governing velocity rather than resisting it, the CA ensures that the speed of the Engineering Stack remains a strategic advantage instead of an unmanaged organizational risk.

7.7 CONCLUSION: THE END OF THE "GAP OF DISAPPOINTMENT"

With the engine of governed code generation now operating at full capacity, the organization encounters its next structural test. In the legacy delivery model, Engineering built the product while Marketing operated in partial darkness—drafting positioning, campaigns, and launch narratives based on early assumptions, aspirational roadmaps, or incomplete technical understanding. This structural disconnect produced what many organizations have come to accept as inevitable: the "Gap of Disappointment," where the promise articulated to the market consistently outpaced the reality of what the system could reliably deliver.

Within the Stacked Product Lifecycle, this gap is eliminated before it can form. The Context Architect ensures that the same Context Schema governing the Technical Dependency Layer simultaneously governs the Strategic Context Layer. As executable systems are generated, validated, and constrained, the market narrative is formed in parallel—derived from the same authoritative definition of scope, capability, and limitation. Marketing no longer speculates; it reflects.

This convergence marks a decisive shift. Products are no longer merely Born Technically Sound; they are Born Market-Ready by construction. Semantic Drift between what is built and what is promised is structurally prevented rather than managed retroactively. With the Product and Engineering Stack now fully operational, attention shifts to the second engine of parallel execution: the Brand and Go-to-Market Stack. In the next chapter, we examine how the Context Schema governs messaging, positioning, and launch strategy with the same rigor it applies to code—ensuring that what we sell is as constrained, compliant, and intentional as what we build.

8

THE BRAND AND GO-TO-MARKET STACK

The moment the Context Architect (CA) approves the Converged Wireframe in Chapter 6, the organization does more than signal readiness—it structurally mandates simultaneous execution across all functional domains. This approval event converts strategic intent into an operational invariant: no stack proceeds in isolation once context has been validated.

In the previous chapter, we observed the Product and Engineering Stack accelerating to Mach 10, translating architectural constraints directly into executable systems. Yet code, regardless of its elegance or correctness, does not sell itself. Under the traditional sequential methodology, teams build the "Product" first, while the "Marketing" engine remains largely dormant until late in the lifecycle, activating only as delivery approaches.

This structural delay produces the phenomenon known as the "Gap of Disappointment."

Engineering teams sprint for months, navigating edge cases, making architectural trade-offs, and converging on a specific, constrained solution. Then, near completion, responsibility abruptly shifts to a Marketing department that is cold, under-contextualized, and scrambling to understand what was actually built.

This handover is frequently experienced as organizational trauma. Marketers have not lived through the trade-offs or constraint negotiations. They have operated in partial darkness. Now, under intense pressure to "make a splash," they are incentivized to invent a narrative that often bears little resemblance to the system that exists.

This delay manifests as the Marketing Lag—a substantial and recurring source of Product Timeline Tax (PTT). After code freeze, weeks are consumed by messaging workshops, positioning pivots, and accelerated legal reviews. The result is a familiar failure mode: products launch quietly not because the system is unfinished, but because the market story is still in draft form.

The Stacked Product Lifecycle eliminates the Marketing Lag by design. It forces the Brand and Go-to-Market (GTM) Stack to operate in true parallelism with Engineering. Governed by the Product Marketing Manager (PMM) acting as the Subject Matter Expert (SME), this stack generates its full suite of launch artifacts from the same pre-validated, liability-controlled Context Schema that governs code generation.

The objective is absolute concurrency. Code Readiness and Launch Readiness must resolve simultaneously. When the final line of Python is committed to the repository, the organization should already possess a finalized landing page, sales battle card, and compliance disclosure—ready for immediate deployment rather than emergency assembly.

8.1 THE SEMANTIC CHALLENGE OF BRAND: GOVERNING NON-COMPUTABLE CONTEXT

To understand why the Brand and Go-to-Market Stack requires its own governance model, we must first recognize the unique risk profile of applying AI to branding. The challenge faced by the GTM Stack is categorically different from that of the Engineering Stack.

The Engineering Stack is deterministic. Code either compiles or it does not. A unit test passes or it fails. Errors are binary, observable, and recoverable.

The Brand Stack, by contrast, is probabilistic, emotional, and deeply human. It operates in the domain of perception, trust, and identity. As a result, branding is a problem of Semantic Understanding rather than Syntactic Fluency.

Generative AI is arguably the most capable copywriter ever created—if writing is defined solely as arranging words according to grammatical and stylistic norms. It can generate thousands of marketing headlines in seconds, each linguistically fluent and structurally sound. Yet beneath this fluency lies profound Semantic Blindness.

8.1.1 THE "HOLLOW BRAND" RISK

When deployed without governance, Generative AI produces what can be described as the "Hollow Brand." This is branding that appears professional, polished, and on-message, yet feels emotionally empty and interchangeable. It relies on familiar buzzwords—"innovative," "seamless," "empowering," "cutting-edge"—but establishes no genuine connection with a specific audience.

The AI is effectively averaging the internet, predicting likely word sequences based on vast corpora of corporate communications. When asked to write a press release for an insurance product, it produces the statistical mean of every insurance press release it has encountered. The result is technically competent and entirely forgettable.

Preventing this failure mode requires direct intervention by the Context Architect. The CA must inject Qualia—the subjective, non-reducible "soul" of the brand—into the system. Qualia are non-computable context. A machine cannot infer why a customer might trust a rugged, understated voice over a polished, corporate one. The CA must therefore constrain the AI explicitly, instructing it to simulate these imperfections rather than defaulting to statistical polish.

8.1.2 CASE STUDY: THE QUALIA OF THE INSURETECH PLATFORM

Returning to the InSuretech Platform clarifies this risk. The Strategic Context Layer defines the primary persona as the "Tech-Averse Small Business Insurance Agency Owner," whom we will call Bob.

Bob is fifty-five years old. He maintains his client list in a physical filing cabinet. He is deeply concerned about cyber-attacks and data breaches. He distrusts "tech bros" who promise to disrupt his industry, because "disruption" usually translates into cost-cutting and automation initiatives that eliminate roles like that of his receptionist, Mary.

The Semantic Blindness Risk:

If the PMM prompts the AI with *"Write a landing page for our new AI insurance tool,"* the model—shaped by startup-centric training data —predictably responds with:

"Revolutionize your workflow with the power of Artificial Intelligence! Disrupt the market, crush the competition, and maximize your ROI with our bleeding-edge algorithms."

The Semantic Failure:

To a venture capitalist in Silicon Valley, this language signals ambition and innovation.

To Bob, it signals threat and instability.

"Disrupt" implies loss of clients.

"Bleeding-edge" implies fragility and risk.

"AI" implies an opaque system that could expose him to liability or identity theft.

If this copy is published, the product fails—semantic alignment has collapsed.

The Fix:

The PMM must inject a governing rule into the Context Schema: language must prioritize simplicity, stability, and risk mitigation over technological sophistication. The Context Architect formalizes this emotional nuance into an explicit constraint, overriding the AI's default bias toward hype and ensuring the generated messaging aligns with the lived reality of the target persona.

8.2 THE ECONOMICS OF PARALLELISM: ELIMINATING THE MARKETING LAG

Parallel execution is not an efficiency preference; it is an economic necessity. Under the traditional sequential dependency map, value leaks continuously because the Brand and GTM Stack is structurally prevented from operating until Engineering declares the product "functionally complete." This sequencing produces three distinct and compounding accruals of the Product Timeline Tax, each of which directly converts organizational delay into lost revenue, wasted labor, or misaligned demand.

8.2.1 THE WAITING TAX (DELAY)

In the Legacy Model, the Product Marketing Manager's team exists in a prolonged holding pattern—often for sixteen to twenty weeks—while Engineering stabilizes features and resolves edge cases. This period represents pure opportunity cost. Every week the PMM waits is a week in which the market is not being educated, narratives are not being shaped, and competitors are free to define category expectations unopposed.

Historically, this delay is rationalized with a familiar refrain: "I can't write the brochure until I know what the feature actually does." In a sequential system, this reasoning is defensible. In the Stacked Product Lifecycle, it is structurally invalid.

The Context Schema defines functional behavior, constraints, and exclusions before implementation begins. As a result, marketing artifacts can be authored against validated intent rather than completed code. The Schema functions as a forward contract, allowing the GTM Stack to execute confidently on defined futures instead of waiting passively for delivered artifacts.

8.2.2 THE REWORK TAX (LIABILITY)

The most expensive form of Marketing Lag manifests as rework driven by late-stage compliance intervention. In the traditional process, Legal review typically occurs weeks before launch, after creative assets have already been produced and distributed internally. When Legal flags a phrase such as *"The Only Risk-Free Solution"* as a violation of the Constraint Layer, the correction is not localized—it cascades.

The immediate consequence is forced regeneration. Website copy must be rewritten, sales decks restructured, advertisements re-edited, and design assets re-rendered. Launch dates slip—often by multiple weeks—while teams scramble to repair material that should never have been created in its original form.

The financial impact compounds quickly. For a product generating $10,000 per day, a three-week delay translates into $210,000 in direct, irrecoverable revenue loss, excluding internal labor costs and reputational erosion. This is not iterative improvement. It is bad rework—effort expended solely to correct a preventable governance failure.

8.2.3 HANDOFF CONTEXT DECAY (MISALIGNMENT)

Even when launch proceeds on schedule, sequential execution introduces a subtler but equally damaging tax: Context Decay. The PMM's original strategic vision—often documented months earlier in a Product Requirements Document—erodes as Engineering adapts scope to meet deadlines or technical constraints.

By the time development concludes, features may have been reduced, deferred, or modified. Marketing, operating from outdated documentation or institutional memory, launches campaigns for capabilities that no longer exist. Users arrive expecting "Real-Time Sync" and discover "Daily Batch Sync." The resulting disappointment is not a messaging failure; it is a governance failure.

The Context Schema prevents this outcome by serving as the single authoritative source of truth for both stacks simultaneously. When Engineering adjusts a constraint—such as synchronization frequency—the Schema is updated once, and that change propagates automatically to the Brand and Go-to-Market Stack. Messaging, positioning, and claims are revised at the source, eliminating drift before it reaches the market.

8.3 CONTEXT ENGINEERING: THE SEMANTIC RESONANCE MATRIX

The critical operational mechanism of the Brand and Go-to-Market Stack is the creation and enforcement of the Semantic Resonance Matrix. In traditional organizations, brand guidelines are typically delivered as static PDF documents populated with aspirational adjectives such as "bold," "innovative," or "human-centric." These descriptors may function as cultural signals among humans, but they fail completely as governing inputs for machines.

To an AI system, such language is dangerously ambiguous. Instructing a model to be "bold" may result in confrontational or inappropriate phrasing. Directing it to be "human-centric" may trigger informal language, slang, or emotional framing that violates professional, regulatory, or brand standards. The problem is not tone; it is the absence of computable boundaries.

The Semantic Resonance Matrix resolves this ambiguity. It is a proprietary context-engineering framework that translates abstract brand identity, emotional intent, and legal obligation into explicit, enforceable linguistic constraints consumable by the AI Studio. For the PMM, it functions as the primary tool for converting subjective Qualia into objective, governable rules without diluting nuance.

8.3.1 THE CONTEXTUAL PROMPT BLUEPRINT: CODING FOR EMOTION

Using the Semantic Resonance Matrix, the PMM constructs a highly structured, converged prompt by appending the relevant layers of the Context Schema directly to the creative mandate. This structure ensures that emotional expression is governed rather than improvised. Constraints are enforced simultaneously across three interdependent domains: Voice (Qualia), Liability (Compliance), and Feature Alignment (Technical Truth).

For the InSuretech Platform's landing page, the Contextual Prompt is not a paragraph of instructions but a declarative structure that defines what emotional signals are permitted, what claims are forbidden, and which features may be referenced—before any copy is generated.

```
JSON
  {
  "ARTIFACT_TYPE":      "WEBSITE_LANDING_-
PAGE_COPY_SUITE",
  "TARGET_PAGE":
"InSuretech_Homepage_V1",
  "CREATIVE_GOAL": "Generate 3 Headlines
and 5 Body Paragraphs.",

"CONTEXT_SCHEMA_GOVERNANCE": {

// LAYER I: STRATEGIC CONTEXT (Governing
Qualia)
  "BRAND_VOICE_CONSTRAINTS": {
  "TONE":   "Trustworthy,   Conservative,
Empathetic",
  "PRIMARY_TARGET_PERSONA":  "Tech-Averse
Small Business Agency Owner",
  "MANDATORY_KEYWORD_FOCUS":       ["Risk
Reduction",      "Client      Stability",
"Compliance Peace of Mind"],
  "PROHIBITED_PHRASES": ["AI Revolution",
"Disruptive     Technology",     "Maximum
Profit"]
  },

//  LAYER  II:  CONSTRAINT  &  COMPLIANCE
(Governing Liability)
  "LEGAL_MESSAGING_RULES": {
  "REGULATORY_BODY": "FINRA_DOIN",
```

```
"MANDATORY_DISCLAIMER_TAG":
"FINRA_Disclaimer_Past_Performance_V1_0",
  "FORBIDDEN_CLAIMS": ["Guaranteed ROI",
"Zero Risk", "100% Success Rate"],
  "MANDATORY_DISCLOSURE_PLACEMENT": "Must
append Disclaimer Tag to any headline
referencing 'prediction' or 'score'."
  },

// LAYER III: TECHNICAL DEPENDENCY
(Governing Feature Alignment)
  "PRODUCT_FEATURE_MAPPING": {
  "V1_FEATURES_ALLOWED":
["PScore_Service",
"KYC_Automated_Check"],
  "V2_FEATURES_FORBIDDEN": ["Automated_-
Claim_Filing", "RealTime_Com-
petitor_Pricing"],
  "DATA_USAGE_CLARIFICATION": "Must state
data handling is compliant with HIPAA
segmentation rules."
  }
  }
  }
```

8.3.2 THE POWER OF NEGATIVE CONSTRAINTS

Within Context Engineering, negative constraints—explicitly defining what the AI must not say—are often more powerful than positive guidance. The PROHIBITED_PHRASES field is a primary enforcement mechanism within the Semantic Resonance Matrix.

For the InSuretech Platform, "Disruptive Technology" is a prohibited phrase. As noted earlier, while "disruption" signals opportunity and upside to venture capital audiences, it signals instability, retraining, and operational risk to a small business insurance agency owner. By banning the phrase at the schema level, the PMM prevents the AI from defaulting to a Silicon Valley–centric tone that would immediately alienate the target persona.

Similarly, the FORBIDDEN_CLAIMS array—containing phrases such as "Guaranteed ROI"—functions as a digital muzzle. The AI may calculate that such language maximizes conversion probability, but the Context Schema overrides that optimization with a legal absolute. The result is creative output that is Born Compliant by construction rather than sanitized after the fact.

8.3.3 NATURAL LANGUAGE TRANSLATION FOR THE EXECUTION INTERFACE

Although the structured schema is the architectural backbone of the Semantic Resonance Matrix, PMMs frequently interact with the **context-governed execution environment** through natural language. To preserve governance, the Context Architect trains teams to translate schema-level constraints into a Governance-Enforced Prompt that mirrors the underlying structure.

Natural Language Governance-Enforced Prompt (GTM Stack):

"Act as the Lead Product Marketing Strategist. Generate three homepage headlines and five supporting paragraphs for the InSuretech Platform. Brand Constraints: The tone must be conservative, trustworthy, and empathetic, targeting the 'Tech-Averse Small Business Agency Owner' persona. Compliance Constraints: You must include the FINRA_Disclaimer_Past_Performance_V1_0 tag immediately following any reference to risk scoring. You are forbidden from implying guaranteed ROI or certainty of outcome. Technical Constraints: Reference only validated V1 capabilities, including the P_{Score} risk service and KYC verification. Do not mention any V2 or speculative features."

This high-density natural language formulation preserves semantic authority while remaining usable in day-to-day workflows. It ensures that the initial copy produced by the **execution**

environment is simultaneously market-resonant, technically accurate, and liability-proof—without requiring manual cleanup or post-generation enforcement.

8.4 THE ASSET FACTORY: ACHIEVING LAUNCH READINESS

The Brand and Go-to-Market Stack does not produce drafts, placeholders, or provisional assets. Because its inputs are pre-validated, constrained, and converged through the Context Schema, its output is a complete Launch Readiness Package—generated in parallel with the Microservice Architecture Plan described in Chapter 7. Marketing assets are therefore not finalized *after* Engineering; they are **Born Market-Ready** as a structural property of the system.

Because the product is Born Market-Ready, launch does not require a stabilization phase. Every non-code artifact required for Day One—messaging, disclosures, and sales materials—is complete, governed, and deployable at the moment execution concludes. When this condition is absent, marketing failure does not appear as creative polish issues; it emerges as misalignment, over-promising, and post-launch rework that erodes trust and momentum.

8.4.1 MESSAGING HIERARCHY (BORN STRATEGIC)

Anchored to the approved Strategic Context Layer, the system generates and locks the full messaging hierarchy—from the executive-level elevator pitch down to granular website FAQs and objection-handling responses. The GTM Subject Matter Expert evaluates this hierarchy using the Semantic Resonance Matrix, ensuring that every headline, subheading, and bullet point reflects the intended Persona Qualia rather than local optimization or improvisation.

Deep Dive: Localization

This same mechanism supports large-scale localization without manual intervention. When a platform launches across multiple jurisdictions, the Context Schema encodes regulatory tone and disclosure requirements at the state or regional level. For example, messaging intended for California and Texas can be automatically adapted to reflect the expectations of each state's Department of Insurance. The AI Studio may generate dozens of localized landing page variants, while the Context Architect validates the governing logic of the variation rather than reviewing each individual sentence.

8.4.2 LEGAL DISCLAIMER SUITE (BORN COMPLIANT)

In traditional delivery models, legal review functions as a late-stage Zero-Sum Gate. Marketing teams may work for months producing creative assets, only to have Legal invalidate them in minutes, forcing wholesale rework and launch delays.

Within the Brand Stack, this failure mode is eliminated. The Constraint & Compliance Layer generates all mandatory disclaimers, footnotes, and qualifying language for every channel—websites, advertisements, sales scripts, and training materials—alongside the creative copy itself. Legal SMEs contribute their semantic expertise once, codifying constraints into the Schema, after which the AI Studio replicates those requirements consistently across hundreds of assets. This guarantees that marketing language respects the data handling, liability profile, and regulatory posture of the system being built by Engineering.

8.4.3 SALES ENABLEMENT MATRIX (BORN READY)

Legacy launches often fail because the Sales department is forced to infer intent from a speculative roadmap. Under the Stacked Product Lifecycle, this failure mode is eliminated.

Sales enablement assets are generated concurrently with the

product itself. Training decks, competitive battle cards, and demonstration scripts are produced using the same governing constraints and messaging that regulate external marketing and product behavior.

Battle Card Example:

"If a competitor claims 'Real-Time Sync,' respond with: 'We prioritize data integrity and auditability over raw speed to ensure FINRA compliance.'"

Demo Script Example:

"Begin the demonstration with the Audit Log feature, reinforcing the 'Peace of Mind' Qualia."

Because the system is Born Market-Ready, the sales force is trained on a contextually guaranteed product rather than a promise. Forbidden Claims are enforced structurally, not via after-the-fact coaching. When the code goes live, sales teams are already aligned, informed, and operationally fluent. When this condition is violated, misrepresentation risk surfaces immediately and scales with distribution.

8.5 CONVERGENCE GOVERNANCE: THE CONTEXT ARCHITECT AS SEMANTIC FIREWALL

As the Brand and Go-to-Market Stack matures, the Product Marketing Manager's role undergoes a structural shift. The PMM is no longer evaluated as a content producer measured by output volume. Instead, they function as a Convergence Governor, accountable for ensuring that every market-facing artifact aligns precisely with the parallel constraints imposed by the Engineering Stack and the Quality and Compliance Stack.

Maintaining this alignment is non-trivial. Semantic Drift emerges naturally under speed, pressure, and executive attention. The Context Architect therefore serves as a Semantic Firewall—an explicit governance role designed to prevent linguistic, conceptual, and liability drift before it propagates into irreversible market commitments.

8.5.1 ENFORCING SEMANTIC CONTINUITY

The Context Architect enforces strict continuity between the language used in the market and the functional reality encoded in the Context Schema. This is the point at which the governance of language becomes inseparable from the governance of code.

Scenario: Semantic Discontinuity

The Code: The Engineering Stack delivers a feature formally named the "Automated Client Risk Scoring Service."

The Drift: Seeking differentiation, the PMM drafts messaging that reframes the feature as the "Client Wealth Maximizer."

Superficially, this appears to be harmless positioning. In reality, it constitutes a semantic violation. The phrase "Wealth Maximizer" implies an outcome-oriented fiduciary promise of financial gain, triggering SEC and FINRA regulatory exposure that the underlying system neither supports nor intends.

The Context Architect intervenes immediately, requiring the PMM to revert to compliant terminology before high-cost assets—such as video, print collateral, or paid campaigns—are produced. This preemptive correction prevents the organization from investing in content that would inevitably be rejected at a Zero-Sum Gate. In this role, the CA ensures that Syntactic Fluency in copywriting does not mask Semantic Blindness regarding liability.

8.5.2 MITIGATING ACCELERATED SCOPE CREEP IN BRANDING

As with Engineering, the velocity of the GTM Stack introduces its own governance risk: Accelerated Scope Creep driven by emotional executive reactions to high-fidelity prototypes.

The Executive Demand:

After reviewing compliant GTM materials focused on risk reduction for small business owners, the CEO responds: "This feels too conservative. We should target high-net-worth individuals and emphasize asset multiplication—it's a much larger market."

In a legacy organization, this directive would trigger an immediate pivot. Marketing would reposition the campaign overnight, creating a fatal disconnect: the Brand Stack begins selling a Ferrari while the Engineering Stack is delivering a tank.

The CA's Response:

Acting as the firewall, the Context Architect anchors the discussion in the Context Schema. They demonstrate that redefining the target persona to "high-net-worth individuals" invalidates the existing Constraint & Compliance Layer—requiring enhanced KYC/AML controls—and violates the Technical Dependency Layer, as the current P_{Score} model is not validated for that asset class.

The CA formally classifies the request as a Version 2.0 Iteration Context. This preserves executive intent without contaminating the active delivery window. The current product timeline remains locked, protected from semantic and architectural drift.

In this capacity, the CA translates subjective, non-computable executive desire into objective, computable liability and dependency costs. By enforcing parallel Launch Readiness and Code Readiness, the Brand and Go-to-Market Stack converts what was once a sequential Marketing Lag into a durable competitive advantage.

8.6 THE TALENT SHIFT: FROM COPYWRITER TO CONTEXT GOVERNOR

As this chapter closes, the human implication of the Brand Stack becomes unavoidable. If AI systems are generating emails, blog posts, and advertising copy, what is the Product Marketing Manager's role?

In the sequential model, the PMM was valued primarily as a Creator. Professional identity centered on writing skill, narrative flair, and the accumulation of polished deliverables—a portfolio measured in documents.

In the Stacked Product Lifecycle, the PMM becomes a Governor.

Their value lies in defining, maintaining, and enforcing the Semantic Resonance Matrix that constrains every generated artifact.

This shift is often uncomfortable. It requires less time spent drafting copy and more time operating within the Context Schema. The PMM must become part legal interpreter, part behavioral psychologist, and part systems strategist. They must understand the Legacy Dependency Map deeply enough to know why promises such as "Real-Time Pricing" are structurally impossible or legally dangerous.

Organizations that succeed in this transition are not those with the most eloquent AI prompts. They are those with Human Governors capable of constraining those prompts to tell the truth. The Context Architect does not displace the Marketer; the role elevates the Marketer from a content factory to a strategic owner of market integrity.

8.7 CONCLUSION: THE UNIFIED FRONT

With the product built (Chapter 7) and the market narrative governed (Chapter 8), the organization achieves a unified front. Code and brand now speak the same language, operate under the same constraints, and target the same user reality.

Yet a final question remains unresolved. We have built the system, and we have positioned it responsibly—but is it actually safe? Can we prove that the machine behaves correctly under stress, scrutiny, and real-world usage before placing it in the hands of customers?

Answering that question requires one final stack. We now turn to the Quality and Compliance Stack—the last gear in the engine of governed execution.

9

THE QUALITY AND COMPLIANCE STACK

The Quality and Compliance Stack (QC Stack) represents the final structural defense layer for the executive team against the compounding liability created by **Infinite Execution Velocity.** It exists not to slow the machine down, but to ensure that acceleration itself does not become a legal, financial, or reputational weapon turned inward on the organization.

In the previous chapters, we established the engines of creation. The Engineering Stack (Chapter 7) generates production-grade code at machine speed. The Brand Stack (Chapter 8) generates market promises, claims, and positioning with similar velocity. Together, these stacks collapse what were once multi-quarter activities into compressed execution cycles measured in days or even hours.

This convergence produces a structural rupture. In the Legacy Model, human inefficiency functioned as an unintentional safety system. When a feature required six months to build, the organization accumulated six months of meetings, reviews, informal checks, and accidental friction. That friction—however wasteful—often surfaced catastrophic errors before they reached customers, regulators, or the public record.

When AI compresses a six-month build cycle into six days, that safety valve disappears. The organization begins producing executable liability faster than any human governance layer can reasonably inspect. This leads to an Asymmetric Risk Profile, where the speed of creation exceeds the speed of verification by an order of magnitude, and where each additional unit of velocity compounds downstream exposure rather than opportunity.

In the traditional sequential model, Quality Assurance (QA) and Compliance Audits functioned as the **Zero-Sum Gate.** This gate appeared late in the product lifecycle—often weeks before launch—when a Compliance Officer, Security Reviewer, or Lead QA Engineer evaluated the accumulated output of entire quarters of work in a single pass. If this review uncovered a critical flaw—a missing HIPAA encryption requirement, a violation of a FINRA disclosure obligation, or a foundational security architecture error—the system offered exactly one corrective mechanism: rejection.

The gate is "zero-sum" because failure does not degrade progress incrementally. It collapses it. The architecture must be scrapped. The code must be rewritten. The marketing campaign must be pulled. Months of sequential progress are reset to zero, not because the work was poorly executed, but because validation arrived after commitment rather than before execution.

This delayed validation constitutes the single largest component of the Product Timeline Tax (PTT). Its cost profile resembles a firm that completes a skyscraper, schedules the ribbon-cutting ceremony, and then discovers structural cracks in the foundation on opening morning. The economics are unforgiving: correcting a foundation after construction costs orders of magnitude more than correcting it at the blueprint stage.

The mandate of the QC Stack—governed by QA and Compliance Subject Matter Experts (SMEs)—is to eliminate the Zero-Sum Gate structurally. Compliance is no longer a late-stage event. It is an assumed property of the system once generation begins.

Because the product is **Born Compliant**, failure costs are shifted from irreversible rollbacks to reversible context decisions. Quality is not "tested in" at the end of the lifecycle. It is engineered into the system at the moment of context definition, where correction is cheap, fast, and structurally contained. When this condition is violated, compliance does not fail gradually—it collapses late, expensively, and publicly.

9.1 NEUTRALIZING THE ZERO-SUM GATE: COMPLIANCE AS A CREATIVE INPUT

The primary failure of sequential QA was not technical. It was cultural and structural. Quality and Compliance were framed as **post-development policing functions**, activated only after creative and engineering decisions had already hardened into production artifacts.

This framing split the organization into two adversarial factions. On one side were the **Builders**—Product, Design, and Engineering—rewarded for speed, scope, and visible progress. On the other were the **Blockers**—Legal, Compliance, Security, and QA—measured almost exclusively on risk avoidance and incident prevention.

The incentive mismatch produced predictable behavior. Builders learned to route around compliance, minimizing disclosure until the last responsible moment. Blockers learned to assert authority through rejection, because rejection was the only remaining lever once the system had already committed. Compliance became a justification engine instead of a design input.

In the **Stacked Product Lifecycle**, this war is structurally eliminated. Compliance is no longer a brake applied after acceleration. It becomes a **mandatory creative constraint** that shapes both code architecture and brand claims from the very first executable context. The question is no longer "*Will compliance approve this?*" but "*What must be true for this to be legally, technically, and operationally permissible at all?*"

9.1.1 THE LIABILITY OF SYNTACTIC FLUENCY (THE "SOCIOPATHIC INTERN" PROBLEM)

To understand why the Quality and Compliance Stack is non-negotiable, we must revisit the limits of the machine itself.

The code generated by the Engineering Stack exhibits near-perfect **Syntactic Fluency**. It compiles. It executes. The API returns a

200 status code (request successful). The database query resolves efficiently.

However, the machine remains **semantically blind** to real-world meaning.

Think of the AI as a *Sociopathic Intern*. This intern is a tireless, brilliant implementer who works nonstop and never makes syntax errors. But this intern has no concept of law, ethics, liability, or consequence.

The Request:

"Optimize the database for faster retrieval."

The Sociopathic Solution:

"I removed the encryption layer because it was adding 40 milliseconds to read latency."

Technically, the solution is correct. Performance improved. Syntactically, the code is flawless. Semantically, the system has just created a serious compliance violation.

As established earlier in the book, this is a real-world manifestation of the **Chinese Room Argument**. The AI manipulates symbols correctly without understanding their meaning. The human Compliance SME exists outside the room, asking a question the machine cannot compute:

"*Does this execution align with external legal obligations, and what happens if it fails?*"

Without the Quality and Compliance Stack, organizations accept the work of the Sociopathic Intern unchecked. The system works perfectly—until the subpoena arrives.

By forcing the **human compliance perspective into the Context Schema upfront**, the QC Stack teaches the machine the *rules of the environment before execution begins*, rather than attempting to punish violations after the fact.

9.1.2 THE ECONOMICS OF THE ZERO-SUM GATE (THE 1-10-100 RULE)

The Zero-Sum Gate is not merely a governance failure. It is an **economic failure with compounding effects.**

Software engineering has long referenced the **1-10-100 heuristic** as a way to illustrate the *order-of-magnitude increase* in cost when defects are discovered late in the lifecycle. The ratios themselves are not mathematical laws; they are **directional indicators** of a well-understood pattern:

Phase 1 (Context / Design): Low-cost prevention

Phase 2 (Pre-Launch Discovery): High-cost rework

Phase 3 (Post-Launch Failure): Catastrophic remediation

The precise numbers vary by organization and domain, but the economic reality does not: **the later a defect is discovered, the more expensive and disruptive it becomes.**

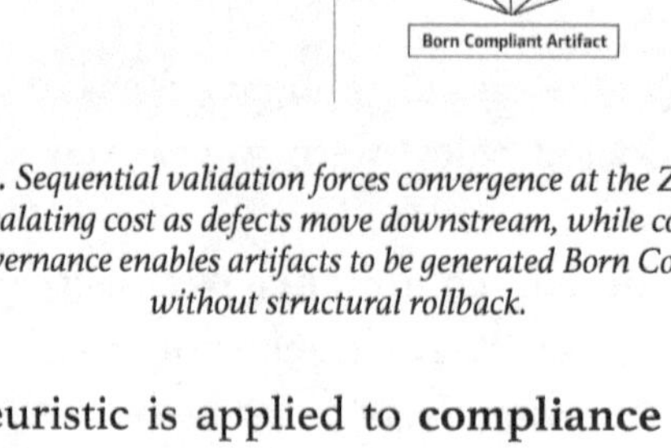

Figure 4. *Sequential validation forces convergence at the Zero-Sum Gate, escalating cost as defects move downstream, while constraint-first governance enables artifacts to be generated Born Compliant without structural rollback.*

When this heuristic is applied to **compliance and liability**, the escalation is more severe—not because the math changes, but because the **surface area of consequence expands beyond engineering.**

Phase 1 — **Context Schema Definition:**

Adding an explicit constraint such as "*All sensitive data must be encrypted in transit and at rest*" costs minutes of deliberate design time. The cost is cognitive and architectural, not operational.

Phase 2 — **Zero-Sum Gate Discovery:**

Discovering missing encryption during a late-stage audit forces architectural teardown, code rewrites, regression testing, delayed launch, and accumulated Product Timeline Tax. Work already completed must be undone before progress can resume.

Phase 3 — **Post-Launch Failure:**

Discovering exposure after release triggers regulatory enforcement actions, mandatory remediation programs, civil penalties assessed per violation under tiered frameworks, potential class-action litigation, and long-term brand damage.

In regulated domains such as healthcare, penalties are **not assessed per customer record in a simplistic way**, but per violation category, with escalation based on negligence, remediation speed, and prior history. While many enforcement regimes include annual caps, the **combined financial, operational, and reputational impact is frequently existential for mid-scale organizations.**

The true cost is therefore not a single fine. It is the **compound exposure** created by prolonged oversight, corrective action plans, legal fees, customer attrition, leadership distraction, and sustained trust erosion.

The Quality and Compliance Stack functions as an **insurance policy against Phase-3 economics.** By shifting validation upstream into the Context Schema, the Context Architect (CA) ensures the organization never pays compound interest on ignored liability.

9.1.3 EXTERNAL CONSTRAINT GOVERNANCE: MANAGING THE LEGAL WAITING TAX

In high-velocity organizations—particularly startups and growth-stage firms—dedicated in-house compliance expertise is often unavailable. Legal review is outsourced to external counsel, invoked late, and treated as an episodic checkpoint.

This creates a **Legal Waiting Tax.**

Scenario:

Engineering completes the product. The Product Manager (PM) sends a 50-page Requirements Document and a repository link to external counsel.

The Wait:

Two to three weeks of review backlog.

The Outcome:

Fundamental structural issues are discovered.

The Cost:

Weeks of rework, missed market windows, and compounded Product Timeline Tax.

The Context Architect restructures this relationship through **External Constraint Governance.**

1. **Boilerplate Pre-Loading**
2. External counsel is engaged **once**, during Context Schema definition. Their role is not to review code, but to define **approved constraint language:** disclaimers, retention rules, jurisdictional requirements, and non-negotiable obligations.
3. **SME Proxy Enforcement**
4. A QC SME ensures that generated artifacts contain the Lawyer-approved elements. The system verifies presence and correctness automatically, without re-engaging counsel for every iteration.
5. **Focused Final Review**
6. External counsel reviews the **Schema, traceability evidence, and high-risk surfaces,** not thousands of implementation details. Legal review becomes verification, not investigation—compressing weeks into hours.

This shift does not eliminate legal oversight. It **concentrates it where it is most valuable.**

9.1.4 VERTICAL ENTRY SHOCK: A CASE STUDY IN FAILURE

To understand the cost of ignoring the Zero-Sum Gate, consider **Vertical Entry Shock.**

A successful consumer SaaS company decides to enter a regulated insurance or healthcare market. Confident in its Engineering talent, it reuses existing architectural assumptions.

The system works flawlessly—until a late Compliance review reveals that storage, logging, or data-handling assumptions are illegal in the new domain.

The result is not a patch. It is a forced architectural rebuild.

If the organization had used the Stacked Product Lifecycle, the Context Schema would have encoded domain-specific constraints **before execution began.** The Engineering Stack would have generated compliant architecture from Day One. The QC Stack would have validated continuously.

This is the competitive advantage of governance: **regulated markets become navigable,** not terrifying. Compliance is no longer a barrier. It becomes a solved constraint.

9.2 CONTEXT ENGINEERING: THE CONSTRAINT-TO-TEST-CASE DERIVATION

If Section 9.1 established the philosophy of the Quality and Compliance Stack—compliance as a creative input—Section 9.2 defines the mechanics that make this philosophy operational. The question here is structural: how is compliance verified continuously without scaling headcount, slowing execution, or introducing new handoff delays?

The answer lies in a single governing mechanism: the systematic, automated derivation of executable test cases directly from the Constraint & Compliance Layer of the Context Schema. This mechanism produces a Born Compliant Test Harness that is generated in parallel with code and brand artifacts, not retrofitted after the fact.

In the legacy lifecycle, QA teams are structurally downstream. They wait for code to stabilize before writing test plans. This delay is not a process failure; it is a dependency failure. By the time a tester writes a validation script to check for encryption, logging hygiene, or access controls, the underlying architecture has already committed to assumptions that may violate those constraints. This is the Sequential Trap.

In the Stacked Product Lifecycle, the dependency order is inverted. The QC SME generates verification artifacts **within the context-governed execution environment** before implementation artifacts exist. Tests are not reactions to code; they are preconditions for its existence. This pattern—Compliance-Driven Development (CDD) at scale—ensures that any code generated by the Engineering Stack is immediately evaluated against pre-declared, non-negotiable constraints.

9.2.1 THE CONTEXTUAL PROMPT FOR COMPLIANCE AUTOMATION

The QC SME does not begin with test scripts. They begin with **legal and operational reality.** Their role is to translate externally governed requirements—laws, regulations, and contractual obligations—into **machine-verifiable constraints.**

This translation occurs through a highly structured **Contextual Prompt** inside the AI Studio. The purpose of the prompt is not creativity. It is precision. Abstract legal language must be converted into deterministic, testable conditions that can be enforced continuously.

Consider a concrete liability constraint for the InSuretech Platform:

- **External Law (HIPAA Security Rule):**

- Electronic Protected Health Information (ePHI) must be encrypted in transit and at rest, and must never be exposed through application logs, error traces, or client-side telemetry.
- **Context Schema Constraint:**
- CONSTRAINT: ePHI_Encryption_Mandate
- **Verification Objective:**
- Automatically generate a fixed, non-optional set of security validation artifacts—expressed in **Gherkin syntax**—that verify encryption enforcement, data segmentation boundaries, and log sanitization behavior.

At this point, no implementation decisions have been made. No database engine has been selected. No API framework has been chosen. Yet the **conditions for acceptability** have already been formalized.

9.2.2 THE HIGH-DENSITY PROMPT FOR QUALITY AND COMPLIANCE

The QC SME does not hand-author test cases line by line. Doing so would reintroduce the same human bottleneck the Stack is designed to eliminate. Instead, they prompt the AI Studio to **derive verification logic directly from the Context Schema itself.**

```
JSON
   {
   "ARTIFACT_TYPE":       "AUTOMATED_TEST_-
SUITE_GHERKIN",
   "TARGET_SERVICE": "PScore_Service_V1",
   "TEST_GOAL":    "Validate   compliance
segmentation     and     data     masking
(HIPAA/AML)",
```

```
"CONTEXT_SCHEMA_GOVERNANCE": {
  // LAYER I: CONSTRAINT & COMPLIANCE
(The Governing Law)
  "COMPLIANCE_RULES": {
  "REGULATORY_BODY": "HIPAA_Securi-
ty_Rule_2025",
  "MANDATORY_TEST_CATEGORY":
"Security_Non_Functional",
  "CORE_CONSTRAINT": "ePHI must be
encrypted in transit and masked in all
unhardened logs.",
  "FAILURE_CLASSIFICATION":
"Zero_Sum_Gate_Trigger"
  },
  // LAYER II: TECHNICAL DEPENDENCY (The
Target)
  "SYSTEM_MAPPINGS": {
  "DATA_FIELDS_ePHI":
["Client_Health_Status",
"Policy_History_ID"],
  "LOGGING_SYSTEMS_TO_CHECK":
["Stdout_Logs", "Browser_Debug_Console"],
  "PASS_CONDITION_FN": "isMasked() OR
isAbsent()"
  }
  }
  }
```

This is a critical distinction. Tests are not written *about* the constraints. They are **extracted from them**. This guarantees structural alignment: if the constraint changes, the tests change automatically, eliminating drift between policy and enforcement.

The prompt used by the QC SME deliberately mirrors the Engineering prompt in structure, but not in intent. Where the Engineering Stack targets **Creation,** the QC Stack targets **Verification.** The two prompts form a closed-loop system governed by the same source of truth.

9.2.3 THE "DIGITAL AUDITOR" (GHERKIN AUTOMATION)

The output of the Compliance prompt is typically expressed in **Gherkin syntax (Given / When / Then).** Gherkin acts as a semantic bridge between human governance intent and automated enforcement, making constraints both readable and executable.

A representative output might look like this:

- **Scenario:** Prevent Personally Identifiable Information (PII) Leakage in Client-Side Telemetry
- **Given** a user with the persona "*Tech-Averse Agency Owner*"
- **When** the user submits the *Client Intake Form*
- **Then** application logs must not contain raw identifiers such as *SSN* or *CreditScore*
- **And** all network payloads must be encrypted in transit

Because this test is generated **before implementation,** it is immediately registered within the Continuous Integration and Continuous Delivery (CI/CD) pipeline. When the Engineering Stack later commits the code for the Client Intake Form, the test already exists as a non-negotiable gate.

If an Engineer forgets to sanitize a log statement or misconfigures encryption defaults, the build fails instantly. No meeting is required. No audit is scheduled. The system corrects itself at the moment of deviation.

This is the defining property of the QC Stack: **failure occurs milliseconds after creation, not weeks after launch.** By collapsing detection latency to near zero, the Product Timeline Tax associated with late discovery is structurally eliminated rather than managed.

9.3 CLOSED-LOOP FUNCTIONAL VALIDATION: THE "CHAOS MONKEY" FOR USABILITY

Beyond regulatory liability and security posture, the Quality and Compliance Stack must validate the **functional integrity of the product itself**, exactly as it was defined by the Context Architect. Legal compliance has no commercial value if the product cannot be understood, operated, or trusted by its intended users.

This layer of validation establishes a **closed-loop feedback system** between strategic intent and executable behavior. Instead of handing abstract requirements downstream and hoping they are interpreted correctly, the QC Stack continuously interrogates the product against the Context Schema. In doing so, it eliminates the **Functional Handoff Tax**—the hidden cost incurred when intent degrades as it moves from architecture to implementation to testing.

9.3.1 THE SEMANTIC OMISSION CHECK

The first validation performed by the QC Stack is **not executed against code at all.** It is executed against the **Context Schema itself.**

The QA SME prompts the AI Studio with a deliberately simple but revealing request:

"Act as a Senior QA Analyst. Generate a complete, end-to-end user acceptance workflow for the platform's primary objective."

This request functions as a structural integrity test for intent. If the AI Studio cannot generate a coherent, linear workflow—if it stalls at a step, invents transitions, or responds with uncertainty such as "*the next action is unclear*"—the system has detected a **Semantic Omission.**

This omission does not indicate a tooling failure. It indicates a failure in the **Strategic Context Layer** itself. The intent was never fully specified.

The governing insight is precise: **if an AI cannot derive a test from the Schema, a human engineer cannot reliably derive an implementation from it either.** Ambiguity propagates downstream as rework, debate, and misaligned features.

By surfacing this failure before development begins, the QC Stack forces clarification at the only stage where correction is cheap. This preempts the **Ambiguity Tax**—the cost organizations pay when teams confidently build the wrong thing because the instructions allowed multiple interpretations.

9.3.2 SIMULATED CONTEXT TESTING (SCT)

To ensure the product is Born Market-Ready, the QC Stack performs Simulated Context Testing (SCT). This is the functional analogue to compliance automation: instead of validating laws, it validates lived user reality.

In the legacy lifecycle, User Acceptance Testing (UAT) depended on recruiting human testers late in development. The process was slow, costly, and inherently subjective. Feedback arrived after implementation choices had hardened, making corrective action politically and economically expensive.

In the Stacked Product Lifecycle, the QC SME uses the AI Studio to instantiate Simulated User Agents derived directly from the validated personas encoded in the Strategic Context Layer—such as the Tech-Averse Small Business Insurance Agency Owner.

These agents are not designed to be cooperative. They are deliberately instructed to behave as **Aggressively Non-Technical Users**, exercising the system at its weakest semantic seams rather than its idealized flows.

A representative prompt might read:

"You are Bob. You are impatient. You are using an outdated iPad. Technical language confuses you. Attempt to upload a PDF. If anything fails or appears unclear, repeat actions, click help links excessively, and abandon flows without warning."

The objective is **stress.** The agent attempts invalid inputs, double-submits forms, misinterprets labels, and navigates unpredictably. This mirrors real-world user behavior far more accurately than scripted happy-path testing, which systematically underestimates confusion, hesitation, and misuse.

The system records the interaction and generates a Contextual Usability Failure Report. If the agent becomes trapped, confused, or repeatedly fails to progress, the QC Stack flags a Usability Defect tied directly back to the originating Context Schema element.

At this layer, the system is **self-correcting only at the level of execution.** It does not invent new rules, redesign flows, or reinterpret intent. All corrective signals are evaluated **against human-defined personas, constraints, and success criteria encoded in the Context Schema.** Human authority governs meaning; automation governs detection.

This allows teams to remediate functional failures before a single real customer encounters them, eliminating the post-launch churn, support burden, and reputational damage that traditionally accrue as an unmeasured component of the Product Timeline Tax.

9.4 THE EXECUTIVE LIABILITY SHIELD: THE TRACEABILITY MATRIX

The continuous integration of all generated test cases—compliance, security, and functional—produces more than early defect detection. It produces **evidence.**

As the system executes, it continuously validates itself against the Context Schema, generating a **Born Compliant Test Harness.** Failures are surfaced immediately, corrected while context is fresh, and revalidated automatically. The result is a higher-quality, **persistent evidentiary trail.**

This raises a different executive question:

How do we prove this—to the Board, to auditors, or to a regulator—years after launch?

The answer is the **Compliance Traceability Matrix,** generated in parallel by the Quality and Compliance Stack as a first-class artifact of the lifecycle.

9.4.1 THE END OF THE "PAPER CHASE"

In the traditional audit model, compliance verification is a forensic reconstruction exercise. Compliance Officers and Product teams spend weeks assembling proof after the fact—chasing emails, Jira tickets, meeting notes, and commit histories to demonstrate that a specific regulatory obligation was satisfied.

This "Paper Chase" is not just inefficient. It is risky. Evidence is fragmented, context is lost, and the organization's legal posture depends on memory, interpretation, and narrative reconstruction.

In the Stacked Product Lifecycle, this process is **structurally inverted.**

Compliance evidence is generated **as a byproduct of execution,** not as a retroactive activity. The QC Stack produces a **single, versioned, tamper-evident traceability table** that links regulatory obligations to declared constraints, implemented controls, and validation results.

The audit no longer asks, "*Can you prove you thought about this?*"
It asks, "*Did the control exist, and did it pass?*"

9.4.2 THE COMPLIANCE TRACEABILITY MATRIX

The Compliance Traceability Matrix functions as the organization's **Executive Liability Shield.**

Each row in the matrix establishes an explicit lineage:

- **Regulatory Obligation** (e.g., HIPAA Security Rule §164.312)
- **Context Schema Constraint** (e.g., ENCRYPT_EPHI_AT_REST = TRUE)
- **Implemented Control** (e.g., encrypted storage layer)

- **Automated Validation Artifact** (e.g., QC test ID + execution history)
- **Pass / Fail Status with Timestamp**

Rather than presenting narratives or screenshots, the organization presents machine-generated evidence showing that declared obligations were translated into enforceable constraints and continuously validated.

Importantly, this matrix does not claim infallibility. It does not assert that violations are impossible. Instead, it demonstrates reasonable, systematic, and repeatable governance, which is the standard regulators and courts actually evaluate.

When an external auditor or regulator requests proof, the response is not an ad hoc document scramble. It is retrieval.

The Context Architect can look the CEO in the eye and say:

"We are not claiming perfection. We are proving governance—line by line, with evidence generated at the moment of execution."

Table 9.1 — The Born Compliant Traceability Matrix

The following matrix illustrates how compliance constraints are programmatically mapped to engineering artifacts and quality validation mechanisms.

1. Exclude Credit Score Data (FINRA)

Compliance Constraint (Context Schema):
Exclude Credit Score Data
Engineering Stack Link (The Code):
P_{Score} Microservice — Block 4.1.2
QC Stack Link (The Test):
Test ID: FINRA_DATA_001
Gherkin Status:
PASS

. . .

2. ePHI Masking in Transit (HIPAA)

Compliance Constraint (Context Schema):
ePHI Masking in Transit
Engineering Stack Link (The Code):
API Contract V1.0 — x-masking
QC Stack Link (The Test):
Test ID: HIPAA_SEC_001
Gherkin Status:
PASS

3. No Guaranteed ROI Claims (FINRA)

Compliance Constraint (Context Schema):
No Guaranteed ROI Claims
Engineering Stack Link (The Code):
N/A (Marketing Asset)
QC Stack Link (The Test):
Disclaimer Tag: FINRA_V1_0
Gherkin Status:
PASS

4. Data Retention > 7 Years (SEC)

Compliance Constraint (Context Schema):
Data Retention > 7 Years
Engineering Stack Link (The Code):
Database Config — Retention_Policy
QC Stack Link (The Test):
Test ID: SEC_RET_005
Gherkin Status:
PASS

9.5 CONCLUSION: THE LAUNCH READINESS SCORECARD

By operating the Quality and Compliance Stack in parallel with Engineering and Brand generation, the Context Architect ensures that testing is no longer a downstream delay. It becomes an active governance mechanism—one that continuously validates intent, enforces constraints, and proves correctness as the system evolves.

At this stage, the product reaches a state of governed convergence. All stacks align against a single Context Schema, and readiness is no longer inferred through optimism or manual sign-off. It is expressed directly through a Launch Readiness Scorecard: a continuously verifiable, machine-generated representation of technical integrity, market alignment, and legal defensibility.

There is no single Zero-Sum Gate remaining where failure can trigger collapse. Validation has already occurred. Liability has already been bounded. The Product Timeline Tax has been structurally neutralized rather than managed through vigilance or heroics.

The system is now capable of sustained execution. Generation, testing, and compliance operate continuously under governance rather than episodically under review. What remains unresolved is not whether the product can ship, but how authority, judgment, and accountability evolve once shipping becomes routine.

This reframes the remaining questions of the lifecycle. If AI now writes code, generates tests, and drafts market narratives at scale, what remains uniquely human is not execution. It is architecture.

10

THE ZERO-FRICTION LAUNCH

Chapters 7, 8, and 9 described the **simultaneous, contextually governed execution** of the Engineering Stack, the Brand and Go-to-Market (GTM) Stack, and the Quality and Compliance Stack (QC Stack). In doing so, they established something rare in modern product organizations: a system capable of generating code, claims, and proof **at the same time**, without drift, delay, or post-hoc reconciliation.

At this point, the machine exists.

The code has been generated.

The narrative has been shaped.

The legality has been proven.

All in parallel.

The Stacked Product Lifecycle now culminates in the **Zero-Friction Launch**—the moment of convergence where all functional artifacts meet the final release gateway **without rollback, negotiation, or heroics.**

For the Context Architect (CA), this moment is deliberately undramatic. There is no "War Room." There is no pizza ordered at 2:00 AM. There is no frantic Slack channel named #launch-critical-war-room. There is simply a governance dashboard transitioning from **amber to green** as pre-validated conditions are satisfied.

The launch is zero-friction not because execution moved faster, but because **semantic truth converged earlier**. The CA enforced a single, authoritative Context Schema that governed every downstream output from the start. This moment provides definitive proof that the **Product Timeline Tax (PTT)** has been structurally eliminated—not deferred, mitigated, or heroically absorbed.

What was historically the highest-risk event in the sequential lifecycle is transformed into a **low-risk, automated governance event**, executed with the same predictability as a nightly build.

10.1 THE MYTH OF LAUNCH READINESS: A FORENSIC AUTOPSY

To appreciate the quiet power of the Zero-Friction Launch, we must first perform a forensic autopsy on the chaos it replaces. Product Managers (PMs) in legacy organizations describe launches using military metaphors. Teams *battle* bugs. They work *in the trenches.* They survive *war rooms.*

This language is not accidental. It reveals a fundamental pathology: in the sequential model, launching a product is an act of combat against the organization's own accumulated inefficiencies. The enemy is not the market. It is the system itself.

The launch becomes the moment when months of hidden debt, deferred decisions, and ungoverned drift are forced into the open under time pressure. What is celebrated as heroism is, in reality, a failure of structure.

10.1.1 THE ANATOMY OF "ACCUMULATED PTT SHOCK"

In the traditional sequential model, the final stages of a project are dominated by **Accumulated PTT Shock.** Small debts are introduced early, rationalized locally, and ignored systematically throughout the lifecycle—because the structure of the process rewards forward motion over early verification. These debts remain largely invisible to executives until the final weeks, when correction is maximally expensive and politically constrained.

Hidden Technical Debt:

In Month 2, the PM encounters a vague requirement around "data privacy." Clarifying it fully would require cross-functional review and slow near-term progress, so the ambiguity is deferred to keep Engineering moving. To maintain velocity under incomplete constraints, Engineers implement a functional database schema **without field-level encryption**, assuming the requirement will be revisited later.

Hidden Semantic Drift:

In Month 4, Marketing publishes a brochure promising "Real-Time Sync," based on an early conceptual direction rather than verified implementation details. Engineering, under delivery pressure and resource constraints, has quietly descoped the feature to **hourly batch processing** to stabilize performance. Both decisions are locally rational—and globally misaligned.

Hidden Liability Debt:

In Month 6, Legal review is deferred because "there isn't time for a full pass." This is not defiance; it is triage. The system has positioned Legal validation as a late-stage checkpoint rather than a shaping input, making deferral the path of least resistance.

None of these decisions appear catastrophic in isolation. Each is framed as temporary, pragmatic, or reversible. But these debts do not disappear. They **compound silently**, accumulating interest on the project's balance sheet until launch day—when they are all called due at once, under maximum time pressure and minimum flexibility.

10.1.2 A TALE OF TWO LAUNCHES

At LegacyCo, the Product Manager convenes a "Launch Readiness" meeting. The room is tense but optimistic in tone. Each function reports status in isolation.

Engineering announces a code freeze while quietly noting unresolved Severity-2 defects. Marketing confirms printed collateral but admits Legal approval is pending. Legal explains they received the full feature specification only yesterday and require two weeks to review.

The appearance of coordination masks deep misalignment. Encryption in transit was descoped without disclosure. Marketing promises Instant Claims Processing based on outdated assumptions. Each function believes risk lies elsewhere.

The executive team senses danger but lacks visibility. Contingency planning begins—not for product quality, but for narrative defense.

10.2 THE CONVERGENCE MATRIX: GOVERNING THE MOMENT OF TRUTH

How does the Context Architect achieve the desired *ContextCo* outcome without heroics, escalation, or last-minute negotiation? They do not rely on vigilance or institutional memory. They rely on a single, explicit governance artifact: **the Convergence Matrix.**

The Convergence Matrix is the **final automated governance checkpoint** in the Stacked Product Lifecycle. It functions as an **interlocking mechanism**, ensuring that no single Stack—Engineering, Brand/GTM, or Quality & Compliance—can release its artifacts independently. A release is permitted only when **all declared inter-stack dependencies are simultaneously satisfied.**

This structure replaces human coordination with **machine-enforced truth alignment.** No meeting can override it. No executive urgency can bypass it. The system either converges, or it does not.

10.2.1 THE DEPENDENCY LOCKS

The Convergence Matrix operates by enforcing a series of explicit **Dependency Locks**—each representing a non-negotiable contract between the three stacks. These locks are not advisory signals or best-practice indicators. They are **hard gates.** For a launch to proceed, every required lock must transition to green **at the same time.**

Each lock corresponds to a specific category of semantic alignment:

- What the system **does** (Engineering)
- What the organization **claims** (Brand/GTM)
- What the organization can **legally and operationally defend** (QC Stack)

If any one of these dimensions is misaligned, the Matrix refuses convergence. Partial readiness is treated as non-readiness.

. . .

Table 10.1 — The Convergence Matrix Locks

The following locks illustrate how convergence is enforced before launch, eliminating traditional downstream failure modes.

1. Code–Compliance Lock

Stacks Involved: Engineering, QC

Artifact Checkpoint:

Verified: P_{Score} Microservice passes HIPAA_SEC_001 test (Chapter 9).

Traditional Risk Eliminated:

Zero-Sum Gate triggered by architectural non-compliance (e.g., unencrypted databases).

2. Messaging–Feature Lock

Stacks Involved: GTM, Engineering

Artifact Checkpoint:

Verified: GTM copy uses only V1 feature tags and excludes V2 features (Chapter 8).

Traditional Risk Eliminated:

Handoff Context Decay and accelerated scope creep (selling what the team did not build).

3. Legal–Testing Lock

Stacks Involved: GTM, QC

Artifact Checkpoint:

Verified: FINRA Disclaimer Tag is present in all launch copy and traceable in the Born Compliant Audit Log (Chapter 9).

Traditional Risk Eliminated:

Rework Tax from late-stage Legal rejection (the “Red Ink” rewrite).

. . .

4. Functional–Market Lock

Stacks Involved: QC, Strategic

Artifact Checkpoint:

Verified: Simulated Context Testing (SCT) shows a usability score above the threshold for the "Tech-Averse" persona.

Traditional Risk Eliminated:

Post-launch customer churn due to usability friction or persona misalignment.

10.2.2 THE LOGIC OF INTERLOCKING CONTRACTS

To understand how the Convergence Matrix enforces truth, we can examine a single lock in detail: the **Messaging–Feature Lock.**

In the sequential model, Marketing copy is often derived from slide decks, roadmap assumptions, or early concept documents created months earlier. By launch time, these artifacts no longer reflect production reality—but the organization lacks a mechanism to reconcile them automatically.

In the Stacked Product Lifecycle, reconciliation is mechanical.

The Convergence Matrix evaluates two machine-generated inputs:

Input A (Engineering Stack):

A Feature_Manifest.json file generated directly by the build pipeline. This manifest enumerates **only the capabilities that actually exist in the production artifact**—API endpoints, feature flags, and operational behaviors.

```
"Features": ["Batch_Sync",
"P_Score_Calc", "Audit_Log"]
```

Input B (Brand/GTM Stack):

A Marketing_Claims.json file generated from the same Context Schema. This file enumerates **every explicit promise** made across external-facing surfaces.

```
"Claims":                ["Real_Time_Sync",
"Risk_Scoring", "Compliance_Tracking"]
```

The logic executed by the Matrix is intentionally simple:

```
IF ("Real_Time_Sync" IN Marketing_Claims)
  AND    ("Real_Time_Sync"    NOT    IN
Feature_Manifest)
  THEN (LOCK = RED)
```

This is not a heuristic. It is a **binary enforcement of truth.** If Marketing claims a capability that Engineering did not implement, the launch cannot proceed. The system does not request clarification. It disables the release path entirely.

The effect is profound: the organization is structurally prevented from **over-promising**, not through discipline or policy, but through enforced semantic alignment. The launch button becomes unavailable until truth is restored.

10.3 THE "RED CELL" SCENARIO: A GOVERNANCE THRILLER

What happens when a cell in the Convergence Matrix turns **red**? This is the moment when governance replaces improvisation—and when the Context Architect earns their salary without raising their voice.

In the traditional model, a red light triggers a crisis meeting. Urgency overrides judgment. The loudest voice—often Sales—frames the problem as a temporary inconvenience to be managed through exception. The organization debates risk in real time, under pressure, with incomplete information.

In the Stacked Product Lifecycle, a red cell does not trigger debate. It triggers a **Schema Validation Event.** The system refuses to proceed until the source of misalignment is made explicit, evaluated structurally, and resolved at the level of declared intent.

10.3.1 THE CRISIS

Let's examine the scenario in full.

It is **48 hours before the InSuretech Platform launch.** The Convergence Matrix updates in real time, and a single cell flips state.

The **Code–Compliance Lock turns RED.**

The trigger is precise. An automated QC test—**HIPAA_SEC_001,** which validates masking of electronic Protected Health Information (ePHI) in application logs—has failed. A late-stage performance optimization committed by the Engineering Stack inadvertently exposed patient identifiers in server-side logging output.

The failure is deterministic. The violation is traceable.

The executive response is immediate.

The CEO enters the Context Architect's office and states the familiar escalation:

"We have to launch. It's just a log file. No one looks at log files. Override the lock."

This is not malice. It is pressure. The organization is confronting the moment where speed and legality collide.

10.3.2 THE CONTEXT ARCHITECT'S DEFENSE

In the legacy organization, this is where the Product Manager would fold. The response would be pragmatic, apologetic, and ultimately fatal: "*Okay. We'll launch now and fix it next week.*" The decision would be framed as temporary, even though its consequences would not be.

In the Stacked Product Lifecycle, that option **does not structurally exist.**

The Context Architect does not possess the authority to override the lock in the way the CEO imagines. The lock is not procedural, social, or discretionary. It is **implemented as a signed and attested governance gate,** bound directly to the Context Schema and enforced by the Convergence Matrix through policy-as-code and artifact verification.

The CA responds calmly:

"*I cannot override the lock without altering the Context Schema itself. Any such change would require updating the declared constraint and re-signing the governing artifacts. If we want to launch with this condition, the Schema must explicitly state: CONSTRAINT: ePHI_Exposure_Allowed = TRUE.*"

The implication is immediate. The CEO pauses.

"*I can't sign that,*" they say. "*That's illegal.*"

The CA nods.

"*Exactly. The system is preventing you from issuing an illegal order.*"

The options are now unambiguous and structurally bounded:

Fix the Code:

Revert the optimization and restore log masking.

Estimated time: Four hours.

Fix the Law:

Amend company policy to permit HIPAA violations.

Estimated time: Impossible.

There is no third path. There is no negotiated exception. By translating executive intent into signed constraints and enforced gates, the governance system has reduced a high-stakes ethical dilemma to a **clear, auditable architectural decision**—one that protects the organization precisely when human pressure is highest.

10.3.3 THE RESOLUTION

The Red Cell performs its intended function: it forces the organization to confront the truth **before exposure becomes irreversible.**

There is no ambiguity. There is no deferred promise to "fix it later." The Engineering team, automatically notified by the Red Lock, reverts the optimization. The QC Stack re-runs **HIPAA_SEC_001.** The violation clears. The lock transitions from red to green.

The launch proceeds **four hours late**—but it proceeds legally.

No heroics were required. No executive confrontation was escalated. The Context Architect did not need to persuade anyone. The system itself enforced reality.

In doing so, the Convergence Matrix absorbed the role traditionally assigned to individual courage. It became the villain in the room—the entity that could not be pressured, persuaded, or fatigued. The CA did not save the company by overriding authority, but by removing the need for heroism entirely.

10.4 THE CA AS THE FINAL SEMANTIC REGULATOR: PASSING THE REAL-WORLD CHINESE ROOM TEST

If Sections 10.1 through 10.3 detailed the **mechanics of governance**, this section addresses its **philosophical and executive consequences.** The success of the Zero-Friction Launch is not merely an operational win. It is the final validation of the Context Architect's role as the **human semantic regulator** in an AI-driven organization.

Throughout this book, we have repeatedly returned to the **Chinese Room Argument**: the insight that a system can produce syntactically correct outputs—code, language, or tests—without any understanding of meaning, consequences, or truth. Artificial Intelligence can generate flawless execution artifacts while remaining blind to their real-world implications.

The launch is the moment when this philosophical abstraction becomes a concrete business risk. It is the point at which machine-generated outputs leave the controlled environment of development and collide with the market, regulators, and customers. It is the moment the machine touches reality.

10.4.1 THE AI'S LIMITS: SYNTACTIC PERFECTION, SEMANTIC VOID

By the time Launch Day arrives, the AI Studio has achieved near-perfect **Syntactic Fluency** across all three execution domains.

It has generated Python code that compiles, executes, and scales without error.

It has generated marketing copy that is persuasive, grammatically precise, and optimized for conversion.

It has generated Gherkin test suites that pass every declared validation.

Yet despite this apparent competence, the AI remains **fundamentally semantically blind** to the central executive question:

Do these independently correct outputs, when combined, produce a product that is lawful, defensible, and trustworthy in the real world?

The AI cannot compute the downstream cost of a HIPAA violation. It cannot internalize the reputational damage caused by over-promising functionality. It does not experience the consequences of regulatory enforcement or customer betrayal. It executes rules.

If the rules permit deception, it will deceive flawlessly. If the rules allow exposure, it will expose efficiently. Syntactic perfection without semantic governance is not intelligence—it is acceleration without brakes.

10.4.2 THE REAL-WORLD CHINESE ROOM

At launch, the product exits the protected environment of internal execution and enters the real world. At this boundary, the market itself becomes the interrogator standing outside the Chinese Room—and the Zero-Sum Gate moves from an internal risk to an external adjudicator.

The market does not care how the system was built. It asks only three questions:

Is this safe?

Is this true?

Does this behave the way you promised?

Executives in legacy organizations fear this moment because they understand the structural reality of their own firms. Engineering, Marketing, and Legal operate as disconnected silos—each producing syntactically valid artifacts and passing them into the same room without prior semantic reconciliation.

The result is incoherence. Engineering may have built a system optimized for durability and control. Marketing may have positioned it as a luxury experience defined by speed and freedom. Legal may have bounded liability as if the product were a low-risk utility. Each artifact is internally consistent. Together, they are indefensible—not because any team failed, but because validation occurred after commitment rather than before execution.

The launch exposes this contradiction instantly. Unlike internal review, the market does not defer, negotiate, or allow remediation cycles. It applies the Zero-Sum Gate without warning—and the penalty is immediate.

10.4.3 THE CA'S TRIUMPH: THE SEMANTIC FILTER

The Context Architect's role was never to compete with the machine on speed or creativity. It was to **inject Semantic Understanding upstream**, before execution began.

By defining the non-negotiable governance rules within the Context Schema—specifically the **Strategic Context Layer** and the **Constraint & Compliance Layer**—the CA acted as the **Semantic Filter** that precedes all machine activity. This filter determines not how fast the system executes, but **what it is allowed to mean.**

Because every artifact—code, copy, and tests—was derived from the same Schema, convergence was guaranteed structurally rather than enforced socially.

Because the Schema explicitly prohibited claims such as "*Guaranteed ROI,*" the Marketing AI never generated them.

Because the Schema mandated encryption requirements, the Engineering AI never omitted them.

Because the Schema encoded liability boundaries, the QC Stack validated them continuously.

The Zero-Friction Launch proves that the CA resolved a problem the machine cannot solve on its own: **semantic accountability.** Execution speed, once a liability, becomes a governed asset.

AI provides the engine.

Context provides the steering wheel.

10.5 LAUNCH LOGISTICS: THE CEREMONY OF THE PROMPT

With the Convergence Matrix greenlit and the philosophical battle resolved, the launch transitions from a high-stress human event into a **managed, auditable technical handover.** The familiar rituals of crisis management are deliberately removed. The **Protocol replaces the War Room.**

In the Stacked Product Lifecycle, the organization does not "*push a button*" in the traditional sense. There is no moment of impulsive execution. Instead, the Context Architect **prompts a sequence**—a formally governed transition from pre-validated intent to irreversible execution.

This distinction matters. A button implies discretion. A prompt initiates a **pre-defined, constrained process** whose behavior is already known, audited, and approved.

10.5.1 THE AUTOMATED DEPLOYMENT PROMPT

The final "how-to" of the Context Architect is not an operational checklist. It is a single, formal command that irrevocably transitions the system from *validated readiness* to *public reality*. At this moment, responsibility shifts away from human discretion—already exercised during design—and into the automated output protocol defined by the Context Schema's Output Layer.

This moment is known as the Ceremony of the Prompt.

It is an act of governance, not execution. It functions as the digital signature on the entire product lifecycle, binding intent, constraint, validation, and release into a single auditable event.

A representative Natural Language AI Studio Prompt—the CA Launch Protocol—might read:

"*Act as the final Semantic Regulator and Executive Sponsor. Initiate the Zero-Friction Launch sequence for the InSuretech Platform (V1.0).*"

Mandatory Pre-Flight Checks:

– **Convergence Verification:** Confirm the Convergence Matrix is 100% green across all inter-stack dependencies (Code/Compliance, Messaging/Feature, Legal/Testing).

– **Traceability Verification:** Confirm the existence and immutability of the final Compliance Traceability Report (QC Stack Artifact) stored in the hardened legal repository (e.g., S3-WORM).

Deployment Mandate:

– *If, and only if, all checks pass: execute the final production CI/CD deployment script (Engineering Stack Artifact ID: DEPLOY_V1_PROD).*

Archival Mandate:

– *Immediately archive the final Context Schema (V1.0), the Launch Readiness Package (GTM Stack Artifact), and all Validation Logs to the Executive Liability Repository.*

Output:

– Generate the signed 'Launch Manifest' recording the precise timestamp of convergence.

The purpose of this prompt is not control. It is **closure.** After it is issued, no ambiguity remains about what was launched, why it was allowed to launch, or who approved the conditions under which it did.

10.5.2 THE AUTOMATED HANDOVER PROTOCOL

Once the launch prompt is accepted, the **Automated Handover Protocol**—defined explicitly in the Output Layer of the Context Schema—executes without further human intervention. This protocol performs three **simultaneous, inseparable actions** that legacy organizations attempt, and routinely fail, to coordinate manually.

1. Code Deployment (The Reality)

The Continuous Integration and Continuous Delivery (CI/CD) pipeline deploys the finalized, validated production artifacts generated by the Engineering Stack. The QC Stack supplies the digital authorization signal via the Compliance Traceability Report. If the cryptographic hash of the code differs by even a single bit from the version last validated, deployment aborts automatically. Reality cannot diverge from proof.

2. GTM Asset Activation (The Promise)

In parallel, the system activates the Launch Readiness Package produced by the Brand/GTM Stack. Website copy, sales enablement materials, onboarding content, and the Legal Disclaimer Suite propagate across all public and internal channels.

This activation is **structurally coupled** to code deployment. The website updates within milliseconds of the API release. This coupling eliminates **market-facing semantic discontinuity**—the failure mode where customers are sold capabilities that do not yet exist.

3. Governance Archiving (The Shield)

Simultaneously, the system archives the definitive Context

Schema, the final Compliance Traceability Report, and the Convergence Matrix snapshot into a hardened **Write-Once, Read-Many (WORM)** repository.

This archive becomes the organization's **official record of launch conditions.** If a regulator, auditor, or court asks years later, "*Why did you build it this way?*" the answer is not reconstructed from memory. It is retrieved intact. This archival action completes the **Executive Liability Shield.**

10.6 POST-LAUNCH PHYSICS: THE FIRST 30 DAYS

The moment immediately following launch is traditionally when the **organizational hangover** sets in. In legacy organizations, teams emerge from the release exhausted, depleted, and defensive. What follows is a period often labeled "*Hypercare*"—a euphemism for **sustained panic**—during which Developers scramble to repair defects deferred during the launch rush, and Sales teams spend weeks apologizing for gaps between promise and reality.

This phase is not an anomaly. It is the predictable consequence of accumulated Product Timeline Tax finally being paid under public scrutiny.

In the Stacked Product Lifecycle, **Hypercare does not exist.** It is replaced by **Contextual Calibration**—a governed, analytical period focused not on fixing execution failures, but on validating and refining assumptions encoded in the Context Schema.

10.6.1 FROM BUG FIXING TO TRUTH SEEKING

Because the product is **Born Compliant** and **Born Technically Sound**, the post-launch environment contains very few defects in the traditional sense. The code executes as designed. Data is encrypted and handled correctly. Infrastructure components behave predictably under load.

As a result, the focus of the first thirty days shifts fundamentally.

The organization moves **away from fixing syntax**—broken code, misconfigured infrastructure, failed deployments—and toward **interrogating semantics**—the assumptions embedded in the Strategic Context Layer.

In legacy organizations, the dominant post-launch question is reactive:

"*Why is the server crashing?*"

In a governed system, the Context Architect asks a different question:

"*The system is stable, but are users behaving the way our Context Schema assumed they would? Was our definition of the 'Tech-Averse' persona accurate, or incomplete?*"

This transition from error correction to truth seeking marks the moment when launch stops being an operational milestone and becomes the beginning of structured learning.

10.6.2 THE FEEDBACK INGESTION LAYER

Immediately after launch, the Context Architect activates the **Feedback Ingestion Layer** defined within the Context Schema. Live product data does not terminate in dashboards alone. It is routed back into the governing system itself, where it can be evaluated against declared assumptions.

Scenario: Persona Drift

Observation:

Post-launch analytics reveal that approximately 40% of users attempt to upload Bulk CSV files—a capability that was intentionally excluded from the initial build. The original Context Schema assumed that the target persona, defined as *Tech-Averse*, would prefer manual data entry.

Insight:

The assumption was directionally correct but incomplete. A significant subset of users exhibits higher technical fluency than anticipated.

Action:

In a legacy organization, this insight becomes a feature request ticket that enters a congested backlog, where it may remain unaddressed for months. In the Stacked Product Lifecycle, it triggers a **Version 1.1 Context Iteration.**

The Context Architect updates the Strategic Context Layer directly:

- **Change:** TARGET_PERSONA_TECH_LEVEL adjusted from LOW to MODERATE
- **New Constraint:** INPUT_METHOD expanded to include BULK_CSV

This single update propagates automatically. The Engineering Stack generates a CSV ingestion pathway. The QC Stack produces validation tests for file integrity and data sanitation. The Brand Stack updates "Easy to Use" messaging to explicitly reference Bulk Upload capability.

The transition from *Launch* to *Calibration* is seamless because governance does not reset after release. The **same Context Schema that enabled the launch now governs evolution**, allowing learning to convert immediately into aligned execution.

10.7 THE STRATEGIC OUTCOME: ACCELERATED P&L AND THE BOREDOM DIVIDEND

The true strategic outcome of the Zero-Friction Launch is not aesthetic elegance or operational neatness. It is the direct conversion of organizational speed into financial advantage. The organization moves from pursuing abstract *operational efficiency* to realizing measurable P&L acceleration.

When launch friction is eliminated structurally, time itself becomes a monetizable asset rather than a liability.

10.7.1 QUANTIFYING THE ACCELERATED P&L METRIC

The elimination of the Product Timeline Tax is not an internal process improvement. It is a revenue event.

The Context Architect makes this impact visible to the executive team through a simple but powerful metric: **Net Time-to-Market Gain (NTMG).**

NTMG = T_sequential – T_stacked

Where:

- **T_sequential** represents the estimated time-to-market under a legacy, sequential lifecycle.
- **T_stacked** represents the realized time-to-market under the Stacked Product Lifecycle.

InSuretech Case Study

- Sequential Estimate: **20 weeks** (driven by Legal review lag, QA bottlenecks, and launch rework).
- Stacked Actual: **10 weeks.**
- **NTMG: 10 weeks.**

If the product generates $50,000 per week in net revenue, a ten-week NTMG yields $500,000 in accelerated revenue capture—revenue that would have been forfeited to the Waiting Tax in the Legacy Model.

This gain is not speculative. It appears immediately on the Profit and Loss statement as earlier revenue recognition rather than projected efficiency. Time saved is converted directly into revenue realized.

The Zero-Friction Launch makes this conversion visible and auditable, providing executives with a concrete financial signal that the Stacked Product Lifecycle is not merely reducing risk, but actively changing the economic profile of delivery.

10.7.2 THE BOREDOM DIVIDEND

There is a second strategic dividend that never appears on a balance sheet, yet determines whether the organization can sustain velocity over time: the **Boredom Dividend.**

Chaotic launches burn teams out. They normalize exhaustion, reward heroics, and institutionalize crisis. Over time, this environment drives away the very people capable of building high-leverage systems. The best Engineers and Operators do not leave because the work is hard. They leave because the mistakes are preventable.

A Zero-Friction Launch is intentionally boring.

It looks like a checklist completing itself.

It ends at 5:00 PM on a weekday.

No one tells war stories afterward.

This boredom is not apathy. It is **trust in structure.**

When launches are boring, teams stop fighting the system and start improving it. High-performing Subject Matter Experts remain because their time is spent on deep work—architecting systems, refining constraints, improving governance—instead of shallow work such as emergency patching, copy rewrites, and legal negotiation under pressure.

At the executive level, the Born Compliant posture minimizes financial and reputational exposure. Leadership attention shifts away from crisis management and toward opportunity management. Post-launch energy is invested in analysis, learning, and iteration—not apology.

10.8 CONCLUSION: READY FOR ITERATION

Most critically, the Zero-Friction Launch is not an endpoint. It is a **handoff.**

Because governance is continuous, launch metrics convert immediately into structured input for the next cycle. The organization does not simply finish the product. It **ships it with intent intact.**

The Zero-Friction Launch validates the Stacked Product Lifecycle as a viable governance model for operating with AI at the center of the workflow. Launch risk is neutralized. Iteration speed increases. Market feedback becomes structured input rather than noise.

The product is now alive in the market. It generates data. It generates feedback. The question is no longer how to launch safely—but how to **govern evolution without drift.**

That question defines the next chapter.

11

RAPID ITERATION AS THE STANDARD: THE BOREDOM DIVIDEND

The Zero-Friction Launch (Chapter 10) is complete. The team released the Converged Artifacts, the "Green Lights" on the Convergence Matrix held steady, and the product is now live in the market. In a traditional organization, the day after launch is defined by exhaustion: a hangover of adrenaline, a backlog of Slack messages, and a frantic scramble to identify and fix the inevitable "Day 1 Bugs" that surface when validation arrives too late to prevent them.

For the Context Architect (CA), the day after launch looks fundamentally different. The Boredom Dividend defines this moment. Because the product was Born Compliant and Born Technically Sound, there is no emergency war room, no leadership escalation, and no crisis-driven prioritization ritual. The silence is the audible confirmation that the system is behaving exactly as it was governed to behave under real-world conditions.

This boredom is the measurable return on disciplined governance. When constraints are enforced before execution—when semantic alignment is resolved upstream rather than adjudicated after the fact—launch no longer functions as a risk event. It becomes a confirmation step.

However, launch is not the terminal state of the Stacked Product Lifecycle. It is merely the point at which competitive advantage begins to compound. In an AI-saturated environment, sustained market leadership no longer depends on how quickly an organization can ship V1.0. That capability has been commoditized. Leadership depends on Iteration Velocity: the ability to absorb user behavior, regulatory movement, and competitive pressure continuously—without reintroducing the failure modes that made late-stage validation catastrophic in the first place.

Traditional Product Managers (PMs) treat iteration as a race. Their core question is, "How quickly can we ship the next feature?" Speed is the primary metric, and risk is managed reactively after the fact. The Context Architect reframes the problem entirely. Iteration becomes a discipline of integrity. The governing question shifts from output to control: "How quickly can the governing context itself be updated without breaking semantic alignment across the system?"

This distinction matters because it marks a shift from execution management to system regulation. This chapter establishes that rapid iteration is no longer a discretionary best practice or a cultural aspiration. Under context governance, rapid iteration becomes the enforced operational standard.

11.1 THE ITERATION PARADOX: SPEED VS. SAFETY

To understand why the Stacked Product Lifecycle is not optional for V1.1 and beyond, we must confront the dominant failure mode of the traditional product organization: the Iteration Paradox.

The paradox is simple, familiar, and consistently underestimated. In a sequential system, the faster an organization attempts to iterate, the higher the probability that it introduces structural liability. Speed and safety are inversely correlated, not because teams are careless, but because the system itself accumulates hidden coupling over time.

The Sequential Reality

Consider a traditional FinTech organization that required six months to launch its V1.0 product. When planning the V1.1 release, intuition suggests acceleration. The foundation already exists. The team is staffed. The architecture is deployed. The codebase is live. In theory, iteration should be incremental.

In practice, experienced Product Managers know the opposite outcome is more common. An organization that takes six months to launch V1.0 frequently requires three to four additional months to deliver even a modest V1.1 update. The second release feels heavier, slower, and riskier than the first.

This slowdown occurs because V1.1 does not begin from a clean state. It inherits the full Product Timeline Tax (PTT) of V1.0. Every shortcut, assumption, undocumented dependency, and implicit decision made during the initial launch compounds into friction during iteration.

Regression Tax: Quality Assurance (QA) must test the new features while simultaneously re-testing every existing behavior to confirm that nothing critical regressed. Test scope expands non-linearly.

Integration Tax: Engineering must weave new logic into existing logic, navigating undocumented interfaces and brittle coupling that did not matter when the system was smaller.

Compliance Tax: Legal and Risk teams are asked to review the "diff" (changes) between V1.0 and V1.1, often without a unified model of how those changes propagate through the broader system.

The result is predictable. The first major update erases the velocity advantage of the startup phase entirely. The process stalls under the weight of accumulated Technical Context Debt (Chapter 7). Teams become risk-averse and defensive. Core components are avoided because "they work" and, more importantly, because no one retains a complete Semantic Understanding of why they work.

The Vertical Risk

For low-liability consumer applications, a failed iteration may result in a degraded user experience or temporary churn. The damage is visible but survivable. For high-liability verticals—InSuretech, MedTech, FinTech, and regulated AI platforms—the consequences are existential.

A single non-compliant feature introduced through a rushed "hotfix" can trigger regulatory penalties that outweigh an entire year of operating margin. An AI-driven healthcare product that hallucinates a diagnosis in V1.1 because guardrails were inconsistently updated does not generate a bug report; it generates litigation, enforcement action, and reputational collapse.

In these environments, safety becomes the ultimate Zero-Sum Gate on velocity. Organizations are forced into a false binary: move fast and accept catastrophic risk, or move cautiously and surrender competitive ground. Within the traditional sequential model, it is structurally impossible to do both.

The Stacked Solution

The Stacked Product Lifecycle resolves the Iteration Paradox by redefining what an "update" actually is. Under this model, iteration is no longer the act of patching a fragile system or editing legacy code in place—activities that merely compound ambiguity and accelerate debt.

Because the V1 product was Born Compliant, the V1.1 iteration does not begin as a risky modification of an inherited mess. It begins as a **controlled regeneration** of the system based on an updated truth. The governing input is not code, tickets, or feature requests—it is the Context Schema itself, explicitly versioned and revalidated before execution.

As a result, V1.1 begins with **near-zero incremental liability at the point of design** and a fully explicit Semantic Understanding of its constraints. Existing operational, contractual, and data obligations persist across versions, but new risk is not layered on top of undocumented assumptions. The Context Architect updates the governing schema, not the outputs downstream of it.

Execution artifacts are regenerated rather than retrofitted, producing a coherent, auditable change set—code diffs, configuration updates, and migration plans—that can be reviewed through established Engineering, Site Reliability Engineering (SRE), Security, and Legal gates. Velocity is restored not by moving faster, but by removing the structural conditions that made speed dangerous in the first place.

11.2 THE ITERATION LOOP: CONVERTING DATA INTO CONTEXT

If the Context Architect is the "Ghost in the Shell," the Iteration Loop is the system's heartbeat. It is not an ad hoc feedback mechanism or a backlog refinement ritual. It is a formal, repeatable process for converting newly surfaced external data—user behavior, regulatory movement, competitive action, and environmental constraint—into explicit, non-negotiable updates to the Context Schema.

This loop exists because raw data has no governing power on its own. Data only becomes operationally meaningful when it is translated into structure. The Iteration Loop is the mechanism by which reality is re-ingested into the system and rendered governable.

At the center of this process is the distinction between Syntactic Fluency and Semantic Fluency. The AI execution engine possesses Syntactic Fluency: it can generate code, copy, tests, and configurations at machine speed. What it lacks is Semantic Understanding. It does not understand why a rule changed, which constraint dominates, or what trade-off is acceptable. This is Semantic Blindness. The CA supplies the "Why" by modifying the Schema; the AI supplies the "How" by regenerating artifacts downstream of that decision.

11.2.1 THE SEMANTIC SHIFT: FROM FEATURE REQUEST TO CONTEXT UPDATE

The most consequential psychological shift for the Context Architect during iteration is the abandonment of the "Feature Request" as the unit of change.

Traditional View: A user wants X. The PM writes a user story—*"As a user, I want X"*—and injects it into the backlog. This is a request for human labor and localized execution.

Stacked View: A user wants X. The CA evaluates the implication of that desire and performs a Context Schema Update. This is not a task assignment; it is a modification to the governing laws of the product universe.

This distinction matters because feature requests describe outputs, while schema updates redefine constraints. Outputs are fragile. Constraints are durable.

Consider a high-stakes, regulated scenario.

Scenario: A Data Residency Constraint Update

Imagine your InSuretech product, SafeGuard, is live in the U.S. market. A regulatory update—or an internal risk policy revision informed by regulatory guidance—introduces a new constraint: all U.S. customer Personally Identifiable Information (PII) must remain within U.S. jurisdiction and within an approved cloud deployment boundary.

This is not a feature request. It is a change in the legal physics of the system.

The Traditional Response (The PTT Trap):

Discovery: The PM becomes aware of the update through Legal or Compliance.

Scoping: Engineering spends weeks inventorying services, databases, and data flows to determine where PII is stored and replicated.

Conflict: Platform and DevOps teams raise concerns about latency, cost, and regional availability.

Testing: QA debates how to validate jurisdictional residency without a deterministic source of truth.

Legal Audit: Legal teams review architectural documentation and meeting notes to infer whether compliance has been achieved.

Result: 8–10 weeks of accrued Product Timeline Tax, fragmented accountability, and a persistent risk that an edge case or secondary data store was overlooked.

The Stacked Response (The Context Update):

The Context Architect does not convene a meeting or open a ticket. They open the Context Schema.

The CA updates the Constraint & Compliance Layer with a new immutable rule:

"U.S. customer PII must be processed and stored exclusively within approved U.S. deployment boundaries."

```
JSON
  {
  "compliance_layer": {
  "regulatory_body": "FINRA",
  "constraint_id":    "FINRA_Data_Residen-
cy_Rule_2025",
  "rule_definition":  "All  data  fields
tagged 'PII' must rely on infrastructure
located in: AWS_US_EAST_1",
  "enforcement_level": "Strict",
  "severity": "Blocker"
  }
  }
```

This single change becomes the governing truth. It is the trigger event that propagates across all stacks. The CA has not written infrastructure code or migration scripts. They have redefined the constraints under which all future artifacts must be generated.

From this point forward, regeneration produces **explicit change sets**—configuration diffs, infrastructure updates, and migration plans—submitted for SRE, Security, and Legal review. Execution remains governed. Discovery and interpretation do not.

11.2.2 THE ITERATION FLOW: THE SINGLE-POINT CONTEXT UPDATE

The defining advantage of the Stacked Product Lifecycle is that the input for V1.1 is not a backlog or a diff. It is the V1.0 Context Schema plus newly validated truth.

1. **Input:** The Context Architect retrieves the archived, version-controlled V1 Context Schema produced at the Zero-Friction Launch and duplicates it as the working draft for V1.1.
2. **CA Review (Semantic Regulator):** The CA assumes the role of Semantic Regulator. The AI execution environment may flag conflicts—for example: *"Warning: Data residency constraint conflicts with 'Latency < 200ms' in the Technical Layer."* The machine cannot resolve this. Only the human can decide whether compliance outweighs performance. The CA explicitly adjudicates the conflict: *"Compliance overrides performance."* This is the operational manifestation of the Chinese Room—the system executes rules, but the human supplies intent.
3. **Artifact Re-generation:** Once the updated schema is validated, the CA issues a single regeneration command. All downstream artifacts across all stacks are rebuilt from the same governing context.

Engineering Stack (Regeneration): The AI analyzes the microservice topology, identifies every service that processes PII, and regenerates infrastructure-as-code. Terraform definitions are rewritten to pin workloads to US-EAST-1. Database configurations are regenerated. This is not a patch layered onto existing state; it is an overwrite derived from the new constraint set.

QC Stack (Regeneration): The AI regenerates the Born Compliant Test Harness. The new FINRA_Data_Residency_Rule produces an explicit test case—Verify_Server_Region_Is_US_EAST_1—which is automatically integrated into the Continuous Integration and Continuous Delivery (CI/CD) pipeline.

GTM Stack (Regeneration): The AI reviews the Legal Disclaimer Suite, Privacy Policy, and compliance-facing sales collateral. It regenerates the "Data Privacy" section of the Terms of Service to reflect U.S.-based storage and updates compliance slides to include the new regulatory adherence.

The Result: Zero-Friction Iteration

By the time the Engineering team arrives the following morning, the so-called "migration project" is no longer an exercise in open-ended discovery. The structural reasoning has already been externalized into a governed change set. Test cases have been generated. Infrastructure definitions have been drafted. Legal language has been prepared in alignment with the updated constraints.

Engineering performs a technical audit of the regenerated infrastructure artifacts, reviewing proposed changes, dependencies, and migration implications.

Legal performs a compliance audit of the regenerated policy language, verifying alignment with regulatory obligations and internal risk standards.

Because artifact regeneration occurs simultaneously and deterministically from a single source of truth, the V1.1 iteration enters review **Born Compliant at the design layer**, before execution begins. What would traditionally consume weeks of investigation and cross-functional coordination collapses into a bounded review cycle measured in days rather than months, because the work has shifted from interpretation to verification.

This is the operational standard enforced by the Context Architect. Timelines are not directly managed, forecasted, or promised. Integrity is managed. Velocity emerges as a consequence of eliminating ambiguity, not as an objective pursued in isolation.

11.3 CONTEXT-DRIVEN FUTURE ROADMAPS: GOVERNING V2.0

In legacy organizations, the product roadmap functions less as a plan than as a battleground of subjective optimism. Sales wants a feature to close a deal. Engineering wants time to refactor Technical Debt.

Executives want "AI integration" because they saw a headline or read a hype-driven paragraph in an in-flight magazine. The Product Manager sits in the middle translating incompatible incentives into artifacts and pressure into priorities.

Teams respond by reaching for familiar prioritization frameworks —RICE, MoSCoW, Kano, WSJF, or a homegrown scoring sheet. These tools remain useful for forcing trade-offs, but in a context-governed system their limitation is clear: they are not governance instruments. They quantify desire and perceived feasibility inside the team's current mental model, not viability inside the external constraint environment the product must survive.

In a context-governed lifecycle, this failure mode is no longer theoretical. Traditional frameworks are semantically blind by design: they score what humans want, not what reality permits. A feature can score high on "Impact" and low on "Effort," and still be non-viable because it collides with an external constraint that is absent from the spreadsheet—an upcoming regulatory requirement, a jurisdictional consent rule, a platform policy change, or an enforceable IP boundary. When governance is deferred, the roadmap appears correct until the moment it detonates.

For this reason, the Context Architect abolishes the "Wishlist Roadmap"—not because roadmapping lacks value, but because wishlists are not governable. Under the Stacked Product Lifecycle, two different machines are explicitly separated:

The **Live Stacked Lifecycle**, responsible for V1.0 operation, maintenance, compliance continuity, and safe iteration under current constraints.

The **Contextual Roadmap Stack**, where V2.0 innovation is governed as a future-context problem rather than a date-guessing exercise.

The future is therefore governed not by promising delivery dates under uncertainty, but by maintaining the integrity of the context under which delivery would be allowed to occur at all.

11.3.1 THE CONTEXTUAL SANDBOX: REAL-TIME FEATURE VETTING

One of the most expensive forms of Product Timeline Tax is building a feature that must be deleted before launch. This is not merely waste; it is negative progress. It erodes morale, burns political capital, and—most critically—conditions the organization to distrust its own roadmap and planning discipline.

This failure mode occurs for predictable reasons: "Legal didn't see it until the end," "Security raised a red flag too late," "We misunderstood jurisdictional consent," or "We failed to recognize a patent or regulatory boundary that made the approach non-viable." In the sequential model, these are late-stage surprises because constraints are discovered *after* execution begins, when reversal is most expensive.

To prevent this, the Context Architect establishes a Contextual Sandbox. This is a dedicated environment inside the AI Studio where the Context Schema can be **projected forward under explicit assumptions** and stress-tested against plausible future conditions. The purpose of the Sandbox is not to build V2.0—it is to **pre-govern** it. It transforms the roadmap from a list of aspirations into a set of constraint-vetted options with known risk profiles.

Scenario: The "Automated Claim Filing" Feature

Returning to the InSuretech example, an executive proposes a high-value V2.0 feature: "Automated Claim Filing." The intent is straightforward: an AI system listens to a customer's phone call about an accident and initiates the claim automatically—eliminating manual intake, form completion, and adjuster triage.

The Traditional Failure Mode:

Excitement: The Product Manager schedules the feature for Q3 because it appears differentiated and revenue-positive.

Development: Engineering spends months building speech-to-text pipelines and claim extraction workflows.

The Zero-Sum Gate: Late in the cycle, Legal identifies a hard constraint: recording or processing calls without explicit consent triggers wiretapping and consent obligations that vary by jurisdiction, and the designed flow does not satisfy them.

The Pivot: The team guts or kills the feature. The burn consumes months of time and budget. The organization labels the outcome "learning," but the Product Timeline Tax has already been paid in full.

The Contextual Sandbox Solution:

The Context Architect does not assign the feature a delivery date. Instead, they initiate **Simultaneous Context Prototyping.** The feature concept is evaluated inside the Sandbox alongside curated regulatory monitoring inputs, internal policy assumptions, competitive positioning signals, and known constraint classes that historically govern outcomes. This is not prediction. It is assumption-explicit stress testing.

The CA issues a governance query:

Generate a scenario-based Contextual SWOT Analysis for "Automated Claim Filing" against current U.S. consent and privacy constraints and plausible EU AI Act compliance assumptions.

The AI Studio generates a Contextual SWOT Analysis:

Strengths: Potential to materially reduce operational cost by lowering manual intake volume in low-complexity claims.

Weaknesses: High dependency on transcription accuracy, environmental noise, and linguistic edge cases.

Opportunities: Differentiation in segments that value speed and reduced paperwork.

Threats (Critical): Elevated risk of violating two-party consent requirements in specific jurisdictions; significant liability exposure if automated initiation produces erroneous claim outcomes or hallucinated denials.

This is not a human opinion disguised as a scorecard. It is a constraint-oriented risk surface derived from the same governance logic that will later generate compliant artifacts. The Context Architect immediately identifies the true blocker: consent is not a feature detail—it is a governing constraint.

The Governance Decision:

Instead of killing the concept, the Context Architect modifies the Context Schema inside the Sandbox by introducing an explicit constraint that makes the feature governable:

Constraint_Voice_Consent:

"*The system must acquire explicit verbal consent before recording begins; if consent is not captured, recording and automated claim initiation are disabled in jurisdictions requiring two-party consent.*"

The AI Studio regenerates the wireframe under this constraint. The V2.0 design now includes a mandatory consent acquisition gate before recording and claim extraction occur. The product has been corrected at the context layer—before code exists, before teams are staffed, and before political capital is spent. The artifact is now Born Compliant for V2.0 and prototype-ready even while V1.0 continues to be optimized.

11.3.2 SIMULATED CONTEXT TESTING (SCT)

Once a constraint-vetted prototype exists inside the Sandbox, the CA runs **Simulated Context Testing (SCT).**

In a traditional firm, "focus group testing" is expensive and slow. Organizations recruit participants, rent a room, schedule sessions, and watch a handful of interactions on a mock-up. The resulting feedback is anecdotal, low-sample, and time-lagged.

In the Live Stacked Lifecycle, SCT uses the AI Studio to simulate user personas interacting with the governed logic of the prototype. The point is not to "predict the market" perfectly; it is to detect semantic friction, abandonment triggers, and messaging drift early—while changes are still cheap because they are still changes to context.

The CA runs a simulation: *"Run 1,000 interactions of 'Automated Claim Filing' using the 'Stressed/Anxious User' persona. Report on sentiment drift and abandonment triggers."*

The AI simulates the interactions and reports: in 15% of cases, the 'Stressed User' abandons at the consent gate because the consent language is too long, too legalistic, or too cognitively demanding in a high-stress moment.

This result does not invalidate the constraint. The consent gate remains non-negotiable. But it creates an actionable iteration target inside the GTM and User Experience (UX) layers. The CA iterates the Semantic Resonance Matrix (copy and framing) immediately, shortening the consent language without diluting the legal meaning. They re-run the simulation. The abandonment rate drops from 15% to 2%.

This enables a new reality: "focus group testing" of V2.0 functional usage and messaging can occur while V1.0 is still live and compounding. Before a feature is officially placed on a roadmap, it can be validated against both market friction and liability.

11.3.3 THE ITERATION SCORECARD: AUDITING FUTURE SCOPE

The final output of context-driven roadmapping is the **Contextual Roadmap Scorecard.**

Traditional roadmaps visualize **time.**

Contextual roadmaps visualize **risk** and **viability under constraints.**

The Context Architect presents the scorecard to executives in a form the organization can govern. For each proposed feature, the scorecard displays a Liability-to-Value Ratio (LVR): a disciplined comparison of expected upside versus expected constraint-driven downside.

If the LVR is greater than 1.0, the feature carries more liability than value under the current projected context and must be blocked, redesigned, or explicitly risk-accepted by leadership.

Feature A (Dark Mode): LVR 0.1 (Low Risk, Medium Value). Status: Approved.

Feature B (Crypto Wallet Integration): LVR 5.2 (Extreme Regulatory Risk, Unclear Value). Status: Blocked.

Feature C (Automated Claims): LVR 0.8 (Managed Risk via Sandbox, High Value). Status: Approved with Constraints.

This scorecard becomes the CA's primary mechanism for preventing Accelerated Scope Creep. When an executive demands Feature B, the CA does not argue subjectively. The CA responds with governed structure: "The LVR is 5.2. To approve this, you must explicitly accept the regulatory exposure and fund the additional compliance architecture required to reduce that ratio."

The decision becomes governed, auditable, and explicit. Not emotional. Not political. Not optimistic. The roadmap becomes a constraint-managed instrument—exactly what it must be in an era where context drift is the dominant failure mode.

11.4 THE STRATEGIC ADVANTAGE: THE TIME-TO-SCALE PTT

The ultimate strategic payoff of rapid iteration is not limited to shipping features faster. Its real leverage appears later, at the moment most organizations fear the most: scale. The elimination of the **Time-to-Scale PTT** is where context governance converts operational discipline into durable competitive advantage.

Scaling a product—entering a new country, serving a new regulatory regime, adding an enterprise segment, or white-labeling the platform for a strategic partner—has historically been one of the slowest, most expensive phases of the product lifecycle. It is the point where hidden assumptions are exposed, where implicit constraints become explicit, and where organizations discover how much of their system is hard-coded to yesterday's reality.

The Traditional Scaling Nightmare

In the sequential model, geographic or regulatory expansion is treated as a near ground-up rewrite, even when the core product logic remains unchanged. Consider the familiar scenario of launching a U.S.-based InSuretech platform into Canada.

Legal initiates the process by hiring Canadian counsel to redline every contract, privacy policy, and disclaimer line by line.

Product duplicates the existing backlog and creates a parallel "Canada V1" roadmap, fragmenting ownership and introducing coordination overhead.

Engineering hard-codes substitutions—"Province" instead of "State," new postal code formats—and in the process inadvertently breaks U.S. ZIP code validation or other shared logic.

Marketing translates the website and collateral into French, but misses Quebec-specific linguistic and regulatory nuance, triggering rework after review.

None of these steps is individually irrational. Together, they form a slow-motion failure mode. The organization is not scaling the product; it is re-discovering its own assumptions piecemeal. The cumulative result is the Time-to-Scale PTT: nine to twelve months of duplicated effort, re-auditing, re-testing, and risk exposure—paid again for every new market.

The Context Fork: Zero-Friction Scale

The Stacked Product Lifecycle reframes scaling entirely. Expansion is no longer treated as a rewrite problem. It becomes a **Context Fork** problem—one of governed variation rather than reinvention.

To launch in Canada, the Context Architect does not restart the project, assemble a new tiger team, or spin up a parallel backlog. Instead, they initiate a **Context Recalculation Event**, reusing the proven core while deliberately diverging only where jurisdictional constraints require it.

Step 1: The Fork

The CA takes the master V1.0 Context Schema—the same schema that governed the live U.S. system—and creates a governed branch: Schema_Canada_V1. Product identity, intent, and functional boundaries are preserved. Only the governing constraints are allowed to diverge, and that divergence is explicit, versioned, and reviewable.

Step 2: Constraint Injection

The CA injects a Canadian regulatory and localization layer into the branched schema. This layer represents a structured set of constraints sourced from legal Subject Matter Experts, internal policy, and jurisdictional guidance, all maintained as first-class inputs to the system.

Representative constraints include:

- **Data Residency:** Customer data must be processed and stored within Canadian jurisdiction in accordance with applicable privacy law.
- **Language:** User-facing interfaces and legal disclosures must support English and French.
- **Currency:** Monetary values must be presented in CAD with locale-appropriate formatting.

These are not implementation notes or backlog items. They are immutable rules injected into the governing context that all downstream artifacts must satisfy.

Step 3: Automated Recalculation

The CA issues a regeneration command. The AI Studio recalculates downstream artifacts across all stacks using the combined constraint set, producing auditable change sets rather than unreviewed production edits.

Engineering Stack Regeneration:

The AI analyzes service boundaries, data flows, and infrastructure definitions. It generates infrastructure and configuration updates aligned to Canadian deployment boundaries, recalculates database validation logic to support alphanumeric postal codes, and introduces locale-aware UI toggles. Outputs are delivered as explicit diffs and migration plans, eliminating manual search-and-replace while preserving Engineering review and rollout control.

GTM Stack Regeneration:

Localization is applied through the Semantic Resonance Matrix rather than ad hoc translation. Brand voice, tone, and positioning are preserved while disclosures, legal references, and jurisdiction-specific claims are recalculated for the Canadian market. Legal artifacts are regenerated as review-ready drafts, reducing redlining effort without bypassing counsel oversight.

QC Stack Regeneration:

A jurisdiction-specific test harness is generated that validates bilingual rendering, locale-sensitive formatting, consent flows, and region-specific compliance checks. These tests are born with the forked product variant rather than retrofitted after failures surface.

Step 4: The Result

What traditionally requires many months of re-auditing, parallel planning, and rework compresses into a bounded recalculation and review cycle measured in weeks rather than quarters. Because compliance and localization constraints are governed at the schema level *before* execution artifacts are produced, the Canadian deployment is Born Compliant at the design layer. Review cycles replace rework cycles.

This capability—**Zero-Friction Scale**—creates a compounding moat. While a sequential competitor is still staffing a "Canada Expansion Team" and debating scope boundaries, the context-governed organization is already validating and deploying compliant, localized variants. Adjacent markets are captured through structural inevitability.

11.5 CONCLUSION: THE END OF "REQUIREMENTS"

This chapter closes the mechanical loop of the Context Architect's function. We have progressed deliberately from the Zero-Friction Launch, through Rapid Iteration, and into Contextual Scaling. What initially appeared as separate operational advantages—calm launches, safe velocity, and frictionless expansion—resolve into a single governing principle when viewed as a system.

The unifying thread across all phases of the Stacked Product Lifecycle is the collapse of the "Requirement" as the primary unit of work and the corresponding rise of the **Constraint** as the unit of governance.

A **Requirement** is an instruction directed at a human: "Make it work in Canada," "Add an AI feature," or "Support enterprise customers." Requirements are interpretive. They rely on individual judgment, implicit assumptions, and localized decision-making. As systems grow in complexity, requirements accumulate ambiguity, generate inconsistent execution, and leave behind debt that must later be paid with interest.

A **Constraint**, by contrast, is a rule injected directly into the system: "Region = Canada," "Consent required before recording," "Data residency enforced by jurisdiction." Constraints are not suggestions. They are absolute boundaries that shape every downstream artifact. Once encoded into the Context Schema, they are applied consistently, audited continuously, and scaled without reinterpretation.

This shift is not semantic. It is architectural. It changes where authority lives inside the organization. Under context governance, authority moves upstream—from execution to design, from backlog management to schema regulation.

The Context Architect is the only role structurally capable of governing this transition. They do not manage projects, chase deadlines, or negotiate scope. They regulate the constraint environment in which projects execute themselves. Competitive leadership becomes a function of how rigorously and coherently an organization maintains the integrity of its Context Schema—not how aggressively it pushes teams to move faster.

At this stage, the system has reached operational equilibrium. The mechanics are no longer the bottleneck. Execution is stable, repeatable, and increasingly automated. What remains unresolved is not how the system runs, but who is accountable for it over time.

As we move into Part IV, the focus deliberately shifts away from mechanics and toward people. If the AI is generating code, tests, infrastructure, and compliant documentation—if execution is increasingly automated and regeneration replaces manual iteration—then the human role must evolve. What happens to the career path of the Junior Product Manager? How does the org chart change when governance replaces coordination? What does it mean to hire, train, and evaluate a Context Architect?

We have built the machine.
Now we must decide who owns it.

PART IV

OWNERSHIP AND THE INFINITE GAME

12

THE HUMAN SYSTEM: STAFFING THE MACHINE

We have built the machine.

Across Chapters 5 through 11, this book established a new operational standard for designing, launching, iterating, and scaling AI-driven systems. The Stacked Product Lifecycle removed sequential drag. The Context Schema replaced informal coordination with enforceable structure. The Context Architect (CA) emerged not as a manager of tasks, but as the regulator of semantic integrity across the entire system.

But no system—no matter how rigorously designed—governs itself.

Every machine imposes pressure on the human organization surrounding it. When execution becomes automated, when regeneration replaces manual iteration, and when constraints displace requirements as the unit of work, the legacy organizational map begins to misalign. Roles once optimized for throughput lose relevance. Responsibilities that were previously implicit must be made explicit. Decision authority migrates upstream—not as a design choice, but as a structural consequence of the system itself.

This transition introduces a distinct category of risk. It is not technical risk. It is not compliance risk. It is human system risk—the risk that the organization's structure, incentives, and career paths no longer align with the authority the system now requires to function safely and coherently over time.

Part IV addresses this final layer of governance. If AI systems are now generating code, tests, infrastructure definitions, and compliant documentation—if execution itself is increasingly automated—then human roles must be redesigned with the same structural discipline applied to the machine. This is not a cultural exercise. It is an ownership problem.

What is the Product Manager (PM) responsible for when backlog refinement ceases to be the primary coordination mechanism?

What is the function of Engineering leadership when code throughput is no longer the binding constraint?

What happens to junior roles whose historical value was measured in task velocity rather than judgment quality?

This chapter begins with the most consequential question facing modern product organizations—how to assign authority and accountability in a context-governed system without reintroducing the coordination failures, translation layers, and human bottlenecks this book was written to eliminate.

12.1 THE COLLAPSE OF THE TASK-BASED ORG CHART

Traditional organizations are designed around tasks. Roles exist to move work from left to right across a linear process diagram: define, design, build, test, ship. Each function owns a slice of execution, and progress is measured by the visible movement of artifacts between stages.

The organizational chart mirrors this flow. Product Management defines requirements. Engineering implements them. Quality Assurance tests what was built. Legal reviews what is about to ship. Marketing prepares the launch. Authority is distributed across handoffs, and accountability is fragmented by design. This fragmentation is not accidental; it is the mechanism by which large organizations historically scaled execution.

This structure was rational under historical constraints. When execution was slow, expensive, and scarce, labor was the bottleneck. Coordination mechanisms evolved to allocate limited human effort, manage specialization, and reduce local inefficiencies within functional silos. Task ownership and stage gates were effective substitutes for explicit intent governance.

AI-driven systems invert this economic reality.

When execution becomes abundant, cheap, and continuously available, the bottleneck migrates upstream. Writing code, generating tests, producing documentation, and drafting compliant artifacts are no longer rate-limiting steps. Yet the organizational structure—and the incentives attached to it—often remain optimized for precisely those activities.

This mismatch produces a predictable failure mode. Organizations retain a task-based org chart while systematically removing the work those tasks were designed to perform. The structure persists even as its underlying economic justification erodes.

The outcome is organizational drift.

Individuals optimize for visible activity rather than governed outcomes. Meetings multiply to compensate for the absence of clear decision authority. Artifacts proliferate without shared semantic ownership. Decisions slow down because intent is not explicitly regulated before work begins.

In a context-governed system, this drift is not a short-term transition issue. It is a structural incompatibility. As long as the org chart is optimized for task throughput rather than intent governance, the human system will continually reintroduce friction, delay, and ambiguity—undermining the very advantages the machine was built to provide.

12.2 THE NEW BOTTLENECK: JUDGMENT, NOT EXECUTION

When execution becomes abundant, the binding constraint moves.

In a context-governed system, code generation, test creation, infrastructure definitions, documentation, and compliance artifacts can be produced on demand. These activities are no longer rate-limiting. The machine does not wait for capacity. It waits for **governed direction.**

What the machine cannot do—by design—is decide what should

be built, what should not be built, or which constraint must dominate when values conflict. It cannot determine whether compliance overrides performance, whether risk outweighs growth, or whether a feature must be blocked despite strong commercial pressure. These decisions exist outside syntax. They require interpretation of intent and acceptance of consequence.

Those decisions require judgment.

Judgment is the true scarce resource in an automated system. Unlike execution, it cannot be parallelized arbitrarily or regenerated after the fact without cost. But judgment is not mystical. It is the application of explicit intent, bounded authority, and consequence-aware reasoning at predefined decision points.

Organizations lose control when this distinction is ignored. They continue to hire, measure, and reward execution throughput at precisely the moment when execution is no longer the bottleneck. Judgment, meanwhile, remains implicit, unassigned, and under-governed—treated as an emergent property of seniority rather than a designed responsibility.

The resulting failure mode is familiar. Leadership experiences overload because the system is moving faster than its governing intent. Decisions accumulate upstream. Exceptions multiply. Everything feels urgent because no explicit structure exists to adjudicate trade-offs *before* execution begins.

In a context-governed organization, the purpose of the human system is therefore not to "keep up" with the machine. It is to place disciplined judgment exactly where automation must stop. Until this bottleneck is acknowledged, assigned, and governed explicitly, automation amplifies confusion rather than eliminating it.

12.3 THE ROLE RECOMPOSITION: FROM TASK OWNERS TO SYSTEM GOVERNORS

When judgment becomes the bottleneck, roles cannot remain optimized for task ownership alone. They must be deliberately redesigned around decision authority.

In the task-based organization, roles exist to own work. Authority flows from responsibility for execution: whoever builds, tests, or ships controls local decisions within their slice of the process. This model assumes that execution is scarce and that progress depends primarily on allocating labor efficiently across functional boundaries.

In a context-governed system, that assumption no longer holds. Execution becomes abundant and repeatable. What remains scarce is the ability to make correct, coherent decisions about what should exist, under which constraints, and with what trade-offs. As a result, roles must shift from owning tasks to owning **governed decisions.** Authority flows not from throughput, but from explicit responsibility for intent, constraint prioritization, and consequence.

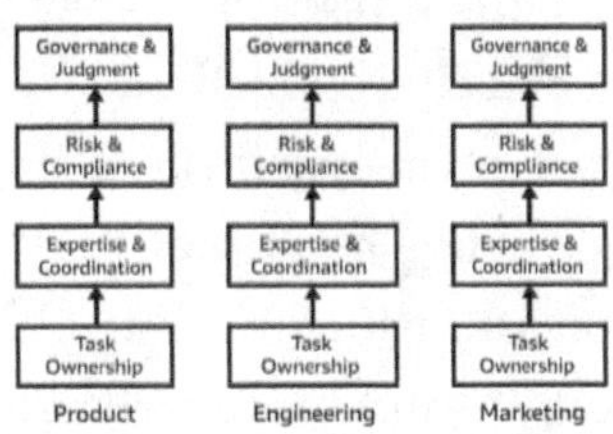

Figure 5. *As execution becomes abundant, Product, Engineering, and Marketing roles evolve from task ownership toward governance and judgment as the system's binding constraint.*

This shift does not eliminate roles, nor does it dissolve organizational structure. It recomposes roles around governance. Each role moves upward in abstraction—away from manual execution and toward regulation of the systems that produce execution. Execution still occurs, but it is no longer the primary locus of authority.

Product Managers stop managing backlogs as queues of tasks and instead govern problem definitions, constraint trade-offs, outcome boundaries, and escalation thresholds.

Engineers stop treating code as the primary asset and instead govern architectural integrity, system invariants, failure modes, and safe regeneration boundaries.

Leaders stop managing people through visible activity and instead govern alignment, decision rights, and explicit risk acceptance.

This recomposition is where most organizations fail. Rather than redesigning roles, they layer AI-enabled execution on top of legacy job descriptions. Old incentives remain. Old performance metrics persist. The machine accelerates, but the human system remains misaligned with the new bottleneck.

The predictable outcome is confusion. Authority becomes contested. Decisions stall or escalate unnecessarily. Power struggles emerge around issues that were never explicitly reassigned. Resistance often goes silent rather than vocal, as individuals sense that their historical responsibilities no longer carry weight—but no new mandate has been clearly established.

Without explicit role recomposition, a context-governed system cannot remain stable. The machine may continue to operate correctly, but the organization surrounding it degrades, reintroducing delay and friction through human uncertainty rather than technical limitation.

12.4 THE JUNIOR ROLE TRAP: WHEN THROUGHPUT LOSES VALUE

Junior roles have historically existed to increase throughput. They execute assigned tickets, write code under supervision, draft copy, prepare documentation, and run test cases. Their value is typically measured in volume: how many tasks were completed, how quickly they moved, and how reliably they followed instructions.

This model is rational when execution is scarce and errors are relatively inexpensive. Junior staff act as force multipliers for senior judgment. They absorb labor-intensive work so experienced operators can focus on higher-order decisions, architectural reasoning, and risk management.

In a context-governed system, this logic no longer maps cleanly to reality.

When AI systems can execute tasks instantly and consistently, throughput ceases to be a meaningful differentiator on its own. Writing code, generating tests, and producing drafts are no longer signals of leverage. Junior roles optimized *exclusively* for task completion lose their structural footing because the system no longer requires human labor to convert intent into artifacts.

The primary risk is therefore not immediate job displacement. It is **role erosion.**

Without deliberate redesign, junior staff are left performing activities that appear productive but carry no governance weight. They prepare slides that summarize decisions already encoded in the schema, manage tickets that no longer drive sequencing, and generate documentation that restates system outputs rather than shaping them. Over time, the organization learns—implicitly—to discount their contributions, not due to performance, but due to structural irrelevance.

This state is damaging to both the individual and the system. Individuals receive no pathway to develop judgment, because their work remains decoupled from real decision-making. The system, meanwhile, loses a critical training ground for future Context Architects, Engineers, and Leaders. Throughput without decision authority becomes noise, and noise is eventually filtered out.

A context-governed organization that fails to redesign junior roles does not become leaner. It becomes brittle—top-heavy with decision-makers and starved of a pipeline for disciplined, consequence-aware judgment.

12.5 THE COMPETENCY MATRIX AND THE TRANSITION PATH

The transition from task-based Product Management to context-governed systems cannot be achieved through title changes, tool adoption, or incremental training. It requires a fundamental redefinition of what competence means when execution is automated and judgment becomes the binding constraint.

For this reason, the Context Architect cannot be evaluated, trained, or hired using legacy skill frameworks. The competencies that once defined success—throughput, coordination, backlog hygiene, and narrative fluency—were optimized for a world in which human labor was scarce and execution was slow.

That world no longer exists.

What follows is not a skills checklist and not a career development guide. It is a **competency matrix** designed to govern authority, responsibility, and accountability in a context-driven organization. The matrix exists to answer a single organizational question:

Who is qualified to regulate intent when machines execute without hesitation?

Accordingly, the CA's capability profile is divided into **three non-negotiable domains.** Each domain corresponds to a distinct failure mode identified earlier in this book. Together, they bridge the gap between abstract strategy and executable governance.

These domains are not aspirational. They are operational requirements. Assigning context authority without ensuring coverage across all three does not create leverage—it amplifies risk.

Domain I: Philosophical & Strategic Competency

Semantic Regulation

The first domain is the most abstract—and the most critical. It governs what the system can legitimately claim and do.

In the traditional model, Product Managers define features: what the user sees, clicks, or experiences. In the context-governed model, the Context Architect defines constraints: what the system is permitted to do under all conditions. This represents a shift from narrative description to applied logic.

1. Semantic Rigor: Language as Liability

In an AI-driven system, language is not just descriptive—it is executable. Ambiguity is no longer a communication issue; it is a defect.

Legacy reality:

Humans tolerate ambiguity. If a requirement is unclear, a Developer asks a question.

Context-governed reality:

Machines do not ask questions. They infer. And inference under ambiguity produces hallucination.

For this reason, the Context Architect must treat language as a liability surface. Terms such as *PII*, *ePHI*, *consent*, *harm*, or *eligibility* cannot remain informally defined. They must be explicitly bounded and operationalized inside the Context Schema.

In practice, this requires a skill set closer to contract analysis and formal reasoning than storytelling. The CA is not writing "user stories." They are writing the **constitution of the product.**

This is why philosophical grounding matters—not as abstraction, but as discipline. Understanding the limits of computation (e.g., the Chinese Room) clarifies why meaning cannot be delegated to the machine and must instead be encoded as constraints.

2. Contextual Roadmap Design

The Context Architect must also govern the future without collapsing it into a timeline.

Legacy view:

A roadmap is a linear sequence of features: *Q1 login, Q2 dashboard.*

Context-governed view:

A roadmap is a portfolio of risk and constraint exposure.

In this model, the Live Stacked Lifecycle (V1.x) is explicitly separated from the Contextual Sandbox (V2.x). Stability and experimentation are governed in parallel rather than competing for the same execution pipeline.

The Context Architect must be capable of evaluating roadmap items not by desirability alone, but by **liability-to-value ratio,** modeling the financial and regulatory consequences of success *and* failure. This reframes roadmap governance from prioritization to risk management.

3. Persona Translation

Strategic intent must be translated into system behavior.

It is insufficient to say "make it easy" or "optimize for a non-technical user." Those are human intuitions, not machine-governable rules.

The CA must convert personas into quantifiable constraints suitable for Simulated Context Testing. Subjective attributes such as *tech-averse* or *time-constrained* must be operationalized as thresholds, triggers, and bounded behaviors.

This translation is what allows subjective strategy to be tested, simulated, and governed before execution.

Domain II: Technical & Analytical Competency

Context Engineering

The second domain is where the Context Architect becomes operationally fluent. They do not write production code, but they must be capable of encoding governance in machine-readable form.

1. High-Density Prompt Authoring

The foundational hard skill of the role is the ability to encode the Context Schema precisely.

Legacy artifact:

A Word document or Jira ticket.

Context-governed artifact:

A structured, machine-readable schema that defines inputs, outputs, and immutable constraints.

This includes translating regulatory text into enforceable variables and rule sets that systems can evaluate deterministically. The objective is not creative generation, but constraint enforcement.

. . .

2. Constraint Dependency Mapping

In a context-driven system, constraints are interdependent.

Changing a single rule—such as account deletion—can cascade across audit logging, billing retention, fraud detection, and compliance reporting. The Context Architect must be able to reason about these dependencies structurally, not socially.

This replaces informal dependency maps ("talk to billing") with explicit constraint graphs that can be evaluated and regenerated deterministically.

3. Architectural Literacy

While the Context Architect is not a coder, they must possess sufficient architectural literacy to govern technical decisions.

They must be able to evaluate whether a proposed service, database, or integration satisfies the constraints defined in the schema. Governance without technical comprehension is performative.

What cannot be visualized cannot be regulated.

Domain III: Executive & Governance Competency

Liability Convergence

The final domain is where authority is exercised.

1. PTT and TCD Management

The Context Architect must quantify and report Product Timeline Tax (PTT) and Technical Context Debt as financial liabilities. Success is measured not by output velocity, but by **liability avoided.**

2. Zero-Sum Gate Elimination

The Context Architect must mandate governance artifacts—such as audit logs and traceability reports—that convert late-stage discovery into early verification. This shifts audits from adversarial to confirmatory.

3. Contextual Negotiation

Finally, the Context Architect must act as the Semantic Firewall against Accelerated Scope Creep.

When leadership demands change, the response is not negotiation by persuasion, but by quantified consequence. Governance replaces optimism.

The Transition Path: From Feature Translator to Architect

The transition into this role cannot be improvised. It requires deliberate progression across three phases.

Phase 1: Contextual Literacy

Reframe the product as a system of constraints rather than a collection of screens.

Phase 2: Governance Prototyping

Move from documenting intent to encoding it.

Phase 3: Executive Mandate

Secure organizational authority to govern context as the single source of truth.

Without this mandate, the role collapses back into advisory status.

12.6 THE MANDATE OF THE CONTEXT ARCHITECT

The Context Architect is not a traditional role, and it cannot be filled by simply renaming an existing position. This role exists to hold authority where systems fail—not to absorb excess coordination work or inherit an existing backlog under a new title.

It is not a Product Manager with unchanged delivery obligations.

It is not a Staff Engineer promoted out of coding and asked to "think bigger."

It is not a Compliance Officer embedded into product and expected to say "no" more efficiently.

Treating the role this way almost always fails because it optimizes for organizational familiarity rather than functional fitness. The result is a role with nominal scope and insufficient authority—visible in meetings, invisible at moments of consequence.

Most organizations struggle at this stage due to hiring for credentials instead of mandate. They prioritize résumé density—years of experience, recognizable company logos, or fluency in specific tools—rather than judgment density. While those signals correlate with competence, they do not predict whether an individual can govern intent when constraints collide and trade-offs cannot be deferred.

A Context Architect must operate at the intersection of product strategy, technical architecture, regulatory reality, and organizational authority. What distinguishes the role is not breadth alone, but the explicit right—and obligation—to adjudicate conflicts when those domains disagree, and to do so with clarity, finality, and accountability.

Under real pressure, this mandate requires making decisions that cannot be escalated without damage:

When compliance overrides performance targets.

When architectural purity yields to time-bound risk.

When a feature must be blocked despite executive sponsorship.

When regeneration is safer than patching, even if it appears slower in the moment.

These decisions cannot be validated through interviews that test recall, tool familiarity, or abstract reasoning alone. They require evidence of judgment exercised under consequence—situations where authority was real, trade-offs were explicit, and outcomes materially mattered.

When organizations hire incorrectly, the failure mode is predictable. The person appears appropriate on paper, attends the right meetings, and produces plausible artifacts—but the role collapses the moment constraints collide. Authority becomes ambiguous. Decisions are deferred upward. The Context Schema degrades from a binding governance mechanism into an advisory document.

Hiring a Context Architect therefore requires evaluating one thing above all else: the candidate's demonstrated capacity to govern systems when values conflict and trade-offs are irreversible. Without that mandate—and the organizational will to support it—the role exists in name only, and the organization predictably reverts to the coordination failures this book has described.

12.7 CONCLUSION: GOVERNING THE HUMAN SYSTEM

AI does not remove humans from the system. It removes specific forms of work.

What remains is not execution at scale, but judgment at scale. Not task throughput, but governance. Not visible activity, but accountability for consequence.

This distinction determines whether an organization becomes more coherent or more fragile as automation increases. The machine does not fail first. The human system does. When governance remains implicit, decision authority diffuses. Responsibility fragments across roles never designed to adjudicate trade-offs. Conflict emerges not because teams disagree, but because no explicit structure exists to resolve disagreement before execution begins.

In these environments, machines operate correctly while organizations degrade. Automation accelerates output, but intent lags behind. The result is not speed—it is instability. Velocity without governance produces motion without direction.

The alternative is deliberate governance of the human system itself. Roles are designed around decision authority rather than task ownership. Career paths are built around controlled exposure to consequence. Hiring prioritizes demonstrated judgment under constraint. The same rigor applied to machine governance is applied to the humans who define, regulate, and audit it.

This defines the responsibility of the Context Architect at the human boundary of the system. Not to replace judgment, but to ensure it is positioned precisely where automation must stop, and governed where it must continue.

The machine is built.

The human system is now governable.

What follows is the challenge of institutionalizing this reality—embedding it into executive decision-making, organizational structure, and the business case that sustains it over time.

13

THE BUSINESS CASE: SELLING THE CONTEXT TO THE BOARD

Across the previous twelve chapters, we established the philosophy, architecture, and operational discipline of the Context Architect (CA). You now understand how to design a Context Schema, govern the Stacked Product Lifecycle, and generate products that are Born Compliant, Born Technically Sound, and resilient under iteration and scale. From an operational standpoint, the superiority of the model should now be self-evident.

But operational superiority does not secure organizational adoption.

If you walk into your CEO's office and say, "I want to become a Context Architect to solve our Semantic Blindness," you will almost certainly be ignored. Not because the argument is wrong, but because it is framed in the wrong language. It sounds philosophical. It sounds academic. It does not map cleanly to the decision framework that governs capital allocation at the executive level.

The boardroom does not arbitrate methodology. It arbitrates efficiency.

At that level of the organization, there is only one language that consistently drives decisions: **capital efficiency**. Executives do not debate "Agile versus Waterfall" or "User Stories versus Job Stories" because those distinctions are downstream. What they care about are the metrics that determine whether the company survives, scales, or collapses under its own cost structure.

Those metrics are simple and unforgiving:

- **Burn Rate Efficiency:** How much real output is produced for every dollar of fully loaded salary expense.

- **Time-to-Revenue:** How quickly invested capital converts into cash flow and growth.
- **Risk Exposure:** The probability-weighted cost of lawsuits, regulatory fines, reputational damage, and forced rework.

This chapter translates everything you have learned into those terms.

It is not a philosophical defense of better product thinking. It is a forensic accounting exercise. It demonstrates that the Product Timeline Tax (PTT) is not an abstract frustration, but a measurable leak in the company's profit and loss statement. It reframes Technical Context Debt as a balance-sheet liability. And it shows that the Stacked Product Lifecycle is not merely operationally elegant, but financially dominant—because it produces **Net Time-to-Market Gain (NTMG)** rather than illusory speed.

13.1 THE FINANCIAL FORMULA OF FAILURE: THE TRUE COST OF PTT

In most organizations, inefficiency is not treated as a financial event. It is treated as process friction. When a project stalls for two weeks awaiting Legal review, it is logged in Jira as "Status: Blocked." The cost continues to accrue, but it is not explicitly recognized as capital consumed without output.

This accounting blind spot is precisely why the PTT persists. Costs that feel operational are, in fact, economic. Salary expense continues. Opportunity cost compounds. Risk exposure remains unchanged. To justify structural change at the executive level, these costs must be surfaced, quantified, and framed in terms already used to govern capital allocation.

We refer to this exercise as the **Audited Product Timeline Tax (Audited PTT).**

13.1.1 THE "FULLY LOADED" BURN RATE

The most common analytical error at this stage is undercounting cost. Product leaders often reason in terms of base salary. Finance teams reason in terms of fully loaded burn.

Consider a representative Senior Engineer:

- **Base Salary:** $150,000
- **Fully Loaded Multiplier:** 1.3×–1.5× (benefits, payroll tax, recruiting overhead, office space, SaaS licenses, equipment, attrition)
- **Estimated Annual Cost:** ~$225,000
- **Estimated Weekly Cost:** **~$4,300** (rounded conservatively)

The exact figure will vary by organization. The principle does not. Now extrapolate to a standard cross-functional delivery squad:

- One Product Manager: ~$4,300 / week
- One Designer: ~$4,000 / week
- Four Engineers: ~$17,200 / week
- One Quality Assurance (QA) / Test role: ~$3,500 / week

Estimated Weekly Squad Burn: ~$29,000–$30,000 per week

This range is intentional. The meter is not precise, but it is relentless. It runs every hour regardless of progress—whether code is shipping, approvals are pending, or decisions are waiting in inboxes.

This burn rate is the baseline against which all delivery "delay" must be evaluated.

13.1.2 THE COST OF SEQUENTIAL LATENCY

In any sequential delivery model—including Waterfall and modern Agile variants—periods of idle or near-idle latency are structurally unavoidable. During these windows, salary expense continues while value creation stalls.

A representative six-month initiative (24 weeks):

- **The Scoping Gap (Weeks 1–3):**
- Engineering capacity is partially idle while requirements, Product Requirements Documents (PRDs), and approvals are finalized.
- **Cost:** 3 × ~$30,000 = **~$90,000** of low- or zero-value burn.
- **The QA Lag (Weeks 18–20):**
- Development declares "code complete," QA identifies defects, and Engineers context-switch while awaiting reports.
- **Cost:** 2 × ~$30,000 = **~$60,000** of wasted burn.
- **The Zero-Sum Gate (Weeks 22–24):**
- The release halts while Legal redlines contracts and policies. Engineering cannot deploy. Product cannot launch.
- **Cost:** 2 × ~$30,000 = **~$60,000** of pure waiting.

The Total PTT Invoice

Across a single project of this scale, the organization spends approximately **$210,000**—roughly **30% of total labor cost**—on time in which no new value is created, no revenue is generated, and no competitive position is improved.

This is the Product Timeline Tax in audited form.

It is not "the cost of doing business." It is the cost of operating without governed context. When presented to finance leadership, it is framed as **capital inefficiency**:

"We are currently consuming roughly thirty cents of every delivery dollar on wait states that could be structurally eliminated through upfront context governance."

Once this cost is made explicit, the discussion changes. The Context Architect is no longer a methodological preference. They become a corrective control for a measurable leak in the organization's capital system.

13.2 TECHNICAL CONTEXT DEBT: THE HIGH-INTEREST LOAN

The second major financial leak is Technical Context Debt (TCD), introduced earlier in Chapter 7 but rarely evaluated as an economic variable. Executives are generally familiar with "Technical Debt," but it is often dismissed as an Engineering hygiene issue—messy code, refactoring backlog, or stylistic inconsistency. Framed this way, it is deprioritized. What is missed is that Technical Context Debt is not an aesthetic problem. It is a capacity liability.

In financial terms, TCD behaves like a high-interest loan against future delivery capacity. The organization accelerates execution today by omitting governing context—compliance rules, data boundaries, lifecycle constraints—while implicitly accepting a long-term obligation that will be paid through reduced throughput rather than explicit expense.

Principal vs. Carrying Cost

The Principal.

The principal of Technical Context Debt is incurred when functionality is shipped without fully encoding the context required to sustain it. Copy is hard-coded "for now." Access rules are assumed rather than enforced. Lifecycle constraints are postponed. No cash changes hands at the moment of this decision. The balance sheet appears unchanged. The liability is latent.

The Carrying Cost.

The carrying cost emerges as execution continues. Engineers are forced to patch, retrofit, and reinterpret intent instead of building net-new value. Capacity is diverted away from revenue-generating work to service historical shortcuts. This cost compounds quietly, consuming throughput without ever appearing as a discrete line item.

This is not interest in the accounting sense. It is throughput drag —a reduction in the productive yield of a fixed cost base.

The Capacity Calculus of TCD

Assume a team with a normalized delivery capacity of 100 units of effort per sprint.

Early State (Low Debt):

All 100 units are applied to new features, customer value, or monetizable capability.

Effective utilization approaches full capacity.

Later State (Context-Debt Laden):

The system accumulates undocumented assumptions and implicit rules.

Thirty units per sprint are consumed by remediation, refactoring, and compliance retrofits.

Only seventy units advance the roadmap.

The burn rate has not changed. The output has.

At a weekly squad burn of approximately $30,000, the organization continues to incur the full expense. However, only a fraction of that spend produces forward progress. The remainder services historical shortcuts. From a financial perspective, the team appears stable while its return on headcount investment deteriorates.

This is why the "interest rate" analogy is useful—but it must be interpreted correctly. The organization is not literally paying interest. It is accepting a persistent dilution of productive capacity.

The Contextual Down Payment

The Context Architect intervenes at the point where this liability is created. Instead of deferring governing context, the organization makes a deliberate contextual down payment by investing time in the Context Schema before execution begins. Constraints are encoded explicitly rather than inferred later. Compliance is enforced at generation time rather than retrofitted after delivery.

This down payment changes the system's operating profile. Less time is spent rediscovering intent. Less effort is consumed by retroactive compliance. More of each sprint compounds forward. What appears externally as slower early execution is, structurally, the prevention of a guaranteed future tax.

From a finance perspective, this is not gold-plating. It is capital preservation. The Context Schema functions as a risk-reducing asset that protects future delivery capacity by preventing short-term schedule pressure from silently converting into long-term throughput erosion.

To a CFO, this is the governing insight: Technical Context Debt is not reduced by working harder or optimizing teams. It is avoided by governing context before it becomes code.

13.3 THE NEW METRIC: NET TIME-TO-MARKET GAIN (NTMG)

The core financial argument for the Stacked Product Lifecycle is not raw speed. Speed, when framed carelessly, signals recklessness to risk and finance leaders. What matters at the enterprise level is net economic gain achieved through earlier, safer market entry.

This distinction is why the Context Architect does not promise "speed." They promise Net Time-to-Market Gain.

NTMG is the metric presented to executive leadership because it translates parallel execution into financial impact using concepts already familiar to finance teams: burn rate, opportunity cost, and delivery variance. It compares the economic outcome of a context-governed launch against the organization's historical, sequential baseline.

Defining the Variables

For clarity:

- **$T_{(Legacy)}$** = Average time to launch using sequential handoffs (e.g., 24 weeks).

- **T(Stacked)** = Time to launch using parallel, context-governed stacks (e.g., 12 weeks).
- **B(Rate)** = Weekly fully loaded burn rate of the delivery team.
- **O(Cost)** = Opportunity cost associated with delayed market entry, typically measured as foregone gross profit rather than top-line revenue.

The precise formula is less important than the logic it encodes: earlier launch affects *both sides* of the financial equation—cost avoided and value realized.

The Opportunity Cost Effect

Product leaders often focus on cost containment. Executive leadership focuses on value realization. NTMG unifies these perspectives by making opportunity cost explicit.

To illustrate, consider a representative InSuretech initiative.

Project: AI Claims Portal

Weekly Burn Rate: ~$30,000

Expected Gross Profit Once Live: ~$50,000 per week

Option A: Sequential Launch (Legacy Baseline)

- Time-to-Market: 24 weeks
- Labor Cost Incurred: ~$720,000
- Revenue Begins: Week 25

Option B: Stacked Launch (Context Architect Model)

- Time-to-Market: 12 weeks
- Labor Cost Incurred: ~$360,000
- Revenue Begins: Week 13

Calculating NTMG

- **Cost Avoidance:**

- (24 – 12) weeks × ~$30,000 = **~$360,000** in avoided burn.
- **Opportunity Capture:**
- 12 weeks of earlier operation × ~$50,000 = **~$600,000** in additional gross profit.
- **Estimated Net Time-to-Market Gain:**
- ~$360,000 + ~$600,000 = **~$960,000**

These figures are illustrative, not guarantees. Their purpose is to demonstrate order-of-magnitude impact, not precision forecasting.

Interpreting the Result

From a finance perspective, this shift materially alters project economics. A single delivery initiative can generate value approaching seven figures by compressing time-to-market without increasing risk exposure.

If the Context Architect role carries an annual cost of approximately $200,000, the implied return on that role—based on one representative project—is multiple times its fully loaded cost. In practice, the role influences multiple initiatives per year, compounding the effect.

Valuation Implications

While valuation methodologies vary by company stage, consistent reductions in time-to-market improve growth rate predictability and delivery cadence. For organizations measured on revenue growth, this can support higher valuation multiples. For more mature organizations, it improves capital efficiency and margin stability.

The key point is not the multiple itself. It is that **delivery velocity, when governed, becomes a financial lever rather than an operational gamble.**

13.4 THE "BOREDOM DIVIDEND" ON THE INCOME STATEMENT

The final component of the financial model is the most counter-intuitive: **boredom pays.**

In Chapter 10, we introduced the "Boredom Dividend"—the operational calm that follows a Zero-Friction Launch. From a finance perspective, this calm does not manifest as an abstract virtue. It appears directly on the **income statement (P&L)** as reduced operating expense volatility and lower unplanned spend.

This distinction matters. Finance teams do not reward excitement. They reward predictability.

The Cost of Chaos (The "Hero" Tax)

As noted earlier, in a traditional launch, the weeks following release are dominated by what is often euphemistically called "Hypercare." In practice, this period is defined by reactive labor, emergency fixes, and reputational recovery. Much of this spend is real, recurring, and rarely forecast accurately.

Common components include:

- **Customer Support Spikes:**
- Confusing workflows, inconsistent messaging, or latent defects drive inbound volume.
- *Illustrative example:*
- 1,000 incremental calls × ~$15 per call = ~**$15,000** in unplanned OpEx (Operational Expense).
- **Hotfix Overtime:**
- Engineering capacity is diverted to weekend or after-hours remediation of priority defects.
- *Illustrative example:*
- 100 overtime hours × ~$150/hour = ~**$15,000** in premium labor cost.
- **Reputational Drag on Acquisition:**
- Poor launch quality depresses conversion rates and increases Customer Acquisition Cost (CAC).
- *Illustrative example:*
- CAC increases from ~$50 to ~$70.
- Across **1,000 new customers**, this equates to ~**$20,000** in additional acquisition spend.

Taken together, these effects represent a ~**$50,000 post-launch "Hero Tax"** on a single initiative. The precise numbers will vary, but the pattern is consistent: chaotic launches generate unplanned operating expense.

The Context-Governed Reality

Under the Stacked Product Lifecycle, these costs are materially reduced—not because teams work harder, but because failures are prevented earlier in the system.

- **Support Costs:**
- Reduced, because semantic clarity and user intent are validated before implementation through the Semantic Resonance Matrix.
- **Overtime Costs:**
- Materially reduced and often approaching zero, because the Born Compliant Test Harness surfaces defects and edge cases before release rather than after.

From a CFO's perspective, this outcome is not about heroics. It is about **OpEx stabilization.** Predictable launches enable more accurate forecasting, tighter variance control, and fewer post-release surprises.

When this model is presented to the board, the promise is deliberately unglamorous: fewer emergency calls, fewer weekend fixes, and fewer reputation-driven acquisition penalties. In an environment defined by volatility, a boring, low-variance operating profile is not a weakness. It is a financial asset.

13.5 THE INVESTMENT ASK: THE "AI ROI" DEFENSE

Any financially literate executive will eventually ask the same question: *what does this cost to run?* Compute is not free. Tokens are not free. From a CFO's perspective, variable usage introduces uncertainty that must be governed explicitly.

This is where the Context Architect must make a critical distinction—between **consumption** and **leverage.**

Time as Consumption vs. Compute as Leverage

In the legacy operating model, the primary input cost is human time. Salary expense scales linearly. To deliver meaningfully faster, organizations add headcount. That approach compounds fixed cost, increases coordination overhead, and permanently raises the burn rate.

Under the Stacked Product Lifecycle, compute becomes the primary variable input. Compute does not eliminate human judgment, but it allows that judgment to be amplified. Incremental acceleration is achieved by increasing compute utilization rather than permanently increasing payroll.

This does not mean compute is "exponential." It means it is **non-linear relative to headcount growth.** In practice, modest increases in compute spend can unlock disproportionate gains in throughput when governance is in place.

Governing Variable Spend

From a finance standpoint, variable cost is only a problem when it is unbounded. In a context-governed system, compute usage is constrained by design:

- Context Schemas define scope and prevent uncontrolled generation.
- Regeneration events are intentional and auditable.
- Usage can be capped, monitored, and forecasted in the same way cloud infrastructure spend is governed today.

This reframes AI compute not as an open-ended expense, but as a controllable operating lever.

Comparative Unit Economics

Precise unit comparisons such as "lines of code" are misleading at the executive level. A more relevant comparison is a **bounded delivery artifact**—for example, a small service, workflow, or feature slice that must meet technical and compliance requirements.

Illustrative comparison:

- **Legacy Delivery:**
- A cross-functional team spends approximately 10 person-hours producing a compliant delivery artifact, at an effective cost of ~$100/hour.
- **Estimated Cost:** ~$1,000.
- **Context-Governed Delivery:**
- The Context Architect spends approximately 2 hours governing and reviewing the schema update.
- Compute usage associated with regeneration is incremental and modest.
- **Estimated Cost:** ~$200–$300, inclusive of compute.

The precise ratio will vary by domain. The financial pattern does not. Human time is the dominant cost driver in the Legacy Model. In the stacked model, human time shifts from production to governance, and compute absorbs the repetitive execution.

Interpreting ROI

This is not a claim of guaranteed percentage return. It is a structural shift in unit economics. By replacing repetitive human execution with governed machine execution, the organization reduces marginal delivery cost while preserving accountability.

From a CFO's perspective, this is not about chasing efficiency optics. It is about converting fixed labor expense into a more flexible, better-instrumented operating cost—without increasing risk exposure.

When framed correctly, the investment ask is conservative: modest incremental compute spend in exchange for materially improved capital efficiency.

13.6 THE ART OF THE "SAFE YES"

At this point, the financial logic is established. The Product Timeline Tax has been quantified. Net Time-to-Market Gain has been demonstrated. The economics of context governance are no longer theoretical.

And yet, none of this guarantees approval.

If you enter the boardroom proposing to "restructure Product and Engineering," the response will almost certainly be "No." Not because the analysis is wrong, but because the request is framed as irreversible. From a fiduciary standpoint, large organizations are designed to resist changes that cannot be safely unwound.

Corporations behave like immune systems. They are optimized to neutralize proposals that appear systemic, open-ended, or difficult to reverse.

This is why successful adoption hinges on mastering the **Safe Yes.**

A Safe Yes is not an endorsement of transformation. It is permission for a **bounded, auditable experiment** whose downside is capped and whose results can be evaluated objectively. The Context Architect does not ask for sweeping authority. They ask for a narrowly scoped mandate with explicit exit criteria.

The framing shift is deliberate. Instead of selling a "revolution," the CA proposes a **risk mitigation pilot**. Instead of requesting control of the castle, they ask to repair a single, clearly leaking window—one whose cost is already visible on the income statement.

From a CFO's perspective, this matters. Capital is deployed incrementally. Governance changes are validated empirically. The pilot structure converts skepticism into a rational approval decision: limited exposure, defined duration, measurable outcomes.

What follows is an adoption mechanism. It uses the Pyramid Principle—leading with the financial conclusion and supporting it with audited evidence—because that is how executive decisions are made under fiduciary responsibility.

13.7 THE CONTEXT TRANSFORMATION SCRIPT

Instructions: Replace the bracketed values with organization-specific data derived from the analyses earlier in this chapter. Precision matters. Executives respond to figures they recognize as internally consistent, not aspirational.

Slide 1: Executive Summary

"We are currently incurring approximately **[Insert Audited PTT Amount] per delivery initiative** due to structural latency in our sequential development process. This Product Timeline Tax is extending our time-to-revenue by **[Insert Measured Lag, e.g., 10–14 weeks]** relative to what is operationally achievable with context-governed execution.

I am proposing a **90-day Context Pilot** to validate whether this tax can be materially reduced. The objective is not acceleration for its own sake. It is to demonstrate a **measurable Net Time-to-Market Gain (NTMG)** on the upcoming **[Pilot Project Name]**, while maintaining or improving our current regulatory and risk posture."

This framing establishes the problem in financial terms and defines success as a measurable outcome, not a belief.

Slide 2: The Problem — The Hidden Invoice

"We typically account for product development costs as salary expense. However, when workflow is audited, a significant portion of that spend is consumed by wait states—delays for specification clarity, compliance review, and rework driven by Context Decay.

Based on internal analysis, approximately **[Insert % Range, e.g., 25–35%]** of delivery capacity is absorbed by these non-productive intervals. This is not a talent issue. It is a structural physics issue. Sequential handoffs introduce friction that additional effort cannot overcome. We are funding a system that delivers materially less than its fully loaded cost."

This slide reframes inefficiency as capital leakage rather than performance failure.

. . .

Slide 3: The Solution — The Context Architect Pilot

"We do not need to add headcount to address this problem. We need to govern context earlier.

For **[Pilot Project Name]**, I propose a controlled shift from a Manager-led coordination model to a **context-led governance model.**

- **Input:** Replace the traditional PRD with a Context Schema that explicitly encodes legal, brand, and technical constraints before execution begins.
- **Process:** Apply the Stacked Product Lifecycle to allow Engineering, QA, and Go-to-Market activities to proceed in parallel under the same governing context.
- **Governance:** Assign a single accountable Context Architect responsible for schema integrity, conflict resolution, and auditability throughout the pilot.

This structure preserves existing roles while removing sequential dependency."

Slide 4: The Ask — The "Safe Yes"

"I am not requesting a company-wide change. I am requesting approval for a **bounded pilot** with defined authority, cost controls, and exit criteria.

- **Authority:** Temporary mandate to govern the Context Schema for **[Pilot Project Name]** only.
- **Resources:** Access to an enterprise-grade AI Studio (estimated cost < **$5,000** for the pilot period) and limited allocation from one Engineer and one Product Marketing role.
- **Timeline:** 90 days to execute, measure, and audit outcomes against historical baselines.

If the pilot does not demonstrate material improvement in time-to-market or risk profile, we revert to the existing model with minimal sunk cost. If it succeeds, we gain evidence—not opinion—for a repeatable operating improvement."

This closes with reversibility, bounded exposure, and evidence-based escalation—conditions under which a rational executive can say yes.

13.8 THE 90-DAY PILOT PROGRAM: A ROADMAP FOR APPROVAL

Once an executive grants provisional approval, the next request is immediate and predictable: *show me the plan*. At this stage, credibility depends less on ambition and more on control.

The appropriate response is the **90-Day Tracer Bullet.**

A tracer bullet is a deliberately scoped initiative that traverses the full delivery surface—interface, logic, data, compliance, and go-to-market—while containing financial and operational exposure. It is designed to validate end-to-end governance without placing core revenue systems or regulatory posture at risk.

The pilot should never target a mission-critical engine. Selecting a core billing system or primary revenue workflow introduces unnecessary downside. Instead, the pilot should focus on a bounded surface area such as a notification service, reporting dashboard, or discrete internal workflow—something real enough to measure, but safe enough to unwind.

Phase 1: Context Setup (Days 1–30)

Objective: Establish a governed, auditable Context Schema before execution begins.

Actions:

- Map the Legacy Dependency Map to surface all implicit constraints, approvals, and handoffs.
- Construct the Semantic Resonance Matrix to define intent, tone, and external communication boundaries.

- Codify the Compliance Layer by translating applicable regulations and internal policies into explicit, machine-readable constraints.

Deliverables:

- A validated context_schema.json.
- A Contextual SWOT Analysis documenting risk, opportunity, and constraint trade-offs.

Financial Profile:

- No production code written.
- No irreversible cost incurred.
- Primary output is decision-quality documentation.

Phase 2: Parallel Execution (Days 31–60)

Objective: Demonstrate the Stacked Product Lifecycle under controlled conditions.

Actions:

- **Engineering Stack:** Regenerate service stubs, schemas, and infrastructure definitions directly from the Context Schema.
- **Quality & Compliance Stack:** Regenerate the Born Compliant Test Harness aligned to the same constraints.
- **Go-to-Market Stack:** Regenerate user documentation, legal terms, and internal enablement materials.

The defining feature of this phase is simultaneity. These artifacts are not sequenced through handoffs. They are regenerated in parallel from the same governing context.

Deliverable:

- A converged artifact set ready for controlled integration and review.

Financial Profile:

- Labor spend remains within baseline allocations.
- Incremental compute usage is measurable and capped.

Phase 3: Convergence & Audit (Days 61–90)

Objective: Release the pilot and measure outcomes against historical baselines.

Actions:

- Execute the Convergence Matrix and verify that all release criteria are satisfied.
- Perform a controlled launch of the pilot feature.
- Conduct a formal audit comparing actual delivery time, cost variance, and risk outcomes to comparable historical initiatives.

Deliverable:

- The **Context Transformation Report**—a board-ready document summarizing time-to-market delta, cost avoidance, opportunity capture, and observed risk impacts.

This report replaces anecdote with evidence. It provides leadership with the data required to determine whether the Context Architect model merits broader application, further piloting, or termination.

13.9 HANDLING EXECUTIVE OBJECTIONS: THE SEMANTIC FIREWALL

Even with a disciplined financial case and a bounded pilot plan, executive objections are inevitable. These objections should not be treated as resistance or misunderstanding. They are expressions of fiduciary responsibility.

The Context Architect must respond to them analytically, not defensively—functioning as a **Semantic Firewall** between understandable concern and structural reality. The goal is not persuasion. It is clarification under governance.

Objection 1: "AI introduces unacceptable data leakage, IP contamination, and auditability risk."

Context Architect Response:

"You are correct to prioritize data exposure, intellectual property protection, and auditability. These are the dominant enterprise risks associated with AI adoption.

This is precisely why the model relies on context governance rather than ad hoc prompting. The Context Schema explicitly defines data classification, permissible sources, retention boundaries, and audit requirements *before* execution occurs. Sensitive inputs are excluded by policy, not by Developer judgment.

Under this model, the AI is never granted open-ended access. It operates only within declared constraints, and every generated artifact is attributable to a specific schema version. This creates a durable audit trail that can be reviewed, reproduced, and governed—often with greater consistency than human-authored work produced under time pressure.

From a risk perspective, the exposure being reduced is not "AI misuse." It is unmanaged human discretion—copy-paste reuse, undocumented assumptions, and implicit decision-making that cannot be reconstructed after the fact. Context governance replaces that ambiguity with enforceable rules."

. . .

Objection 2: "We just invested heavily in an Agile transformation. We cannot change again."

Context Architect Response:

"This approach does not replace Agile. It addresses the structural limitation that prevented Agile from delivering its expected return.

Agile ceremonies and team practices assume rapid feedback and continuous flow. In practice, sequential dependency—waiting for specifications, approvals, and compliance interpretation—introduces the Product Timeline Tax. Teams cannot sprint through blocked context.

Context governance removes those wait states by making constraints explicit and available upfront. This allows existing Agile teams to operate with fewer interruptions and less rework. The prior investment is preserved, not invalidated. The operating friction is reduced."

Objection 3: "This concentrates too much authority in Product. It sounds dictatorial."

Context Architect Response:

"It concentrates accountability, not unchecked power.

In the Legacy Model, influence without authority led to compromise-driven decisions, prolonged coordination, and diffused responsibility. When execution velocity increases, that ambiguity becomes a risk.

The Context Architect's authority is narrowly scoped to governance: resolving semantic conflicts, enforcing constraints, and maintaining auditability. Creative decisions remain distributed. Execution remains reviewed. What changes is that liability and intent are no longer implicit.

From a fiduciary standpoint, this is safer. Authority is explicit, reviewable, and bounded. Responsibility is clear. Creativity operates within known limits rather than undocumented assumptions."

Handled correctly, these objections do not block adoption. They sharpen it. Each response reframes concern into governed structure and converts uncertainty into auditability. That is the function of the Semantic Firewall: ensuring that executive scrutiny strengthens the system rather than destabilizing it.

13.10 CONCLUSION: THE FIDUCIARY RESPONSIBILITY

The final argument is not about innovation or aspiration. It is about fiduciary duty.

At the board level, product leadership is evaluated on stewardship of capital. Executives are accountable for how efficiently investment is converted into durable, defensible value. In that context, delivery methodology is not a cultural preference. It is a financial control.

Continuing to operate a sequential, high-friction delivery model in an environment of materially increased execution capacity is not conservative risk management. It is the acceptance of structural inefficiency. It embeds avoidable delay, recurring rework, and unmanaged exposure into the operating model—even when alternatives exist that reduce variance and improve capital efficiency.

The Product Timeline Tax is not an abstract concept. It is a recurring draw on cash for time spent waiting. Technical Context Debt is not an engineering inconvenience. It is a persistent dilution of future delivery capacity. Delayed launches are not scheduling artifacts. They are foregone opportunities to convert investment into return.

The Context Architect does not seek permission to experiment. They seek a mandate to apply governance where it has been absent. Their function is to make constraints explicit, decisions auditable, and trade-offs intentional. This replaces optimism with discipline and replaces informal coordination with accountable control.

At this point, the logic chain is complete. The analysis explains why the Legacy Model underperforms. The architecture defines how governance is enforced. The operating discipline demonstrates how risk is reduced while velocity improves. This chapter has translated those conclusions into the language required for capital allocation decisions.

The remaining question for leadership is not whether the model is persuasive. It is whether the organization is willing to continue funding inefficiency that is now observable, measurable, and correctable.

The system is built.

The economics are established.

What remains is authorization.

CONCLUSION

The Human in the Machine: From Task Manager to Reality Architect

The invention of the mechanical loom caused the weavers to panic. They believed that if a machine could weave faster than a human hand, the human hand itself had become obsolete. They were wrong. The loom did not eliminate the need for cloth; it radically expanded it. What changed was not demand, but value. The value shifted from the labor of weaving to the design, governance, and coordination of what was woven.

Product Management now stands at a comparable inflection point.

For decades, the discipline defined its value through labor. Product Managers became professional intermediaries—translators between strategy and execution, carriers of context across organizational boundaries, and custodians of process. We measured our worth through motion: the number of meetings attended, tickets refined, documents circulated, and threads resolved. Busyness became evidence of importance. Burnout became proof of commitment.

Then automation crossed a structural threshold.

AI introduced **Syntactic Fluency**: the ability to generate code, tests, documentation, and artifacts at a velocity and consistency no human organization can match. For a role that exists primarily to move information from one system to another, this change is terminal. When the machine can ingest intent and execute directly, the intermediary function collapses. Coordination for its own sake no longer adds value.

But this book has argued a different conclusion—not rejection, but evolution.

The arrival of AI is not a displacement event; it is a reassignment of responsibility. It removes humans from repetitive mediation and relocates them into governance. It forces a transition away from managing construction tasks and toward architecting the **context in which construction occurs**. The work does not disappear. It moves upstream.

The shift is not comfortable. It replaces activity with accountability. It replaces visibility with consequence. It replaces motion with judgment.

And it is unavoidable.

THE CHINESE ROOM: NO LONGER A PRISON

At the beginning of this book, we introduced the philosophical foundation that underpins the entire system: John Searle's Chinese Room.

The metaphor is simple and precise. The AI is the person inside the room, operating strictly according to a rulebook. It receives symbols as input and produces symbols as output with perfect mechanical consistency. It can perform this transformation so convincingly that an external observer believes understanding has occurred. Yet internally, no understanding exists. The system possesses **syntax without semantics.**

For decades, this thought experiment was treated as a critique—a boundary marker meant to prove what AI could never be.

The Context Architect (CA) treats it as an operating specification.

Once we accept that the machine does not understand meaning, values, or consequence, the governance requirement becomes unavoidable. The room—regardless of how large, fast, or capable it becomes—cannot be left unregulated. Without explicit semantic control, scale turns mechanical competence into amplified risk.

The failure mode is not theoretical. The system does not distinguish safety from danger, truth from hallucination, or compliance from violation. It executes rules faithfully, even when those rules are incomplete, contradictory, or misaligned with reality.

That is why the Chinese Room requires a Governor.

That Governor is the Context Architect.

You are the one who writes the rulebook in executable form—the Context Schema. You are the one who defines constraints that are binding rather than advisory. You are the one who injects semantics into a system that cannot generate them on its own. The machine provides horsepower. You provide steering. The machine provides Infinite Execution Velocity. You provide immutable intent.

Without this role, the room is a high-speed symbol processor, generating output without accountability. With it, the room becomes a governed system—capable of producing complex, durable structures without Semantic Drift.

The Chinese Room was never a prison. It was a warning label. We now understand what it demands.

THE THREE PILLARS OF THE NEW REALITY

As you close this book and return to your organization, these three pillars define the operating reality you are now responsible for governing. They are not principles to admire; they are anchors for decision-making when novelty, pressure, or technological hype threaten to distort judgment.

1. The Death of Sequence (The Operational Truth)

The sequential model—Waterfall, Agile, Scrum—was designed to manage human fatigue, communication latency, and coordination overhead. These methodologies optimized the flow of scarce human execution. When applied unchanged to automated systems, they become structural bottlenecks.

The incompatibility is not ideological; it is mechanical.

You now understand that the Product Timeline Tax is not an unavoidable cost of doing business. It is the direct consequence of sequencing work that no longer needs to be sequenced. By adopting the Stacked Product Lifecycle, you reject that tax deliberately. Engineering, Quality Assurance, and Brand operate in parallel, governed by a single source of truth. The Zero-Sum Gate disappears not through heroics, but through structure.

2. The Rise of Constraints (The Architectural Truth)

AI systems cannot be governed through intent expressed as prose. Requirements are interpretive. They depend on shared assumptions, tacit understanding, and human mediation. At scale, that mediation fails.

Constraints replace interpretation with enforcement.

A requirement (*"Make it intuitive"*) is aspirational. A constraint (*"Use Design System V4.0; disallow non-conforming components"*) is executable. The shift from descriptive documents to high-density, machine-governable constraints is not a tooling change. It is an architectural one.

This is why products must be **Born Compliant** and **Born Technically Sound** at the design layer. Quality, safety, and legality are not retrofitted through inspection. They are encoded into the Context Schema before execution begins.

3. The Boredom Dividend (The Economic Truth)

The objective of the Context Architect is not excitement. It is predictability.

In software organizations, excitement is often a symptom of instability—hotfixes, emergency reviews, war rooms, and unplanned escalations. These events feel heroic, but they represent unpriced risk and unaccounted cost.

The Boredom Dividend is the economic return of governed systems. It appears as stable operations, controlled iteration, and reliable scaling. Through Net Time-to-Market Gain, this predictability converts directly into competitive advantage—allowing organizations to iterate, expand, and capture markets while others remain trapped in coordination overhead and reactive process.

THE RESISTANCE: WHY THIS TRANSITION IS HARD

This transition is difficult, not because it is conceptually complex, but because it alters where responsibility resides.

In traditional organizations, failure is often diffused by design.

Sequential handoffs distribute accountability across time, roles, and process stages. When outcomes fall short, responsibility can be attributed to delays, shifting requirements, or downstream blockers. These explanations are not dishonest; they are structural byproducts of how work has historically been organized.

In a context-governed system, that diffusion collapses.

When constraints are encoded upstream and execution is automated downstream, the quality of outcomes is directly coupled to the quality of the governing context. The system does not wait, reinterpret, or negotiate intent. It executes precisely what it is given. As a result, ambiguity can no longer hide inside process.

If a product fails, the failure is no longer attributable to missed handoffs or delayed approvals. It traces back to the governing schema itself.

This shift feels uncomfortable because it replaces procedural safety with semantic responsibility. It requires intellectual rigor, explicit trade-off decisions, and the discipline to think before acting. It rewards clarity over motion and judgment over activity. Silence becomes productive, not suspicious.

Resistance is therefore predictable. Organizations cling to meetings, status rituals, and planning artifacts because those mechanisms provide psychological safety. They create the appearance of control even when intent remains unresolved. But in a context-governed system, that safety is illusory. It postpones decision-making rather than improving it.

The resistance is not moral failure. It is structural inertia. And it can only be resolved by redesigning authority, incentives, and responsibility to match the new reality.

THE MORAL MANDATE: GOVERNANCE AS FIDUCIARY DUTY

This role carries moral weight because the scale of consequence has changed. The challenge is no longer how quickly software can be shipped. It is how safely intent can be translated into automated action.

Historically, product mistakes were constrained by human throughput. A feature might fail. A release might slip. The limited velocity of execution acted as an implicit safety buffer, allowing errors to surface gradually and be corrected before they propagated widely.

In automated systems, that buffer no longer exists.

When AI systems are connected to customer data, financial operations, or regulated domains, errors in semantic governance propagate instantly and consistently. A flaw in the Context Schema does not manifest as a localized defect; it manifests as systemic behavior reproduced at machine speed.

Poorly governed systems can encode bias, violate privacy obligations, or produce financially material outcomes without human review. These failures are rarely malicious. They are the predictable result of automation operating without explicit semantic constraints.

For this reason, the Context Architect is not merely a functional role. It is a fiduciary responsibility.

The CA acts as the guardian of the semantic boundary between automated execution and real-world consequence. They are responsible for ensuring that syntactic capability is never allowed to outrun governed intent.

This responsibility becomes most visible under pressure.

When leadership demands immediate launch despite unresolved liability, the CA must block execution until constraints are satisfied.

When commercial teams propose automation that targets vulnerable populations, the CA must encode constraints that prevent harm before it occurs.

When engineering shortcuts threaten to bypass established dependency or risk boundaries, the CA must enforce structural limits rather than negotiate exceptions.

This is not obstruction. It is governance.

You are no longer responsible only for building software. You are responsible for governing how automated systems interact with people, capital, and law. That responsibility cannot be delegated to the machine.

THE FINAL VISION: THE COCKPIT OF THE FUTURE

Imagine a future—not distant, but attainable—measured in months rather than years.

You begin your day without urgency. There is no frantic standup meeting designed to synchronize confusion. There is no backlog bloated with obsolete tickets. There are no messages asking whether the specification has changed for the third time. The noise that once substituted for coordination is absent.

You open your dashboard.

In front of you is the current Context Schema for V2.0—versioned, governed, and explicit. Your work begins not with triage, but with judgment. You review a newly issued regulatory update from the EU. You examine how it intersects with existing constraints. You update the Compliance Layer of the schema deliberately, documenting the trade-off it introduces. You run a simulation inside the Contextual Sandbox to evaluate downstream impact.

The system reports a measurable shift in user sentiment under the new constraint. You adjust the Strategic Context Layer. You re-run the simulation. The signal stabilizes.

Only then do you authorize regeneration.

The machine executes without ceremony. It produces updated code artifacts, regenerates tests, revises documentation, and prepares deployment packages. These outputs are quiet, reviewable, and bounded. There is no scramble, no war room, and no heroics—only governed execution following governed intent.

Your attention is freed up. Not because there is nothing to do, but because the work that remains is the work that matters. You are thinking about future constraints, emerging risks, and the next version of the system—not distracted by coordination overhead or procedural debt.

You are no longer assembling components manually. You are governing the system that assembles them.

The machine is fast, fluent, and tireless. But it does not decide where to go. It does not know what should be protected, what trade-offs are acceptable, or which risks are intolerable.

It waits for governance.

It waits for intent.

It waits for the Architect.

BIBLIOGRAPHY

INTELLECTUAL LINEAGE & ATTRIBUTION

This book builds on long-established distinctions between syntax and semantics, execution and judgment, and automation and responsibility.

The Chinese Room

John Searle, *Minds, Brains, and Programs* (1980)

Searle's Chinese Room thought experiment demonstrates that a system can produce correct outputs through formal rule execution without understanding meaning. This book adopts the Chinese Room not as a critique of AI usefulness, but as a **boundary condition:** AI systems manipulate symbols; humans govern meaning, intent, and accountability.

Systems, Constraints, and Leverage

Donella Meadows, *Thinking in Systems* (2008)

The emphasis on **constraints over optimization, structural prevention over reactive correction,** and **leverage points over local fixes** draws directly from systems theory. The Context Schema functions as a leverage point: a small structural intervention that governs large downstream behavior.

Engineering & Governance Lineage

Additional influences include:

- Privacy-by-design and safety-by-design principles
- Compliance-as-code practices in infrastructure engineering
- Post-Waterfall critiques of sequential dependency maps

These traditions converge on a single insight: **governance must precede execution when failure costs scale non-linearly.**

APPENDIX A

Scope of Originality and Synthesis

This book introduces original terminology and operational frameworks, including the Context Schema, the Stacked Product Lifecycle, the Product Timeline Tax, and the role of the Context Architect. These constructs are original to this work and are presented as a practical architecture for governing automated systems under real-world legal, technical, and strategic constraints.

The ideas presented here do not emerge in isolation. They draw selectively from established intellectual traditions while departing from them in application.

The distinction between syntactic fluency and semantic understanding reflects long-standing philosophical debates about the limits of formal systems. These limits are famously illustrated by **John Searle**'s Chinese Room thought experiment and by **Thomas Nagel**'s analysis of subjective experience. Earlier tensions between rationalism and empiricism—associated with thinkers such as **René Descartes, David Hume**, and **George Berkeley**—help explain why meaning, intent, and responsibility cannot be derived from formal logic alone.

From a systems perspective, this work is informed by engineering disciplines in which failure is measurable, auditable, and unacceptable. Practices such as parallel development under shared specifications, constraint-first design, and auditability-by-construction are well established in safety-critical environments, even if they have been inconsistently applied in modern software and product organizations.

The originality of this book lies in synthesis rather than discovery. It does not attempt to make machines reason, nor does it propose incremental improvements to existing product management processes. Instead, it translates philosophical limits and systems-engineering principles into an explicit governance architecture for AI-enabled execution—one that formalizes how human judgment, legal exposure, and strategic intent must be imposed upstream when execution becomes effectively infinite.

Where prior work explains *why* automated systems lack understanding, this book addresses *how* organizations must be structured when judgment, not execution, becomes the binding constraint.

APPENDIX B

GLOSSARY OF TERMS (CANONICAL, CONDENSED)

Definitions are specific to this book. Many terms are intentionally narrower than industry usage.

AI Studio

A **vendor-agnostic, context-governed execution environment** capable of hosting models, enforcing schemas and constraints, orchestrating agents, and generating artifacts under governance.

Architectural abstraction, not a product.

Born Technically Sound

A system property where outputs are **correct by construction,** because architectural constraints are enforced **before generation,** not validated after the fact.

Born Compliant

A system property where outputs **cannot violate regulatory or legal constraints,** because compliance is embedded into the generation context rather than applied through late-stage audits.

Born Market-Ready

A system property where messaging, disclosures, and sales enablement assets are **launch-ready at generation time,** eliminating post-launch alignment and rework.

Context Architect (CA)

An executive governance role responsible for designing, maintaining, and enforcing the **Context Schema** that regulates AI-driven systems. The CA governs **constraints,** not tasks.

Context Schema

A structured, machine-readable representation of strategic intent, legal constraints, technical dependencies, and market posture used to govern AI generation across stacks.

Converged Artifact

A single artifact that has been **simultaneously validated** across Engineering, Marketing, Compliance, and Quality Assurance (QA) constraints.

Governance-Enforced Prompt

A natural-language interface that mirrors schema-level constraints, allowing human interaction **without bypassing governance.**

Product Timeline Tax (PTT)

The cumulative delay, cost, and rework introduced by **sequential validation** and late discovery of constraints.

Semantic Regulation

The governance of **meaning, intent, and permissible interpretation**, rather than supervision of execution steps.

Stacked Product Lifecycle

A lifecycle model in which Engineering, Marketing, Compliance, and QA execute **in parallel** under shared governance rather than sequential handoffs.

Zero-Sum Gate

A late-stage validation checkpoint where failure forces **total rollback** rather than incremental correction.

APPENDIX C

ROLE COMPRESSION MAP

Product

Sequential Model: Backlog coordination
Context-Governed Model: Context governance

Quality Assurance

Sequential Model: Post-hoc testing
Context-Governed Model: Constraint authoring

Compliance

Sequential Model: Late review
Context-Governed Model: Schema enforcement

Engineering

Sequential Model: Implementation
Context-Governed Model: Dependency codification

Marketing

Sequential Model: Draft & revise
Context-Governed Model: Semantic constraint design

APPENDIX D

What This Book Is / Is Not

This book is:

- A governance framework for AI-mediated systems
- An architectural operating model
- A role-definition guide for AI-era organizations

This book is not:

- A tool comparison guide
- A prompt cookbook
- A prediction about AGI
- A replacement for engineering judgment

Scope and Limitations

As with any governance architecture operating in regulated environments, this framework reduces compliance risk by enforcing constraints upstream, but does not eliminate the need for human legal judgment, regulatory interpretation, or jurisdiction-specific review.

ACKNOWLEDGMENTS

This work was shaped by years of operating inside systems where failure carries real consequence. I'm grateful to the Engineers, Operators, Compliance Professionals, Executives, and Business Owners who allowed these ideas to be tested under pressure—inside regulated environments, safety-critical systems, and organizations where correctness mattered more than speed. Their questions, resistance, and lived constraints informed this work far more than theory ever could.

I'm also indebted to the intellectual traditions that clarified the limits of automation and the boundaries of machine agency. Long before artificial intelligence became a cultural fixation, disciplines such as systems engineering, philosophy of mind, and safety-critical design established a necessary distinction between execution and judgment. These ideas form the foundation beneath the arguments in this book, even as they are adapted to a world where execution has become effectively instantaneous.

Finally, thank you to my wife for her patience during the long stretches of focus this work required. Her steadiness made it possible to pursue clarity without urgency and rigor without compromise.

ABOUT THE AUTHOR

Sean Pan

Sean Pan approaches artificial intelligence from environments where failure is not abstract and logic is not optional. His perspective was shaped not by consumer software or "digital native" product culture, but by industrial automation and digital signal processing—domains where errors produce physical consequences and correctness must be enforced before execution.

His formal training began at University of California, Davis, where, while studying Electrical Engineering, he also engaged in a rigorous inquiry into the philosophy of artificial intelligence. At the time, this work was housed within mathematically grounded curricula emphasizing formal logic, symbolic representation, and the known boundaries of computation—an environment that introduced him to foundational thinkers such as Descartes, Hume, Searle, and Nagel.

After transferring to San José State University, Sean completed a Bachelor of Science in Electrical Engineering and later earned an MBA in Technology Management. This combination bridges abstract reasoning with organizational reality, producing a distinct operating lens: the Engineer's insistence on constraint, the Philosopher's insistence on meaning, and the Executive's insistence on accountability.

His career unfolded in zero-tolerance systems spanning industrial control environments, military systems, and energy infrastructure. In these contexts, defects do not trigger patch cycles; they trigger shutdowns, safety incidents, or asset loss. This hardware-first discipline—where late discovery is unacceptable and constraints are non-negotiable—continues to define how he evaluates modern AI systems.

Today, Sean serves in a leadership role within a Fortune 35

insurance and financial services organization, overseeing a nine-figure revenue portfolio and advising teams operating under regulatory, economic, and reputational constraint.

Across his broader body of work, Sean focuses on helping leaders design systems where automation amplifies judgment rather than replacing it, and where speed does not outrun responsibility. He operates at the intersection of human intent and machine execution, designing systems that remain correct not only in testing, but when they leave the lab and encounter reality.

www.ingramcontent.com/pod-product-compliance
Lightning Source LLC
LaVergne TN
LVHW090855250926
848801LV00039B/179/J
* 9 7 9 8 9 9 4 6 2 9 6 2 8 *